COHABITATION WITHOUT MARRIAGE

To our respective spouses Vivien and Adrian

Cohabitation without Marriage

An Essay in Law and Social Policy

MICHAEL D. A. FREEMAN
University College London
and
CHRISTINA M. LYON
University of Manchester

Gower

Published by
Gower Publishing Company Limited,
Gower House, Croft Road, Aldershot, Hants., England.

British Library Cataloguing in Publication Data

Freeman, Michael D.A.
Cohabitation without marriage.
1 Unmarried couples–Legal status, laws, etc.
I Title II Lyon, Christina M.
342.61'6 K675

ISBN 0–566–00455–0

Printed and bound in Great Britain by
Biddles Ltd, Guildford and King's Lynn

Contents

Preface

Ten years ago it would have occurred to few writing in the area of the family, whether as sociologists or lawyers, to have included a chapter on the phenomenon of cohabitation outside marriage. Sociological treatises of the time usually devoted some space to the problems of legitimacy within the social structure of Latin America or the Caribbean; legal texts rarely raised the issue of cohabitation beyond mention in the odd footnote. The change has been enormous. Rarely can social change have occurred with such rapidity. Cohabitation outside marriage is, of course, not new. Nevertheless, there can have been few developments relating to the organisation of the family as dramatic as the rise in incidence of cohabitation outside of marriage in the 1970s. Statistics are difficult to establish: there is bound, as with crime, to be a dark figure. Reliable statistics, however, indicate that *3 per cent* of women were cohabiting in Great Britain in 1980. In figures this means that about a third of a million women under 50 were cohabiting outside marriage in 1979. The percentage in the USA is similar. It is higher in France *(5 per cent)* and is of the order of one in eight in Denmark and Sweden. The prophets of doom are having a field day: they see marriage declining and read this as a sure sign that society is in decay too. But marriage remains popular. In England, indeed, the number of marriages celebrated has begun to increase once again. That this is partly attributable to the high number of divorces does not matter: it points to the popularity of marriage as an institution.

Cohabitation has arrived or reappeared. With it have come a plethora of books on the subject. They range from guides for those 'about to' to collections of conference papers and legal texts. A journal *(Alternative Lifestyles)* has also emerged. We are offering another book on the subject because we believe we have something different and valuable to contribute. We approach the subject as lawyers but as lawyers interested in social policy: hence the sub-title of the book. We are interested in the law as law but we are also interested in the organisation of the family and society and in the light that a study of law throws on this. We do not concentrate on the legal solutions provided by one legal system. Our point of departure is the English system but references will be found to developments in the United States, to other common law countries, to Scandinavia (particularly Sweden), to France, Yugoslavia and Latin America. Cohabitation is, we believe, an interesting test case for theories about women and the family and women and the state. We take a feminist stance. We are concerned that women should not be 'protected' by having marriage thrust upon them willy-nilly. Despite pressure groups which argue to the contrary, current laws and policies relating to women in marriage do not favour them. To believe that they do is to ignore the structural dependence of women in marriage. Developments in the law relating to cohabitation tend to treat cohabitation more and more like marriage. We believe that the autonomy of cohabiting couples should be respected, and we deprecate these developments.

The book began as a paper at a Ford Foundation Conference held in London in 1978. It developed through a short article published in the *New Law Journal* in 1980. The book itself was written mainly in 1980 and 1981. The book is co-authored and each of us is jointly responsible for the book as a whole. Michael Freeman took primary responsibility for Chapters 1, 2, 5 and 8 and Christina Lyon for the remainder. Insofar as legal developments in England are concerned, we take account of all developments up to the end of 1981. Our discussions of developments in other countries are more by way of trend than detail and necessarily are not as immediately up to date.

The book was typed with her usual competence, patience and humour by Eleanor Maloney and both of us are extremely grateful to her for preparing a clean typescript out of a sometimes very untidy manuscript. Our thanks are also due to our respective spouses, Vivien Freeman and Adrian Lyon who suffered, as the intimate family usually does, the traumas associated with the research and writing of the book.

1 March 1982

M.D.A. Freeman
C.M. Lyon

1 Introduction

Cohabitation is not a new phenomenon, though sociological and legal interest in it may be. There is documentation throughout history of heterosexual mates living together without legal sanction. There is no doubt that in terms of history the concept of family antedates that of marriage.[1]

Today, throughout much of the world, data indicate that more individuals are cohabitating outside marriage than before. We know that there is more cohabitation today than twenty, even ten years ago.[2] But we do not know whether cohabitation is more prevalent today than it was in past ages, for we have only the flimsiest of pictures of the organisation of family life in earlier periods of history.[3]

Despite the existence of cohabitation throughout history, though in a variety of forms, sociological research has, until recently, been very limited. Students of the subject have had to rely on journalistic accounts in the popular press. These have often not risen above the sensational. They have rarely been objective: cohabitation emerges from them as a form of deviance. This is beginning to change and cohabitation is for the first time being studied seriously. There is now even a journal, *Alternative Lifestyles,* which since its inception in 1978 has attempted to examine 'holistically and systematically . . . the complexity of intimate behaviors within and beyond conventional conceptions of marriage and family'.[4] National and international congresses[5] have focused their attention on the phenomenon. So have the legislatures and law courts of many countries. Until sociologists became interested, until law-making bodies turned their attention to it, there was little need to be precise about cohabitation. As a result, it was neither operationalised for empirical inquiry nor systematically defined in a conceptual sense. A statutory definition of cohabitation is still awaited, at least in Britain.[6] Perhaps it is unattainable or even undesirable, for being unduly restrictive. Judges too need to experiment! But researchers have found it necessary to define, rather more loosely than lawyers would, what cohabitation means and it is to some of these definitions that we now turn.

What is cohabitation?

The term 'cohabitation' may be applied to married as well as unmarried couples. Thus, Trost[7] notes that the term 'syndyasmos' was coined by the Hungarian Löcsei to refer to both married and unmarried cohabitation. It means those varieties of enduring living arrangements between men and women. Cohabitation is, though, more commonly used to refer to non-legalised pair-bond relationships. In this book cohabitation will not be used to refer to marriage.

The Swedish taxation system has long known a definition of cohabitation, one of the few definitions to be encoded in a statutory provision. Cohabitation is there defined as entailing 'long-lasting common life'.[8] This is not further defined. It is restricted to those who have or have had children together or have been married to each other. But what is 'long'? And 'long' from whose perspective? That of the parties (who may not agree) or the taxation authorities? The definition of cohabitation was also discussed by a Swedish government committee which was examining a proposal to make state loans to families starting a new home. According to Trost, its definition would be roughly: 'a man and a woman living together under marriage-like conditions'.[9] But, we may ask what these are. Despite this difficulty, Trost himself defines cohabitation as 'living together under marriage-like conditions but without a marriage'.[10] In a later article he argues 'that a phenomenological definition may suffice for certain purposes, for example sociological enquiry'.[11] But he agrees that this has two major problems: (i) where each partner perceives the relationship differently; (ii) where some authority has to determine whether cohabitation exists for a particular purpose.

All, or nearly all, definitions refer to relationships between the sexes. Homosexual or gay cohabiting arrangements exist, and have increased in number, but consideration of them is outside the scope of this book.[12]

A common feature of definitions is the emphasis on the sharing of common living facilities for the purpose of satisfying certain family functions. The relevant functions differ from one piece of research to another. Some stress economic functions ('common habitat duties and responsibilities of housekeeping')[13], others sexual imperatives. Some include also childbearing and rearing, including socialisation and control. There is need to distinguish cohabitation from a casual sexual relationship. To one researcher cohabitation meant 'living together in a relatively permanent manner similar in many respects to marriage but without legal or religious sanctions'.[14] Macklin's studies of cohabitation among unmarried college students in the United States were the first explicitly to use the time dimension as a key factor in conceptualising cohabitation relationships. She defines cohabitation as 'shar[ing] a bedroom and/or bed with someone of the opposite sex to whom not married, for four or more nights a week for three or more consecutive months'.[15] The definition was specifically geared to living patterns of college students and took account of the fact that many went home for weekends. Macklin also attempted a typology of cohabitation:

Type A – relationships in which a bed or bedroom was shared for at least four nights a week for three or more consecutive months.
Type B – relationships in which a bed or bedroom was shared less than four nights a week for three or more consecutive months.
Type C – relationships in which a bed or bedroom was shared for four or more nights a week for less than three consecutive months.
Type D – relationships in which a bed or bedroom was shared for less than four nights a week for less than three consecutive months.

Other researchers have not utilised a time dimension as a critical criterion. But it is a factor that courts certainly think ought to be taken into account.

Thus, in recent years English courts have distinguished 'permanent' quasi-marital relationships from 'casual or intermittent' ones.[16] Back in 1950, twenty years was held by the Court of Appeal not to be enough. The couple was said to be 'masquerading . . . as husband and wife': to say 'that they were members of the same family seems . . . an abuse of the English language'.[17] By 1975 the same court, though not the same judges, had no difficulty in construing the word 'family' to include a woman who had lived with a man for twenty-one years. Significantly, the judges took account of the way that the word 'family' had changed in meaning according to the understanding of the ordinary man using the word in its popular sense.[18] But, more recently, a relationship which had existed for five years did not lead the court to infer sufficient permanence to attach legal consequences to it.[19] There were other considerations in this case, to which further reference is made in Chapter 4.

It is, we think, important to distinguish long-term, regular relationships from short-term, transient or transitory ones. It would, we think, be a distortion of language to include casual encounters within the notion of cohabitation. Cohabitation must be distinguished from fornication, from adultery, and from other relationships which are intended to satisfy only such limited needs as sexual ones. This is not to say the law should not recognise that legal consequences may attach even to casual, impermanent relationships. This legal systems have done and continue to do. Thus, the liability of the father of an illegitimate child to pay maintenance to support that child when his paternity has been established on the initiative of the mother is recognised in all, or nearly all, legal systems.[20] Adultery remains a fact upon which divorce proceedings may be founded in many systems, even though there has been a move away from offence-based divorce laws to no-fault systems.[21]

It is not easy to give a precise definition of what is meant by cohabitation. Cole views 'the cohabitation relationship as a special type of primary relationship in which the partners meet socioemotional, sociosexual, sociophysical and socioeconomic needs and maintenance functions'. His view implies that the relationship covers 'a relatively large degree of interpersonal commitment in order to meet interpersonal need and support system functions'.[22] Cohabitation as a life-style is transitional for many individuals. Many today form cohabiting relationships and then marry the partners with whom they have cohabited. But cohabitation is also not uncommon among the middle-aged who are separated or divorced, as well as among the elderly who are widowed. Cohabitation does not fulfil the same needs for all who cohabit.

Sociologists and others who research cohabitation can make do without a precise formal definition. They may even resort to what has come to be called 'grounded theory'.[23] But the law needs to be more precise. On the other hand, it needs to avoid undue rigidity. It would be wrong for a legislature to stipulate a given period of time as a prerequisite to the acquisition of some status arising out of cohabitation. We argue anyway in this book that contract is a more important notion than status and that autonomy of the parties should be recognised wherever possible.[24] Despite this, a definition of our subject matter is called for. We understand by cohabitation *a stable, more or less permanent, relationship between two persons of the opposite sex who are not married to each other (though one or both may be married to someone else) and who share living facilities.* They may or may not have children; she may or may not take his surname; they may or may not have entered into a formal contractual relationship. The flexibility of cohabitation is one of the attractions which it holds out.

The name of those who cohabit – a note on terminology

A variety of labels has been used to refer to an unmarried heterosexual couple who share a common bedroom. 'Living together',[25] 'living together unmarried',[26] 'two-step marriage',[27] 'live-ins',[28] 'consensual unions',[29] even 'companionate marriage'[30] and 'trial marriage'.[31] Today most agree on the label 'cohabitation'. But what are we to call those who cohabit?

To call them 'unmarried persons' or 'unmarried partners', as one legal commentator does, [32] is not always even accurate, for they may be married to another person, and it certainly does not take us very far. It avoids the issue: we do not, for example, call children non-adults. For a time 'the inaccurate but expressive phrases "common law wife" and "common law husband" '[33] came into general use to describe them. These expressions are now less often used, which is fortunate as they technically refer to a person married according to one of the non-statutory methods of contracting a marriage. 'Common law marriages' in this sense cannot be contracted in this country[34] but may in certain limited circumstances be contracted abroad and recognised in England.[35] But they are instances of marriage, not cohabitation: the incidents which attach to them are those of marriage.

Other legal commentators as well as journalists and many others still refer to the female partner as a 'mistress'. Consistency demands that they refer to the male as a 'lover' or even, to capture the flavour of an earlier age, as a 'paramour'. Few, of course, do.[36] This is not surprising. 'Mistress' is a wholly sexist notion in this context, essentially encapsulated in Lord Kilbrandon's description in 1978 of 'a woman installed in a clandestine way by someone of substance normally married for his intermittent sexual enjoyment'.[37] 'Mistress' is not even an accurate depiction, for the word primarily means a woman in a position of authority or control, a head of household, an owner (usually of an animal) or a teacher. Insofar as the word came to connote an unmarried partner, it stresses exclusively the illicit sexual relationship which was considered to be its central feature. Most men who had 'mistresses' in an age when that was the customary designation probably did not cohabit with them at all. They lived with their wives and fornicated with their 'mistresses'.

The word 'cohabitee' is also commonly used today. It has been said that it is 'much too ponderous'.[38] It certainly lacks the colour of 'mistress'. But perhaps the principal objection to using it, apart from the fact that it is grammatically inaccurate, is that male partners are rarely referred to as 'cohabitees'. Thus, it is said that 'cohabitee' is, like 'mistress', a word with explicitly sexist imagery. This is unfortunate, for there is no reason why the term should not be employed to describe both male and female partners. But, it is true, hitherto it has not. Most writers on the subject accordingly prefer instead the rather ugly expression 'cohabitants'. We use this word in this book. It seems unlikely, however, that 'cohabitant' will easily or readily become part of common usage. 'Jim, this is my cohabitant' seems no more likely to roll off the lips at a party than does 'Jim, this is my mistress'. Why, indeed, it may be asked, 'my' anything? Many who cohabit do so explicitly to avoid proprietary notions associated with marriage.[39] But few have been able to shake off social conventions entirely and the search for a way of describing the person with whom one lives outside marriage goes on. Pat Clayton's recent *The Cohabitation Guide* contains an amusing scenario centred on this particular dilemma.[40] It is not one from which we need extricate ourselves in this book. What those who cohabit call their partners is not our concern. We use the term 'cohabitants' more for convenience than out of conviction. Perhaps in time a more suitable word will emerge.

Cohabitation: its historical context

The rising popularity of cohabitation, to which reference is made in Chapter 3, must be placed into historical context. There is more cohabitation today than ten years ago. The 1979 *General Household Survey*,[41] which included a new question about cohabitation, shows that 20 per cent of women marrying in the late 1970s lived with their husbands before marriage and 3 per cent of single women over 17 were living with someone 'as man and wife'. These figures may represent a 100 per cent increase over a decade.[42] But how many cohabited in past ages?

To understand this question some light must be thrown on the institution of marriage as it has emerged and has been controlled. In England shortly before the Norman Conquest, casual polygamy was general.[43] There was easy divorce and the practice of concubinage was widespread.[44] In the Early Modern period, 'marriage was an engagement which could be undertaken in a bewildering variety of ways and the mere definition of it is fraught with difficulties'.[45] Family structures must be understood in relation to property rights.[46] To the minority with property, marriage was a private contract between two families relating to a property exchange.[47] The contract would also commonly provide for some financial protection for the bride if her husband died or deserted her. For the propertyless 'it was a private contract between two individuals, enforced by the community sense of what was right'.[48] A church ceremony was an optional extra and considered both expensive and otiose, given the widespread resort to divorce by mutual consent and remarriage. It was only in the thirteenth century that the Church succeeded in acquiring control of marriage law.[49] The principle of the monogamous, indissoluble marriage was established. The Statute of Merton of 1236 excluded the illegitimate from the inheritance of property.[50] Incest was defined and prohibited[51] and fornication and adultery punished in the ecclesiastical courts.[52]

By Tudor times marriage was fairly well defined. In the later seventeenth century, however, clandestine marriages were still widespread and there is evidence that the children born of unions forged by irregular weddings were not baptised as bastards.[53] Until Lord Hardwicke's Marriage Act of 1753 there were numerous ways of entering into marriage. Stone describes them thus:

> For persons of property it involved a series of distinct steps. The first was a written legal contract between the parents concerning the financial arrangements. The second was the spousals (also called a contract), the formal exchange, usually before witnesses, of oral promises. The third step was the public proclamation of banns in church, three times, the purpose of which was to allow claims of pre-contract to be heard (by the seventeenth century nearly all the well-to-do evaded this step by obtaining a licence). The fourth step was the wedding in church, in which mutual consent was publicly verified, and the union received the formal blessing of the Church. The fifth and final step was the sexual consummation.[54]

In ecclesiastical law the spousals were as legally binding as the church wedding. This was not regarded as a sacrament until 1439.[55] Indeed, it was only after the Reformation (at the Council of Trent in 1563) that the Catholic Church first required the presence of a priest for a valid and binding marriage.[56] The Anglican church did not, of course, adopt this innovation, with the result that things were left in considerable confusion. But gradually in the sixteenth and seventeenth centuries both clergy and laity came to regard the wedding in church as the key ceremony. Lawyers did not. As far as they were concerned spousals before witnesses were sufficient.[57] Spousals could take two forms: the contract *per verba de futuro* (an oral promise to marry in the future) and the contract *per verba de praesenti.*[58] The former, if not followed by consummation, was an engagement which could be legally broken by mutual consent. If followed by consummation, it was legally binding for life. But it also meant that 'each partner was at liberty to go to bed with the other directly a match had been decided upon, though a church wedding was still in the future'.[59] The latter (an exchange of promises before witnesses) was regarded in ecclesiastical law as an irrevocable commitment which could not be broken and which nullified a later church wedding to someone else.[60]

Matters were further complicated by canons of 1604[61] which stipulated that a church wedding had to take place between the hours of 8 am and noon at the church at the place of residence of one of the spouses, after the banns had been read for three consecutive weeks. They further forbade the marriage of minors (that is those under 21) without the consent of parents or guardians. Such marriages were illegal but were nevertheless valid. A commerce developed whereby unscrupulous clergymen, operating in districts outside superior ecclesiastical supervision, married anyone for a fee without asking any questions. The most flourishing trade of all was done by certain decadent or profligate clergymen in the Fleet district of London.[62] 'Many drunken, hasty and exploitative unions were . . . sealed in these sordid surroundings, and once performed they could never be dissolved. These venal clergymen were also prepared, for a fee, to backdate a registration to legitimize children already born, or even to supply a man for a woman seeking a husband in a hurry.'[63]

Lord Hardwicke's Marriage Act of 1753 put an end to these practices.[64] From 1754 only church weddings,[65] and not verbal spousals, were legally binding. A prior oral contract was no longer a cause for the annulment of a later marriage in church. A number of other reforms tightened up the law, the enforcement of which was transferred to the secular courts. Purely civil marriage was not recognised in England until the Marriage Act of 1836.

In this context cohabitation did not have the meaning it has today. In pre-modern times consensual unions were common. Laslett in *Family Life and Illicit Love in Earlier Generations* produces entries in the parish register of Llanelian in Denbighshire relating to one Edward Parry, who is listed for successive years (1685 and 1686) as living with his 'concubine'.[66] There is no reason to believe that such an entry is that uncommon. Marriages were contracted late and normally broken early. There was to all intents and purposes no law of divorce before 1857.[67] But there were functional substitutes: death, bigamy, disappearance, even wife sale, the last reported instance of which is as late as 1887.[68] In Stone's words, in the pre-modern family marriage was a 'transient and temporary association'.[69] People lived together before marriage and lived with others when marriages broke down. The line between marriage and cohabitation was not so clearly drawn as it is today.

Some indication of sexual activity outside marriage in the past may be gauged from the ratio[70] of illegitimate births. There are parish registers from the reign of Elizabeth I in Lancashire and Cheshire[71] recording similar percentages of illegitimate births (9 to 10 per cent) as exist in this country today.[72] There is no simple relationship between sexual activity and illegitimacy, as Shorter[73], Laslett[74] and others[75] point out. Illegitimacy figures indicate a brief, insignificant rise between 1550 and 1650, an enormous rise in illegitimate births and pre-marital pregnancies in the century from 1750, and a steady increase during the period

1955–1970.[76] But changes in the extent of illegitimacy are not connected in any straightforward way. Thus, for example, figures were low in Puritan times, but so they were in the Restoration period which followed.[77] Simply then to relate illegitimacy figures to attitudes or social controls will not do. That the number of illegitimate births plummeted in the period 1850–1940 may be attributed to growth of, and improvement in, contraceptive practices. There was, as Shorter points out,[78] a simultaneous decline in marital fertility. Similarly, 'rates of both bastardy and pre-marital pregnancy climbed in Anglo-Saxon and Scandinavian countries after 1945, principally as a result of the improved biological capacity to conceive, which in turn came from a better diet'.[79] It was not until the late 1950s that actual patterns of sexual behaviour among the unmarried significantly changed.

Illegitimacy statistics are then only a rough indicator of sexual activity outside marriage. Laslett points out[80] that a large number of circumstances has to obtain before a birth could be marked as 'natural' or 'spurious' or 'base' in a parish register (or after 1838 in the books kept by the Registrar-General).

> A man and a woman, both fecund and not married to each other, though not necessarily unmarried, had to be in association. Sexual intercourse had to take place at a time and under circumstances when conception was possible, and without successful contraceptive measures. Spontaneous abortion must not have occurred during pregnancy, and no effective act of deliberate abortion either. No marriage must have taken place between the parties before term – that is, where they were both at liberty to marry each other. The child must have been born alive, and have survived birth for the period of time (which might be weeks or even months) which elapsed before baptism or registration came into question.[81] This means that the baby must have been in sufficient health to survive the most dangerous days of its existence (especially for unwanted infants) and that no one should have disposed of it, either at parturition or subsequently, by violence or by deliberate neglect. Finally (in the era before official registration) the child must have been taken to the church for the ceremony of baptism and the act of christening. When it came to making the entry in the register the parson or his parish clerk must have felt obliged to set down the tell-tale description of the baby's social and legal status. After civil registration began, the official responsible must have got this information out of the reluctant mother. Sexual intercourse between associating individuals not recognised as spouses to each other cannot have led to a recorded illegitimacy unless every one of these conditions had been satisfied.[82]

Illegitimacy rates are accordingly an underestimate of the 'true' figures.

Even so, they reveal that something like one in thirty-three registered births in the early seventeenth century was illegitimate and that about one in eighteen was in the early nineteenth century. Laslett shows in *Family Life and Illicit Love in Earlier Generations*,[83] how illegitimacy comes in waves with climaxes about 1600 and a second one in the 1840s. He also reveals a dip in the 1810s and a generally downward tendency in the ratio during the years from the 1800s to 1831.[84]

Illegitimacy did not mean in past ages what it means today because marriage had not acquired its contemporary meaning. Today marriage is an official act, 'a public and a punctual act'.[85] But this conception of marriage is relatively recent, more so in Scotland where 'marriage by habit and repute' still lingers on.[86] Before what has to be recognised as a major shift, marriage was less a registered act than 'a condition, a state of affairs recognised by the consent of the community . . . It thus belonged to the community to recognise marriage – or to refuse and to oppose it'.[87] It follows that in this type of marriage what constituted illegitimacy lacked rigour and precision.

> There was no mathematical moment after which it was legitimate to sleep together. People passed from 'courtship' to 'final conjugality' through a series of stages of consents and agreements, and also of ceremonies . . . The situation changed when the Church, the state and progress of the law combined to make marriage what it is today: a public, punctual, written act.[88]

The relationship of the state to the family is problematic and largely a phenomenon of this century. It is depicted in Chapter 2 and no more will be written of it here.

The historical context of cohabitation is important. Contemporary critics of the 'living together' phenomenon of today, the self-styled prophets of doom, lack historical insight into developments of the family. The contemporary concept of marriage is a product of history, of a process that owes as much to the community itself as it does to controls exercised by the church or the state. Furthermore, it is a process which is not yet complete nor ever will be. In these terms the cohabitation experiments of today may be seen as attempts to challenge the implicit assumption that current notions of marriage are naturally 'given' and are thus beyond the reach of critical opinion. Cohabitation experiments may cause marriage to change, although in the short term any changes that do occur are likely to be imperceptible. But will marriage be made more like cohabitation or will the consequences of cohabitation be assimilated to those of marriage? In this book we argue that an attempt, conscious or not, is currently being made in England and other countries to treat cohabitation like marriage.[89] The development is a vertical rather than a horizontal one, proceeding *ex cathedra* rather than from within the community. Whether such an assimilation is justifiable is one of the major concerns of this book. We doubt it for reasons which will become apparent in the course of the book.

Notes

1 See E. Westermarck, *The History of Human Marriage,* Macmillan, 1921, p. 72.

2 See *post,* p. 56.

3 As to which, see E. Shorter, *The Making of the Modern Family,* Basic Books, 1975; P. Laslett and R. Wall (eds), *Household and Family in Past Time,* Cambridge U.P., 1972; P. Laslett, *Family Life and Illicit Love in Earlier Generations,* Cambridge U.P. 1977; P. Ariès, *Centuries of Childhood,* Jonathan Cape, 1962; L. Stone, *The Family, Sex and Marriage in England 1500–1800,* Weidenfeld and Nicolson, 1977 (revised, abbreviated edition, Penguin 1979); and E. LeRoy Ladurie, *Montaillou,* Scolar Press, 1978.

4 Published by Sage Publications: edited by Roger Libby of the Centre for the Family, University of Massachusetts.

5 It was the subject of the Third World Conference of the International Society on Family Law in Uppsala in 1979. The papers from this conference are published as J. Eekelaar and S. Katz (eds), *Marriage and Cohabitation in Contemporary Societies: Areas of Legal, Social and Ethical Change; An International and Interdisciplinary Study,* Butterworths, 1980.

6 Cf. Lord Widgery CJ in *R v S.W. London Supplementary Benefit Appeal Tribunal ex parte Barnett* (1973) unreported (but in M. Freeman, *Family Law,* Butterworth, 1976, p. 106): 'We have been invited to give some guidance upon the phrase "cohabitating as man and wife", but for my part it is so well known that nothing I could say about it could possibly assist in its interpretation hereafter'.

7 'Married and Unmarried Cohabitation: the Case of Sweden, with some Comparisons', *Journal of Marriage and the Family,* 37 (1975), 677–82.

8 See J. Trost, 'Cohabitation Without Marriage in Sweden' in Eekelaar and Katz, op. cit., note 5, pp. 16, 21.

9 *Idem.*

10 *Op. cit.,* note 7, p. 677.

11 *Op. cit.,* note 8, pp. 21–2.

12 But see K. Plummer, *Sexual Stigma: An Interactionist Account,* Routledge and Kegan Paul, 1975. See also *Bramlett v Selman* 597 S.W. 2d 80 (1980).

13 *Per* L. Hickrod, quoted in C.L. Cole, 'Cohabitation in Social Context' in R. Libby and R. Whitehurst (eds), *Marriage and Alternatives,* Scott, Foresman, 1977, pp. 62, 65.

14 *Per* S. Lautenschlager, quoted *idem.*

15 'Heterosexual Cohabitation among unmarried College Students', *Family Co-ordinator,* 21 (1972), pp. 463–72; 'Cohabitation in College: Going Very Steady', *Psychology Today,* 8 (1974), pp. 53–9.

16 *Per* James L.J. in *Dyson Holdings Ltd. v Fox* [1975], 3 All E.R. 1030.

17 In *Gammans v Ekins* [1950], 2 All E.R. 140 *per* Asquith L.J. at p. 142.

18 In *Dyson Holdings Ltd. v Fox* [1975], 3 All E.R.1030 at pp. 1033,1035.

19 See *Helby v Rafferty* [1978], 3 All E.R., 1016.

20 See as to the English position Affiliation Proceedings Act 1957, amended by Affiliation Proceedings (Amendment) Act 1972 and Domestic Proceedings and Magistrates' Courts Act 1978.

21 This has gone further in many systems than it has in England, where adultery plus the petitioner finding it intolerable to live with the respondent is a fact upon which irretrievable breakdown of marriage may be presumed (see Matrimonial Causes Act 1973, s.1 (2) (a)). It is significant that over a quarter of petitions in England are still based on adultery.

22 *Op. cit.,* note 13, p. 66.

23 See B. Glaser and A. Strauss, *The Discovery of Grounded Theory,* Aldine, 1967.

24 *Post,* p. 204 *et seq.*

25 *Per* J. Lyness, M. Lipetz and K. Davis, 'Living Together: An Alternative to Marriage', *Journal of Marriage and the Family,* 34 (1972), 305–11.

26 *Per* R. Whitehurst in R. Libby and R. Whitehurst, *Marriage and its Alternatives,* Scott, Foreman, 1977.

27 *Per* M. Mead, 'Anomalies in American Post Divorce Relationships', in P. Bohannan (ed.), *Divorce and After,* Doubleday, 1970, p. 107.

28 *Per* N. Clatworthy, 'Living Together', in N. Glazer-Malbin (ed.), *Old Family/New Family,* Van Nostrand, 1975, ch. 3.

29 *Op. cit.,* note 14.

30 *Per* B. Lindsey and W. Evans, *The Companionate Marriage,* Brentanos, 1928.

31 *Per* M. Berger, 'Trial Marriage: Harnessing the Trend Constructively', *Family Co-ordinator,* 20 (1971), 38–43.

32 S. Cretney, *Principles of Family Law,* (3rd ed. 1979) Sweet & Maxwell, p. 244.

33 *Per* Bridge LJ in *Dyson Holdings Ltd. v Fox* [1975], 3 All E.R. 1030, 1036.

34 Since Lord Hardwicke's Act of 1753.

35 See *Wolfenden v Wolfenden* [1946] P.61; *Taczanowska v Taczanowski* [1957],2 All E.R. 563; *Lazarewicz v Lazarewicz* [1962] P.171.

36 But see P. Howard, *Words Fail Me,* Hamish Hamilton, 1980. His essay 'Shack-up à son goût' notes some 30 expressions used.

37 In *Davis v Johnson* [1979] A.C. 264, 338–9.

38 By P. Clayton, *The Cohabitation Guide,* Wildwood House, 1981, p. 18.

39 See *post,* p. 51.

40 *Op. cit.,* note 38, p. 18.

41 See A. Brown and K. Kiernan, 'Cohabitation in Great Britain: Evidence from the General Household Survey', Office of Population Censuses and Surveys, 1981.

42 See *post,* p. 57.

43 On polygamy and Christianity see J. Cairncross, *After Polygamy was made a Sin: the Social History of Christian Polygamy,* Routledge and Kegan Paul, 1974.

44 *Idem.*

45 *Per* L. Stone, *The Family, Sex and Marriage in England 1500–1800,* Weidenfeld and Nicolson, 1977, p. 30.

46 See an interesting interpretation of this in C. Creighton, 'Family, Property and Relations of Production in Western Europe', *Economy and Society,* 9 (1980), pp. 129–67.

47 As it remained until well into the nineteenth century. See H.J. Habbakuk, 'Marriage Settlements in the Eighteenth Century', *Transactions of the Royal Historical Society,* 32 (1950) pp. 15–30.

48 *Per* L. Stone, *op. cit.,* note 45, p. 31.

49 See R.H. Helmholz, *Marriage Litigation in Medieval England,* Harvard U.P., 1974; J. Scammell, 'Freedom and Marriage in Medieval England', *Economic History Review,* 2nd ser., *XXVII* (1974), p. 530.

50 See R.H. Helmholz, 'Bastardy Litigation in Medieval England', *Amer. J. of Legal History,* 13 (1969), pp. 360–83.

51 See F. Pollock and F.W. Maitland, *History of English Law* (2nd ed., 1968), Cambridge University Press, vol. II, p. 543. It only became a secular criminal offence in 1908 with the passing of the Punishment of Incest Act 1908. See, for a discussion of its origins, V. Bailey and S. Blackburn, 'The Punishment of Incest Act 1908: A Case Study of Law Creation', *Criminal Law Review* (1979), pp. 708–18.

52 See F. Pollock and F.W. Maitland, *op. cit.,* note 51, p. 543.

53 See P. Laslett, *Family Life and Illicit Love in Earlier Generations,* Cambridge U.P., 1977, p. 131.

54 *Op. cit.,* note 45, p. 31.

55 *Idem.*

56 See J. Bussy, 'The Counter-Reformation and the People of Catholic Europe', *Past and Present,* 47 (1970).

57 *Op. cit.,* note 45, p. 32.

58 But, as Maitland notes, 'of all people in the world lovers are the least likely to distinguish precisely between the present and future tenses' (*op. cit.*, note 51, p. 368).

59 *Per* P. Laslett, *op. cit.*, note 53, p. 129.

60 This was part of Henry VIII's argument in his attempt to extricate himself from his marriage to Catherine of Aragon. She had contracted to marry Henry's brother, Arthur. See H.A. Kelly, *The Matrimonial Trials of Henry VIII*, Stanford U.P., 1976.

61 See R. Helmholz, *op. cit.*, note 49, pp. 75–9.

62 See G.S. Alleman, *Matrimonial Law and the Materials of Restoration Comedy*, Univ. of Pennsylvania, 1942; and M.D. George, *London Life in the Eighteenth Century*, Kegan Paul, 1925 (reissued by Penguin, 1966).

63 *Per* L. Stone, *op. cit.*, note 45, p. 53.

64 An Act for the Better Preventing of Clandestine Marriages, 26 Geo II, c. 33.

65 Quakers and Jews were exempt from this provision.

66 *Op. cit.*, note 53, p. 121.

67 Before which time an Act of Parliament was necessary. On the prehistory of divorce see O.R. McGregor, *Divorce in England*, Heinemann, 1957.

68 See G. Mueller, 'Inquiry into the State of a Divorceless Society', *University of Pittsburgh L. Rev.*, 18 (1957), pp. 545–578; and C. Kenny 'Wife-Selling in England', *Law Quarterly Review* 45 (1929), pp. 494–7. The most famous example is the fictional one in Thomas Hardy's *The Mayor of Casterbridge*, first published in 1886.

69 *Op. cit.*, note 45, p. 55.

70 The difference between this and 'rate' is explained in Laslett, *op. cit.*, note 53, pp. 120–1.

71 See P. Laslett, *op. cit.*, note 53, p. 104.

72 12 per cent in 1980. See *Social Trends*, no. 12, HMSO, 1981, Table 2.17 (p. 39).

73 *The Making of the Modern Family*, Basic Books, 1975, ch. 3.

74 See particularly *Bastardy and its Comparative History*, Arnold, 1980.

75 For example, S.F. Hartley, 'The Amazing Rise of Illegitimacy in Great Britain', *Social Forces*, 44 (1966), pp. 533–45. See also her *Illegitimacy*, Univ. of California Press, 1975.

76 See Shorter, *op. cit.*, note 73, pp. 87–103, 113–124.

77 See, as to this, K. Wrightson, 'The Nadir of English Illegitimacy in the Seventeenth Century', in P. Laslett *et al.*, *Bastardy and its Comparative History*, Arnold, 1980, p. 176.

78 *Op. cit.*, note 73, pp. 89–90.

79 *Idem*, p. 90.

80 *Op. cit.*, note 53, p. 108.

81 B.M. Berry and R.S. Schofield, 'Age at Baptism in Pre-Industrial England', *Population Studies*, 25 (1971), pp. 453–65.

82 *Op. cit.*, note 53, p. 108–9.

83 *Idem*, p. 113.

84 Since this is a book about cohabitation and not the phenomenon of illegitimacy, the reasons for this are outside our scope. But see the essays in P. Laslett, K. Oosterveen and R. Smith, *Bastardy and its Comparative History*, Arnold, 1980, as to this, particularly those in Part I of the book.

85 *Per* P. Ariès 'Marriage', *London Review of Books*, 2, no. 20, p. 8 (16 October–5 November 1980).

86 *Idem.*

87 *Idem.*

88 *Idem.*

89 See *post*, p. 67 *et seq.*

2 The Family, Women, the State and the Law

The family is a near universal[1] but it has not always been as it is now. The 'cereal packet norm'[2] is of relatively recent vintage. It attained its fullest flowering in late Victorian times. It is based on the concept of the companionate marriage, in which the union is one of two individuals rather than two lineages, on the child-centred household,[3] on the quasi-emancipation of women (to which further reference is made in this chapter)[4] and on the structural isolation of the nuclear family from the kinship system and society in general. The emergence of alternative life-styles, of which cohabitation is just one, can be seen as an indication of the decay of this concept. It can also be viewed, and this is how we interpret it, as a further stage in the development and recognition of individual autonomy.[5]

The emergence of the modern bourgeois family

The family is not a pre-given entity. It does not exist other than as an 'ideological construct'.[6] The structure of the household, concept of kinship and the ideology of 'the family' itself have varied enormously in different types of society. Some insight into these changes is to be found in Jean-Louis Flandrin's *Families in Former Times: Kinship, Household and Sexuality.*[7]

He argues, from a study of French dictionary definitions of the term 'family', that in the sixteenth, seventeenth and eighteenth centuries the two elements of the term, kinship and co-residence, were clearly dissociated. 'The word "family" more often referred to a set of kinsfolk who did not live together, while it also designated an assemblage of co-residents who were not necessarily linked by ties of blood or marriage.'[8] He shows that in the seventeenth century it was common to include in the 'family' all members of the household who were subject to the authority of the male head. Only in the eighteenth century did the concept begin to be restricted to those members of the household who were related by blood. Flandrin argues that over this period the concept of the family was restricted to kin relations. Only later did it also come to embrace co-residence in a household. The earliest definition located by Flandrin which emphasises 'persons of the same blood living under the same roof, and more especially the father, the mother and the children'[9] dates from 1869.

It is also now clear that it was inaccurate to speak of the family in past times for another reason. There was not one family but several. The household structures of different social classes were different.[10] Poster generates four models of family structure, from a history of the European family: the bourgeois family in the mid-nineteenth century, the aristocratic family of the sixteenth and seventeenth centuries, the peasant family of the sixteenth and seventeenth centuries, and the working-class family of the early industrial revolution.[11] On much there is still controversy but one thing at least is clear: the modern family arose among the bourgeoisie in Europe around 1750. In Poster's words:

> The bourgeoisie developed a family form in sharp contrast to that of the aristocracy and the peasantry, indeed, in sharp contrast to what this group itself experienced before the eighteenth century. During the early stages of the industrial revolution the working class had a unique family structure which, in the course of the next two centuries, became more and more like that of the bourgeoisie. During the same time period, much of the old bourgeoisie lost its control of property, becoming skilled salaried labor and hence resembling the working class.[12]

Flandrin cites an encyclopaedia entry in the eighteenth century which demonstrates explicitly the difference between the bourgeoisie's ideology and practice on the one hand and that of the aristocracy and the poor on the other:

> Pride has . . . decreed in our language,[13] as in past times among the Romans, that the titles, the great dignities and great appointments continuously held by people of the same name should form what one calls the *houses* of the people of quality, whereas

> one describes as *families* those of citizens who clearly distinguished from the dregs of the populace, perpetuate themselves in an Estate, and transmit their line from father to son in honourable occupations, in useful employments, in well-matched alliances, a proper upbringing, and agreeable and cultivated manners.[14]

Families, as Michèle Barrett puts it, are in these terms 'an achievement of industriousness, respectability and regulation'.[15] That we can speak of 'the family' today is the result in part of the eclipse of the aristocracy[16] but is more fundamentally the product of the gradual bourgeoisification of the working class. The working class 'acknowledged the moral legitimacy of the bourgeoisie by adopting its family structure . . . The transformation of working class family structure is', Poster argues most persuasively, 'one of the unwritten aspects of the political success of bourgeois democracy'.[17] The lawyers' response to cohabitation today, to treat it as equivalent to marriage, is reminiscent of this process, though it is a true example of the bourgeois family ideal being 'imposed', whereas the earlier example is more one of adoption than imposition.[18]

The family as a refuge

In pre-capitalist societies and in the early stages of capitalism work and family life overlapped. The household was the basic unit of production: the home was a place of work. There was no clear distinction between the role of the worker and of what we should call the family member. There was no reason why there should be: many members of the 'family' were strangers in blood. With industrialisation and capitalist production the nature of work and family life changed radically. This is not the same thing as saying that these changes were the necessary outcome of capitalist relations of production, as some Marxists would so interpret them.[19] Productive work came to be located in the factory. Work increasingly became routine and offered little satisfaction to most workers. At first women and children were used by the factory system,[20] but increasing industrialisation brought unemployment and women were driven into dependence upon husbands. This outcome was not inevitable. It would be wrong to argue that capitalism requires the separation of home and workplace so that the relegation of women to the home and their exclusion from wage labour is an effect of it.

> A more historical approach . . . indicates that this situation developed in a long and uneven process, one element of which was the struggle between male and female workers in which the better-organised male

craft unions succeeded in over-riding the interests of women workers . . . So although the general tendency towards the separation of home and workplace has proved oppressive to women, this is because the problem so starkly posed – who was to be primarily responsible for childcare? – was resolved, according to an ideology of gender that pre-dated capitalism, in the interests of men.[21]

Women's work was increasingly restricted to looking after husband-workers and producing children.

Eli Zaretsky, in *Capitalism, the Family and Personal Life,* [22] has described how at the same time the family became idealised, as did the familial role of women, and the home became a refuge from the demands of capitalist society, 'a separate realm from the economy',[23] a private place to which people, but especially men, could withdraw. In Christopher Lasch's graphic phrase, the family became a 'haven in a heartless world'.[24] 'The family', Lasch has written, 'found ideological support and justification in the conception of domestic life as an emotional refuge in a cold and competitive society.'[25]

The family (the bourgeois family, that is) was thus exalted. A 'cult of domesticity'[26] or 'true womanhood' was engendered, according to Carl Degler,[27] by women themselves. It confined women to the home but at the same time made them moral arbiters of the family and of whatever else touched its interests. Degler shows how women turned the 'cult of domesticity' against itself and laid the foundation of modern feminism. He argues, following Kraditor[28] and Cott,[29] that demands for the recognition of married women's property rights, for divorce laws favourable to women, for sexual self-control on the part of men, for acknowledgment of the woman's greater stake in regulating pregnancy as well as for reforms in the larger social sphere, particularly in matters relating to social purity such as liquor traffic and prostitution, all arose from the logic of domesticity itself.

The connection between the 'cult of domesticity' and the quasi-emancipation of women has also been noted by Jacques Donzelot in *The Policing of Families*.[30] He argues that 'birth control and the "liberation" of women rested on women's old social vocation, on their function as ambassadresses of culture.'[31]

Controlling families

Donzelot also perceives what Degler would not appear to see: that women's role as cultural missionaries was to some extent the deliberate creation of doctors seeking to make wives and mothers agents of medical influence. The emotional intensification of family life had led to conflict. The nascent psychological sciences sought to explain this, to prevent it and, where that was impossible, to iron it out. As Lasch has argued: 'to be enlightened members of the professional classes – and this includes most feminists – knowledge of this kind promised a preventive science of sexual and social control, which could be used among other things to civilise the poor, to subject them to new controls sincerely disguised as benevolence, and thus to integrate them more fully into the emerging industrial order'.[32] Women saw the advantage of professional intervention in family life: it undercut patriarchal authority, though, of course, at the same time it helped erode the traditional prerogatives of women. Thus, as Ehrenreich and English[33] have also shown, women welcomed the substitution of doctors for midwives in childbirth.

The result was that professionals continually expanded their jurisdiction over family life. Patriarchal authority may have suffered, though the extent to which it did may be exaggerated. But so did the authority which women formerly had exercised themselves. It was, it was believed, all 'for their own good'. Lasch has surely put his finger on it when he claims that in 'allying themselves with the helping professions, women improved their position in the family only to fall into a new kind of dependence, the dependence of the consumer on the market and on the providers of expert services, not only for the satisfaction of her needs but for the very definition of her needs'.[34]

It is easy to see how society came gradually to be governed by doctors, psychiatrists, social workers, juvenile court personnel, criminologists, etc., in brief by the modern apparatus of resocialisation. The 'helping professions' during the first third of this century came to see themselves as doctors to a sick society. In early modern times, Philip Rieff[35] has observed, the church or cathedral stood as the symbolic centre of society; in the nineteenth century the legislative chamber replaced it and, in our time, the hospital has replaced this. The growth of the 'therapeutic state'[36] has had a profound effect on the family.

It is common to read of the family losing its functions in the twentieth century[37]. What is meant is that the family is ceasing to carry out tasks that have been associated with it since the rise of the bourgeois family. In reality it is not so much that the family has lost its functions, but rather that they have been taken over by society playing the nurturing mother. To socialisation of production, Lasch believes we should add, 'the socialisation of reproduction'[38]. This, he rightly claims, 'proletarianised parenthood, by making people unable to provide for their own needs without the supervision of trained experts'.[39] Some early proponents of rights for children[40] exemplified this approach. Thus, Jenkin Lloyd Jones argued that all children were children of the state: 'the state is but the coordinated parentage of childhood, yielding to the inexorable logic of civilisation that will compel co-partnership, co-operation, corporate life and conscience'.[41] The leading American feminist, Charlotte Perkins Gilman, expressed similar sentiments in a book published in 1903.[42] There are many examples of the philosophy in practice. The development of a system of compulsory education[43] is one example; the emergence of a system of juvenile justice is another.[44] Its emphasis was on child-saving.[45] Reformers argued that the juvenile court was to be a friend of the juvenile offender as well as a confederate of his family. Donzelot exposes this as 'pious representations . . . of reasons that are much less "democratic" '.[46] He sees intervention in the family as a 'depoliticising strategy'.[47] It was inspired by a fear of class conflict. It belonged to the general attempt to control the poor. It was the liberal state's answer to socialist propaganda. It aimed to convert political debates into administrative procedures. The language used may have been that of hygiene and health, but political considerations were never far below the surface.

Liberals (Donzelot shows in France, Lasch in the United States, but they refer to a process common in the Western world at the time) tried to steer a course between what they saw as the Scylla of conservative paternalism, which upheld the family as the foundation of the social order so that every change was seen as a threat to social integrity, and the Charybdis of socialism, which wanted to replace parenthood with the state. But 'in the end', Lasch notes, 'they outflanked their adversaries by creating a therapeutic state which left the family more or less intact yet subjected to nonstop supervision'.[48] This century has witnessed the 'triumph of the therapeutic'.[49] The liberal state is furnished with a system of indirect controls, which preserve the appearance, even some of the reality, of private initiative but encase it within an overarching structure of professional supervision. The therapeutic apparatus, in these terms, leaves the family 'always "justified" in theory and always suspect in practice'.[50]

The position of women today

The position of women in society today is closely related to their role within the family. An understanding of woman's oppression accordingly requires a description and analysis of the position of women in today's privatised family. As Mary McIntosh rightly has observed, 'ultimately the very construction of men and women as separate and opposed categories takes place within, and in terms of, the family'.[51] Women are expected to be dependent on men. Their role is geared to the household. They are responsible for child care, as well as for the care of the aged and handicapped. Their domestic labour is seen as non-productive, not real work.[52] Women, particularly married women, have to be housewives: if they do not carry out the service roles depicted here they are 'bad' housewives, but housewives nevertheless. Furthermore, as Kate Millett noted, 'sex role is sex rank'.[53] 'As long as woman's place is defined as separate, a male-dominated society will define her place as inferior'.[54]

In fact most women are also engaged in remunerative employment. For well over a century, women have constituted about a third of the formal labour force in Great Britain.[55] In 1980, for example, 39.4 per cent of those formally engaged in remunerative work were women.[56] In the period up to the Second World War the typical female worker was single and young. Since that time there have been large increases in the number of older married women who undertake paid employment outside the home. In 1977 50 per cent of married women did.[57] The Department of Employment projection for 1981 was 51.9 per cent.[58] Nearly 70 per cent of married women between 35 and 54 are working in remunerative employment. By 1991 the DOE has estimated that there will be over seven million married women in a labour force of 28.7 million people.[59] In fact that figure is an exaggeration of the true one because of the large increase in unemployment.

The Department of Employment[60] attributes the big increase in the number of women working to several factors: the declining birth rate (it fell by 25 per cent between 1971 and 1975); changes in attitudes among both men and women towards women's paid employment, in part the product of legislation such as the Equal Pay Act 1970 and Sex Discrimination Act 1975; a big increase in part-time employment opportunities (in 1975 there were four and a quarter million part-time workers, nearly one million more than in 1971, all but 700,000 of whom were women and 80 per cent of the women were married).[61] Forty-one per cent of women in paid employment work part-time.[62] Women workers are not dispersed throughout all sections of the economy, but are heavily concentrated in four occupational groups:[63] clerical workers; service, sports or recreational workers, mainly cooks, canteen assistants and office cleaners; professional and technical workers such as teachers and nurses; and shop assistants. It is noticeable that women are over-represented in work which resembles domestic work in the house: ideological divisions within the family are reproduced in the labour market. To Sally Alexander[64] this represents an extension of the division of labour of the patriarchal family. Nor is this new. Evidence from the early Victorian period indicates similar work patterns[65] and Alice Clark's *Working Life of Women in the Seventeenth Century* suggests that even when goods were being produced in the household there was a division of labour by gender.[66] Divisions of work tasks then antedate capitalism.[67] Capitalism is nevertheless a watershed for it divided the workforce into wage earners and those dependent upon the wage of others. In Michèle Barrett's words, 'capitalism did not create domestic labour, or the "feminine" areas of wage labour, but it did create a set of social relations in which pre-existing divisions were not only reproduced but solidified in different relations in the wage-labour system'.[68] Divisions of work tasks along gender lines also exist in countries such as the Soviet Union[69] and China,[70] which have undergone revolutionary transformations and which, even if not socialist, certainly have economic formations rather different from those in Western Europe.

Most women are employed on the labour market at some time. A study of women's employment in Britain conducted in 1965 revealed that only 2.4 per cent of women between 16 and 64 had never had paid work.[71] Women work after marriage, usually until shortly before the first child is born, and they are now returning to work more quickly than in the past. One reason for this is necessity. It has been estimated that in 1971 the number of poor two-parent families in Britain with fathers in full-time employment would have already nearly trebled if the father's earnings had not been supplemented by the mother's.[72]

Children are a major restraint on women's work patterns. Children of five and over are at school for some 199 days a year. But the school day is shorter than the normal working day. Alternative child care facilities are not well-organised. The majority of women who work part-time do so because of child care responsibilities. Some give up work altogether during the school holidays. Women's family responsibilities do not cease once their children have grown up. Apart from a continuing commitment to care for their husbands, middle-aged women may well acquire the responsibility of caring for a sick or elderly relative.[73] This too can have a detrimental effect on the employment opportunities of middle-aged women. In addition to children and elderly relatives, domestic responsibilities can affect the part women play in the labour market. These include not just household chores, for even with the growth of the so-called 'symmetrical family'[74] women do the bulk of these, but such matters as transporting children to and from school. Perhaps one-third of married women in Britain with children under 10 have the use of a car.[75] Men are more likely to drive to work. Their very mobility increases their job opportunities.

A lot of women still do paid employment in the home.[76] One estimate puts the number at a minimum of a quarter of a million.[77] Home workers are paid very low wages and usually work on a piece-rate basis. They are a marginal occupational group in relation to the wider economy, but the work they do may be all that is available for people who occupy a marginal position in the labour market. Many are young mothers with pre-school children; others are handicapped. Many homeworkers are members of ethnic minority groups.

As already noted, a high proportion of women in employment are part-time workers. It is still legal in Britain to pay part-time employees at a lower rate of remuneration than full-time employees, because wage rates are not one of the matters to which the Sex Discrimination Act 1975 applies. This is the province of the Equal Pay Act of 1970. This Act, however, only applies where men and women can be directly compared and can be said to be doing 'like work'.[78] But many women are found in occupations in which women predominate. The Employment Appeal Tribunal has upheld the payment of a lower hourly rate to part-time employees.[79] There is a great deal of evidence that women's domestic commitments are being used to prevent any lessening of differences between men's work and women's work. The TUC favours the retention of restrictions on night work for women.[80] So long as such restrictions remain, it is easy for employers to continue to pay their female work-force less. It would not be difficult to criticise the TUC, but it is not merely being patriarchal, nor does it wish to protect women's welfare. It is concerned with protecting male employment. Its attention is focused on a 'family wage'[81] for a male breadwinner, not equal pay for women workers.

Women workers are paid less. No matter how it is calculated there are considerable differentials between the pay of the two sexes. The gap is narrowest when average hourly pay is calculated. In 1976 women earned 75.1 per cent of what men earned, though by 1980 the proportion had slipped, despite the implementation of the Equal Pay Act in December 1975, to 73.5 per cent.[82] The gap is larger if gross weekly earnings are considered. In the public sector these were 65.4 per cent of men's pay in 1974, 72.1 per cent in 1976 and 69.3 per cent in 1980.[83] The discrepancy is greater in the private sector, where women's rates have never reached 60 per cent of male earnings: they were 57.8 per cent in 1980.[84] It is also greater as one goes down the occupational scale.[85] Furthermore, the gaps are increasing despite equal pay legislation.[86] Many employers have undertaken 'regrading' exercises to remove the possibility of comparison between male and female work. The courts have upheld such grading schemes. 'If it were to go forth that these grading schemes are inoperative and operate against the Equal Pay Act', said Lord Denning, MR, in *National Vulcan Engineering Insurance Group Ltd. v Wade* in 1978, 'it would be . . . disastrous for the ordinary running of efficient business'.[87]

One of the reasons why the gap between weekly rates is so much greater than that between hourly rates is that men work overtime and acquire bonuses for shift work and like duties.[88] This raises the issue of protective legislation, to which further attention is given later in this chapter.[89]

Women are not only subject to low pay. They are also more dispensable and are less likely to be unionised. They are accordingly less secure. Women are being made redundant at roughly three times the rate of men.[90] They are less likely to occupy senior grades or to be found in the higher professional occupations.[91] Since women are often not eligible for unemployment benefit, many who are out of work do not register, particularly in the United Kingdom. Actual statistics of female unemployment are, therefore, a gross underestimate. Nevertheless, the percentage of women among the registered unemployed is high and is increasing. In the United Kingdom it increased from 20.5 per cent in 1975 to 27.9 per cent in 1977. In West Germany the equivalent figures are 42 per cent and 49.8 per cent, and in Denmark 29.3 per cent and 42 per cent.[92] Between 1976 and 1977 female unemployment in the EEC increased by 15.4 per cent and male unemployment by 6.8 per cent.[93] Werneke attributes this in the main to the concentration of women's employment in a narrow range of jobs, often of an unskilled or semi-skilled nature.[94] A better indicator of female unemployment in the United Kingdom is the *General Household Survey,* since this gives information on those seeking work who are not registered as unemployed. From this Bruegel calculated an increase between 1974 and 1976 of 10 per cent for men and 28 per cent for women.[95]

In trying to understand the position that women occupy in the labour market as a secondary labour force,[96] it is difficult to avoid the conclusion that family structure and the ideology of domestic responsibility are significant factors. Michèle Barrett puts it this way:

> It is clear . . . that women's involvement in the highly exploited areas of part-time work and home-work is the direct consequence of their responsibility for child care. This type of work is not only most convenient for a worker with responsibility for children, it is often (in the absence of nursery or after-school provision) literally the only work available. In addition to this, the categories of work primarily undertaken by women have clearly been constructed along the lines of an ideology of gender which poses servicing and caring work as pre-eminently 'feminine'. Furthermore, the construction of a family form in which the male head of household is supposedly responsible for the financial support of a dependent wife and children has militated against demands for equal pay and equal 'right to work' for women. The 'right' of married women to take jobs at the expense of male workers has frequently been explicitly challenged . . . Family responsibilities play a direct role in the structure of women's wage labour and in setting limits on women's participation.[97]

But the process is not one-way. The weak position of women on the labour market has the effect of reinforcing their subordination in the home. The notion of the 'family wage' has as its concomitant female dependence. A privileged male wage has usually meant an underprivileged female one. Women's wages are generally seen as supplementary to those of husband wage earners, even by many women workers themselves.

The 'family wage' notion is usually justified in terms of the sexual division of labour. It is thus said to rest on a fair distribution of responsibilities between the sexes, to uphold complementarity of roles. But the sexual division of labour is, as Maxine Molyneux notes, 'more than a mere technical division in that it helps to enforce relations of domination and subordination creating structures of privilege and discrimination'.[98] Women are expected to perform household duties even when they are employed on the labour market. Most are poorly paid. These two considerations together act as a deterrent to women seeking remunerative employment and encourage them to seek fulfilment in the home. Female unemployment is also frequently justified by invoking the 'family wage' notion: it is important, wherever possible, it is argued, that the family income continues to be provided by its 'head'. An effect of this ideology is that women are not expected to enter the labour market but to become housewives and mothers, or at best part-time workers earning 'pin-money'. Both their formal and informal education and training tend to be oriented towards these skills and expectations.[99] This in its turn is reinforced by the sexual division of labour, which, as noted already, allocates women in the main to jobs designed to utilise their 'natural', 'feminine' capabilities.

The arrangement is one from which both men and the state benefit. A debate, which will not be pursued here,[100] has arisen as to whether, in Barrett's words, 'women are principally oppressed as *wives,* from which child-care and other domestic responsibilities follow, or as *mothers*'.[101] It must also be borne in mind that the confinement of women to the domestic setting may be beneficial in certain conditions and not others. Thus, in periods of rapid accumulation or severe labour shortage, as in war, it may be advantageous to socialise domestic labour so as to release women to work in industry. In this sense women have often been called a 'reserve army of labour'.[102] But merely to talk of them in these terms lacks explanatory value, for the question 'Why should *women* be seen in this light?' would still need to be posed. Further, if it is conceded that the domestic labour arrangement is one from which the state profits, some qualification of this is required, for it is clear that what may be true of the general interests of capital may not necessarily be true of specific capitals.[103]

Law and ideological practice

We have been talking of the state, but where does the legal system come in? This book is a treatment of family law. On the whole, family lawyers have tended to believe that the law does not play an active role in regulating family relationships. 'The normal behaviour of husband and wife or parents and children towards each other', wrote Sir Otto Kahn-Freund, a distinguished comparative family lawyer, 'is beyond the law – as long as the family is "healthy". The law comes in when things go wrong.'[104] In the same book John Eekelaar wrote of 'English practice', which, he said, 'has been to refrain from formulating general principles as to how families should be managed'.[105] Seven years later, he wrote, in *Family Law and Social Policy,* of the law's 'minor role in creating conditions which are hoped to be conducive to the successful creation of families'.[106]

This view distorts reality. It is clear, and we provide evidence here, that not only does the law serve to reproduce social order,[107] but it actually constitutes and defines that order. The law is a 'cultural underpinning'.[108] The legal form is one of the main forms of social practice through which actual relationships embodying sexual stratification have been expressed. Law defines the character and creates the institutions and social relationships within which the family operates. This is not to state that the legal system alone reproduces the ideology of the family. Other elements which play at least as important a role have been discussed earlier in this chapter. The evidence is, however, that the legal system is constantly recreating a particular ideological view of relationships between the sexes, best expressed as an ideology of patriarchalism.[109]

That law operates as a form of ideological practice is an idea found in the writings of Engels[110] and one which attained its fullest flowering in those of Antonio Gramsci[111] and, to a lesser extent, Louis Althusser.[112] Such a view has gained currency in the last decade largely through its propagation by the Warwick school of social historians, E.P. Thompson,[113] Douglas Hay[114] and others, as well as in the writings of critical legal theorists.[115] One of us has tried to take this approach in looking at domestic violence and the remedies constructed in an attempt to alleviate that problem.[116] It was there argued that legal structure and ideology implicitly supported wife battering, that all women were potential victims, and that the battle that had to be fought was not one to achieve superficial changes supportive of the overall ideology but was one to challenge the ideology itself.[117]

An excellent example of a study of law as ideological practice is Douglas Hay's account of criminal law processes in eighteenth-century rural England.[118] He is concerned with an apparent paradox. The century witnessed both an enormous expansion in the number of capital offences, particularly offences against property, but at the same time there was a weak and declining enforcement of the law, frequent acquittal of defendants on technical grounds, as well as frequent pardons or commutations of the death sentence. The gentry resisted advice that more attention be given to detection of crime and certain but graded sentences. Hay shows that this resistance, though seemingly irrational, is explicable if we appreciate that the social function of the criminal law was not the management of crime but the sustenance of the moral authority of the gentry and the creation of a complex and richly articulated system of social relationships of personal dependence that constitutes the structure of power. This 'allowed the class that passed one of the bloodiest penal codes in Europe to congratulate itself on its humanity . . . The law', Hay continues, 'was important as gross coercion; it was equally important as ideology. Its majesty, justice and mercy helped to create the spirit of consent and submission'.[119]

Hay sees the functions and strength of ideology as two-fold. First, 'its effectiveness lies . . . in its very elasticity, the fact that men are not required to make it a credo, that it seems to them the product of their own minds and their own experience'.[120] Secondly, its strength lies in its generality. 'Provided that its depths are not explored too often or by too many, it remains a reservoir of belief throughout society and flows into the gaps made by individual acts of protest'.[121] So, Hay adds, 'those using it are concerned above all with surface appearances'.[122] It is Hay's argument that the ideology of the law was crucial in 'sustaining the hegemony of the English ruling class'.[123] Just as the criminal law processes throw light on eighteenth-century English society, so a study of the relationship between the law and the family today gives us insight into contemporary patriarchalism.

Women, law and ideology

There are many justifications posited for treating men and women differently in law.[124] These may rest on sex differences but it is usually gender role differences that are called upon to justify differential treatment. But the law itself is a major instrumental force in constructing the gender role differences themselves. 'Legal institutions support the ordering of society on a gender role basis . . . The law defines and reinforces gender roles for individuals which do not necessarily have an inevitable connection with sex differences'.[125] Very few of the rights and duties of husband and wife, and still fewer of cohabitants, are laid down in legislation in Britain[126] (though in other countries there is a code detailing a normative relationship),[127] but there is a consensus among lawyers, judges and governmental bureaucrats about the nature of family relationships. Diana Leonard Barker comments that 'the lack of specification reflects the totality of the relationship . . . and that it is a relationship of *personal* dependency'.[128] 'Women cannot be at one and the same time married, as we understand marriage, and independent', Elizabeth Wilson observes, speaking of the cohabitation rule[129] as a particular instance of this 'general principle'.[130]

Women are supposed to be dependent and to lack power and control over themselves. Their domestic work, as already noted, is seen as non-productive. There are ideals to which a 'good wife'[131] must conform. Her status, her standard of living, her expectations, her life-style, her identity almost, are governed by her husband and, as we demonstrate in this book, even by her cohabitant as the law gradually assimilates the rights and obligations of quasi-marital relationships to those of marriage. Married women are not autonomous individuals, but are defined in legal institutions in terms of marriage.

There is no better illustration of this relationship, particularly since it demonstrates direct intrusion by the state apparatus, than in fiscal policies and social security arrangements.[132] These affect the economic dependence of women at every turn. Men and women are not treated equally by them. Both are stereotyped, and discrimination is a necessary concomitant of this, for a large number of women do not fit the female stereotype upon which such laws and other institutional arrangements are predicated.[133] Assumptions about the place of married women derive from economic and demographic concerns of the 1930s,[134] though they are rooted in an ideology which developed in the nineteenth century with industrialisation. The woman's place is in the home, and this cult of domesticity is supported throughout in the tax and social security systems.

The law in Britain relating to national insurance, pensions, supplementary benefit, sickness and unemployment benefit, family income supplement and income tax are all based on stereotypical sex classifications which impute a dependent role to women.[135] The system makes the assumption that women's earnings are supplementary to the male breadwinner, and women and children dependent on the man's income. The social security system strengthens the subordinate position of women as domestic workers inside the family and as a secondary labour force outside it. They are largely excluded from independent rights to benefits because they are assumed to be dependent on their husbands' incomes. Women who do not conform to the norm of dependence on men are often relegated to a low level of benefits. At the same time social security policies nurture the position of women as low-paid, casual or part-time workers, or even homeworkers with low pay and insecurity. Land and Parker have commented that 'in reading the social security legislation it would be hard to deduce that the "typical" family consisting of a man in full-time employment, the woman as a full-time housewife, and two dependent children has been at any point, a minority of families'.[136] In fact 10 percent of families conformed to this stereotype in 1971. It has been estimated that, in the same year, the number of poor two-parent families with fathers in full-time employment would have nearly trebled if the father's earnings had not been supplemented by the mother's.[137] Further, Louise Hamill has estimated that seven million working wives contribute on average 25 per cent of the family income.[138]

In fact a lot of women are not dependent on men. There are wage earners who do not need, and many widows, separated and divorced women and unmarried mothers who do not have a man to support them. But, as Ginsburg notes, 'support of these women by the state has been such as to encourage, if possible, the renewal of dependence on men and to discourage the break-up of marriage by rendering single motherhood less eligible and attractive.'[139] Unsupported women (that is those not barred by the cohabitation rule)[140] tend to fall back on supplementary benefit, but supplementary benefit authorities, and before them the poor law, have consistently attempted to shift the burden of support from the state (or parish) to 'liable relatives'. They have attempted to re-establish economic dependence on husbands and fathers. In fact the authorities have had little success. Thus, the cost to the state of providing benefits where there were 'liable relatives' was £345 million in 1977 and only £29 million of this sum was recovered from 'liable relatives'.[141] Not surprisingly, many women are not especially co-operative in helping the authorities to establish paternity or locate a separated husband. The invitation to re-establish dependence is quite properly rejected by many women. This is not entirely true, for when a marriage breaks up there are implicit pressures on a woman to remarry. Having been (if that is the case) a housewife for a number of years, a woman has decreasing value on the labour market. Thus, as Christine Delphy has noted,

> from the woman's standpoint, marriage creates the conditions for its own continuation and encourages entry into a second marriage if a particular union comes to an end . . . For the majority of women the contrast between the standard of living that they enjoy while married and that which they can expect after divorce simply redoubles the pressures in favour of marriage or remarriage depending on the circumstances.[142]

The roots of the social security system are embedded in the Beveridge report, published during the Second World War. Women are not treated equally in this. Man and wife were seen 'as a team'.[143] The married woman was to be treated as a dependant of her husband, and as entitled to economic support by him, both for herself and their children. Thus, it was argued that 'it should be open to any married woman to undertake [paid employment] as an exempt person, paying no contributions of her own and acquiring no claim to benefit in unemployment or sickness'.[144] Those who opted to contribute were to receive benefits at a reduced rate. For Beveridge, 'maternity [was] the principal object of marriage'[145] and his proposal that maternity benefit should be higher than normal unemployment or disability benefit (though, as Wilson says, 'reproduction was . . . tacitly defined as a disability')[146] was adopted by the legislature in 1948, though repealed in 1953. A number of Beveridge's reforms have succumbed to recent reforms. Women entering employment now have to pay full contributions and can receive full benefits. The new state pension scheme has introduced protected state pension rights for women: years of 'home responsibility' count as contribution years. There are new maternity rights for women, though these are mainly conditional on contributions, continuity and hours of employment, thus excluding the majority of mothers from them. But increasing formal recognition of equality can obscure discriminatory structures which continue to exist.[147]

For all the reforms, the social security system still embodies the concept of women's dependence on men and emphasises their maternal and domestic duties. Of the countless examples that remain, three will be illustrated.

Perhaps the most notorious principle of the social security system is the cohabitation rule. It has been described by Ginsburg as 'the implicit reinforcement of patriarchy within the social security system'.[148] The rule, which applies to a wide range of benefits, though criticism tends to centre on its application to supplementary benefits, where it is policed most stringently, states that where a husband and wife live together as members of the same household, their requirements and resources shall be aggregated and treated as the husband's. Only he then may claim the relevant benefit. Though this is susceptible to criticism, it is the extension of the rule to men and women who 'live together as a man and wife' that has provoked most censure.[149] What is meant by 'cohabitation' is not defined in statute or case law.[150] A number of considerations are taken into account in considering whether a man and a woman are living together as man and wife, though more than a lurking suspicion remains that the primary consideration in the minds of officials and investigators is a sexual relationship between the couple. The now defunct Supplementary Benefits Commission itself admitted that 'in the last resort, it is a matter of personal judgment'.[151]

The cohabitation rule is symptomatic of the ideology structuring family relationships, for it makes the assumption that if a man lives with a woman, he supports her. The rule is often justified on the basis that an unmarried couple should not get more favourable treatment than a married man and his wife would.[152] This is in many ways a bootstrap argument, for it assumes and does not question that marriage should contain a breadwinner and a dependent. In this sense the removal of the cohabitation rule would reveal starkly the dependence and inequality inherent in the marriage relationship. This aside, the way the rule operates, a married woman is treated 'more favourably' than her cohabitating sister.

The rule puts women, who are often in tenuous personal and economic circumstances, into a position where it is difficult for them to establish stable relationships with men. It subjects them to widespread invasions of privacy from those policing the system. It is also thoroughly anomalous. A man has no obligation to maintain a woman with whom he is living even if he has fathered children by her,[153] though he may be compelled to support any such children through affillation payments.[154] In other words, a cohabiting woman has no legal means of compelling support. On the other hand, a married man gets a tax allowance for his wife, irrespective of whether there are dependent children: a man receives no tax allowance for the woman with whom he cohabits. Whilst the cohabitation rule succours the institution of marriage (in itself a strange moral argument), it undoubtedly also reinforces the ideology of dependence which so permeates the legal system and its administration.

A second disturbing example of the partiality of the social security system is the way in which family income supplement (FIS) operates. This is a means-tested benefit which heads of families in employment may claim so long as their income does not come above a certain level.[155] It is graded to take account of the number of children in the family. A woman who is a lone parent may claim FIS provided she works twenty-four hours a week. Indeed, a high percentage of FIS claimants are single mothers.[156] Otherwise only men may claim this benefit. This means that in a family where the man stays at home and the woman works, the couple will not qualify for FIS. This refusal to accept women as economic supporters is to be expected from a system which categorises them as dependants. Where a couple are living together, only the man may claim FIS and he can claim it only if he is in full-time work (defined for these purposes as thirty hours a week). The discriminatory rule has now been recognised as such by Parliament and will change in November 1983.[157]

A third example of arrangements which embody notions of dependence is to be found in several statutory provisions governing tax and social security. As already indicated, a married man gets a tax allowance for his wife. It is assumed that a wife 'or some female person' should care for a man's children and do his housework. An additional personal allowance is paid where wives are incapacitated.[158] But married women with incapacitated husbands are denied this additional allowance. As Katherine O'Donovan has noted:

> The allowance reflects the assumption that it is a married woman's unpaid job to care for children and that if she cannot do so, her husband is entitled to financial assistance for someone else to perform the job. In contrast, a woman on her own, even if working, is not considered by the courts as in need of an allowance for a substitute childminder.[159]

There are similar examples in other social security provisions. The invalid care allowance is not paid to married women. This can only be because they are expected to do such work without compensation. Where additions for adult dependants are given to those who get the allowance, these are limited to a wife or 'some female person . . . who . . . has care of a child or children of the beneficiary's family':[160] in other words, a male dependant with care of children is excluded. It is also notable, though perfectly consistent with a system which emphasises women's domestic duties, that a disabled married woman is not eligible for the non-contributory invalidity pension 'except where she is incapable of performing normal household duties'.[161] This test has been described as an 'unjust and illogical anachronism'.[162] The assumption behind the 'household duties' test is that a married woman is by definition a 'housewife', who is dependent on her breadwinner husband for financial support and whose contribution to the family is the unpaid work she does in the home. Indeed, the 1974 White Paper[163] which first proposed a non-contributory invalidity pension for married women says as much. The retention of the 'normal household duties' test is virtually impossible to defend but it limps on.[164] It remains one of the most stereotypical sexist of social security provisions.

These examples illustrate the way in which fiscal policies and social security arrangements impose a particular structural form, patriarchy,[165] on social relationships between men and women. The writings of Albie Sachs, discussing the reasoning used by the judiciary in the nineteenth and early twentieth centuries to deny women rights to participate in the professions and in public affairs, demonstrate the use of a strikingly similar ideology. For sixty years the judiciary strongly denied that women were 'persons'. They even accepted the absurd argument that 'women were "persons" for the purpose of legal disabilities but "non-persons" for the purposes of legal rights'.[166] A change came in 1929.[167] Sachs suggests that there is no explanation of the change in terms of judicial reasoning, in 'legal logic'.[168] He and Joan Hoff Wilson argue that 'a study of sexism in the legal systems of Britain and the United States . . . explodes the notion that legal systems evolve according to inherent principles of logic and procedure'. They continue:

> . . . the structures of the law were part of the wider social structures rather than apart from them. The inequality in public life which the women complained about was as present inside the legal system as outside of it, while the stake which the male judges had in maintaining gender exclusiveness was in some ways more direct than any interest they might have had in maintaining race or class inequality.[169]

They show how it was the prevailing concept of 'womanhood' that determined how the courts would decide the arguments. The judges put forward a theory of sexual complementarity, but Sachs and Wilson argue that this was 'merely a gracious way of explaining female subjection'.[170] The judges couched their language, their justifying reasoning, in terms of refinement, decorum and delicacy. They stressed that women were not being deprived so much as exempted. The exemption was said to be based on respect. The clearest statement of this is Willes J's judgment in *Chorlton v Lings*.[171] 'Far from being impartial arbiters', Pearson and Sachs argue, '. . . the Judges appear to have been part of the very problem the women and their male supporters were complaining about . . . The judges believed in the principle of gender exclusiveness, and said as much, both on and off the Bench.'[172]

The bias in the 'persons' cases which glares at us today was just as clearly impartial justice to the judges and the majority of society 100 years ago. 'What was self-evident truth to feminists, however, was manifest absurdity to most judges.'[173] How, then, is this particular change to be explained? Sachs argues that 'what had altered was the "ideology" of the judges'.[174] It is not necessary here to examine why this had altered. But what the history of the male monopoly cases puts beyond question is the way that judicial reasoning both reflected dominant male interests and reinforced patriarchalism.

Not that it is unusual for judicial modes of reasoning to define issues in terms favourable to dominant groups. There can be few better examples of this than Lord Denning MR's reasoning in the leading case of *Wachtel v Wachtel* in 1973.[175] Earlier, extra-curially, Lord Denning had warned of the dangers of women being given equality. He had pointed to what he saw as the Roman example.[176] In *Wachtel* Lord Denning MR defended the resuscitation[177] of the 'one-third rule' as a starting-point for the reallocation of assets on divorce in this way:

> When a marriage breaks up, there will thenceforward be two households instead of one. The husband will have to go out to work all day and must get some woman to look after the house – either a wife, if he re-marries, or a housekeeper, if he does not. He will also have to provide maintenance for the children. The wife will not usually have so much expense. She may go out to work herself, but she will not usually employ a housekeeper. She will do most of the housework herself, perhaps with some help. In any case, when there are two households, the greater expense will, in most cases, fall on the husband than the wife.[178]

Of course, this reasoning is totally unrealistic. Most men whose marriages founder do not employ housekeepers, and, even if this argument were relevant, it would not explain why wives are not allowed the value of their housekeeping services. The fact that a wife will not employ a housekeeper hardly seems a justification for cutting down on her share. Lord Denning's reasoning makes a number of assumptions, and none of them are right. The first is that all women perform household duties and that no men do housework, and the second is that only fathers maintain their children. Mothers who do not take remunerative employment do so in kind rather than in cash. Indeed, they often forgo paid employment and lose promotion to do so. The third assumption is that housework is not real work. Lord Denning MR is the most influential of contemporary English judges. He thinks, and so do many of the public, that his decisions are some form of 'wives' charter'.[179] It is as well to remind ourselves of E.P. Thompson's insight that 'the dominated and oppressed have often perceived their grievances in legal terms and articulated their needs and interests in terms of rights thought to be promised or owed by law'. In fact, he adds rather wryly, 'some of them had the impertinence, and the imperfect sense of historical perspective, to expect justice'.[180] Thompson is making the point, expressed throughout this section, that if law is to be effective in its function as ideology it must appear to be just. Indeed, he notes that this cannot be the case where it does not uphold 'its own logic and criteria of equity; indeed, on occasion, by actually *being* just'.[181]

Lord Denning's reasoning in *Wachtel* was not just, though other parts of his judgment dealing with a woman's contribution to the welfare of the family and his comments on the effect of adultery on financial provision are instances of actual justice, in Thompson's terms. Lord Denning MR's reasoning otherwise is an apt example of what has been called 'repressive benevolence'.[182] There have been a number of reforms in the recent past. For example, the duty to maintain is now mutual.[183] But this, like many other changes, remains only formal until women are given substantial equality. Even today, so long as they are living together, the law refuses to intervene in a married couple's financial relationship. It supports the notion that the husband sets the standard of living.[184] The wife, in other words, may be a dependant, but the legal system shows marked reluctance to afford her economic protection during marriage. Conditions of domestic production remain outside the purview of the law.

A limited exception is the rule contained in the Married Women's Property Act 1964 [185] that money derived from an allowance given to the wife by the husband or anything bought with that allowance is shared equally by the spouses. The Act only applies if the housekeeping allowance is provided by the husband. Cases have indicated that if the wife gives money to her husband for use in the home, she is deemed to give it to him as the head of the family, so that the money becomes his.[186] It is doubtful, to say the least, that the courts would take such a view today, though the cases remain interesting for their ideological assumptions. But it is not only the gender assumption of the 1964 Act which invites critical comment. It is also significant that the Act, despite these assumptions, does nothing to compel a husband to make his wife any allowance. It concentrates instead on penalising a thrifty wife by compelling her to share half what she saves, or buys with what she saves, with her husband. In past times women managed the domestic economy.[187] The allowance system itself is thus a relatively recent innovation, and the 1964 Act now enshrines it.

Many more examples could be given to illustrate the point. More significant is the fact that in England today (and English law is not untypical) there is but one type of marriage. Its nature is not negotiable. Rights and obligations are fixed by operation of the law, not by agreement between the parties. Lenore Weitzman has, with considerable justification, described the conception of a single structure for all marriages as 'tyrannical'.[188] We view with some alarm the increasing tendency to treat cohabitation as if it were marriage. It seems that many who avoid marriage because of its ideological notions of subordination and dependence find the consequences attaching to marriage thrust on them whether they like it or not, almost as if, as one critic notes, women were being told that they were not allowed to escape by cohabiting.[189] The extension to relationships outside marriage of 'marriage-type' law merely reinforces the outmoded views discussed in this section and transfers their application to settings where they are even less appropriate.

Protective legislation

However, it is common to find arguments which support such an extension based on the idea that such an assimilation will protect cohabitants,[190] especially female cohabitants. We here examine the ideological assumptions underlying protection.

Annika Snare and Tove Stang-Dahl see talk of the law as a protector of women's integrity as a myth. Referring to the state's role, they use the suggestive phrase the 'coercion of privacy'.[191] They see the family as a private prison for women. The state, they argue, need not use formal methods of repression and control when women are constrained by a more primary and informal control within the family. The relegation of women to the private sector, documented in Snare and Stang-Dahl's article, is significant also as it becomes an alternative to granting women greater public rights. Albie Sachs, whose exposure of the myth of male protectiveness has already been referred to, draws attention to this idea in his discussion of the Married Women's Property Act of 1882. This allowed married women to retain control over their own property. Sachs argues convincingly that:

the law went some way towards protecting wives from being abused inside the home; it did not create opportunities for them to be useful outside the home. A curb on spending by husbands was not the same as a licence to earn independently by wives. Thus the destiny of woman as wife rather than as independent person was enhanced rather than reduced by the Act.[192]

The question whether the law protects or controls women must be raised. An obvious comparison are the measures which purported to protect children, such as the invention of the juvenile court[193] and intelligence testing.[194] Just as child-saving has often been a cloak to control a 'problem population',[195] so it seems legislation to protect women may also be.

In their rather different ways the Victorian conservative judge Sir James Fitzjames Stephen and the American actress Mae West understood the meaning of protection. To Stephen 'submission and protection' were 'correlative'. Withdraw the one', he argued in *Liberty, Equality, Fraternity* (a polemical attack on Mill), 'and the other is lost, and force will assert itself a hundred times more harshly through the law of contract than ever it did through the law of status'.[196] Mae West noted that 'every man I meet wants to protect me. Can't figure out what from'.[197] Jalna Hanmer has shown how violence or its threat is used to control women both within and outside the home. Women, for example, are taught to avoid certain areas. 'Urban space for women is compartmentalised, to deviate from women's allotted space is to run the risk of attack by men.'[198] The fear of violence, particularly rape, has the effect of driving women to seek protection from men, of making them dependent. There is a certain irony here, for women are supposed to feel safer in the company of husbands and boy friends, though the evidence suggests that they are more likely to be attacked or raped by them than by the dangerous strangers whom they are taught to fear.[199] 'Chivalry', Susan Griffin has noted, 'is an age-old protection racket which depends for its existence on rape.'[200] She equates it with the sort of relationship the Mafia established with small businessmen in the United States earlier in this century.

The problematic nature of protection is strongly to the fore in legislation regulating employment conditions of women (and children), which is usually called 'protective legislation'. Whom does this legislation protect? It was introduced in the nineteenth century 'reform era', not in all areas of work but rather, it has been argued,[201] in areas where there was competition with male workers. Angela Coyle has called protective legislation a 'protection racket'. It did not

> bring women equal pay, it did not bring equality and it has not provided adequate protection at work . . . The very existence of

legislation serves as a recognition of . . . inequality . . . The problem with the current legislation is that it does not genuinely 'protect' women but rather operates paternalistically to reinforce women's conditions of inequality.[202]

Protective legislation may now be repealed, but why was it passed (and when challenged in the United States upheld as constitutional)?

On the face of it, limiting the hours of female labour was not in the immediate interests of capital. But it was of concern that if women were worked too hard they would be unable to produce the next generation of workers. 'No individual firm would benefit from stopping the exploitation of female labour, but the state under pressure from the "Ten Hours" movement, as well as from elements of the bourgeoisie, was able to restrict hours of work, especially for women and children.'[203] The state, in other words, as the 'ideal collectivity of capitals',[204] had to concede limitations on hours of work to ensure the reproduction of labour power.

Another interpretation of the origin of protective legislation, which is sometimes posed as an alternative view and sometimes a supplementary one, stresses that such legislation was supportive of the interests of male workers. It suggests that working men were fearful that women would infiltrate industry, taking men's jobs (women being cheaper and more pliable) and causing lower rates of pay for all. Not only would this be a disaster in terms of men's position within commodity production but it would also liberate women from dependence on men and obliterate gender labour divisions in the home. Heidi Hartmann argues that women and children in the labour force 'undermined authority relations'. She continues:

Not only were women 'cheap competition' but working women were their very wives, who could not 'serve two masters' . . . While the problem of cheap competition could have been solved by organising the wage-earning women and youths, the problem of disrupted family life could not be. Men reserved union protection for men and argued for protective labour laws for women and children.[205]

On the other hand, as Jane Humphries shows in her study of the 1842 Mines Regulations Act,[206] which she agrees may be an atypical instance, hewers neither individually nor collectively feared competition from female labour and many had an interest in the retention of female and child labour underground as it increased their family's income. Despite this 'male colliers almost universally wanted state intervention to regulate the labour of women and children, and the overwhelming majority of hewers believed that women should be prohibited from working below ground'.[207] She also shows that the other strand in the Hartmann 'patriarchy first'[208] approach, which emphasises patriarchal privileges in having wives at home, is inconsistent with the realities of collier life. 'Existing theorisations', she concludes, 'have proven inadequate to the understanding of an important historical example.'[209] Her conclusions are rather negative, though she draws attention to the contradiction between the exploitation of women workers and the sex role standards prevailing among the bourgeoisie, 'themselves conditions of existence of the *sexual* oppression of women within that class'.[210] Insofar as this might suggest that the legislation supports the transformation of working-class family structure to something like that found in the bourgeoisie, it reinforces a view presented earlier in this chapter.[211]

That this discussion should end inconclusively does not matter greatly. What it has demonstrated is just how problematic protective legislation is. It may be that a multi-dimensional explanation is called for. It may be that different historical examples will stress different features. There seems little doubt, however, that the primary motivating force in protective legislation was not to protect women's welfare.

In the United States similar legislation was challenged as to its constitutionality. In *Lochner v New York* (1905),[212] legislation limiting hours for male bakers had been held to violate constitutional rights of personal liberty and liberty of contract. But in *Muller v Oregon* (1908),[213] the Supreme Court, fortified by the famous Brandeis Brief, held that similar legislation designed for the protection of women 'may be sustained, even when like legislation is not necessary for men and could not be sustained'. In Joan Hoff Wilson's words: 'women have continued to experience economic discrimination because the Supreme Court presumed to establish policy on the basis of quasi-scientific data and its own "common knowledge" about the nature of women'.[214] What appeared as a great improvement ended up clearly as a mixed blessing. The *Muller* decision was welcomed at the time, not least by feminists, some of whom were driven into a state of complacency, convinced that activism was unnecessary as the courts would take care of their needs. In retrospect it was a most retrogressive decision.

Protective employment legislation is likely to disappear quite soon. In 1979 the British Equal Opportunities Commission submitted a report to the government proposing the removal of much of it controlling the conditions of work for women, though retaining it for young people. It argues:

> that the hours of work legislation constitutes a barrier – often an artificial one – to equal pay and job opportunities for women. So long as this legislation remains as it is at present, women as

workers will be disadvantaged. Therefore we cannot accept the retention of legislation in its present form, because discrimination will continue to arise out of it.[215]

Unfortunately, much that is problematic is not questioned by the EOC. For example, their report 'poses the question of shift work as a *choice* for women to make, rather than recognising the economic circumstances which *force* people into the night shift'.[216] There is a strong case for making work conditions equal by extending protective legislation to male workers, but that is hardly likely.

Protective legislation, including the debate surrounding its history and present uses, presents in sharp perspective some of the issues that arise in the protection of women. We insist that these must be explored. Protection of women (and children for that matter) is a problematic notion and one too often taken for granted.

Notes

1 One deviant society were the Nayars. See K. Gough, 'The Nayars and the Definition of Marriage', *Journal of the Royal Anthropological Institute,* 89 (1959), pp. 23–34.

2 *Per* E. Leach, 'Ourselves and others' (3rd Reith Lecture), *The Listener,* 30 October 1967, p. 695.

3 Emphasised by R. Fletcher in *The Family and Marriage in Britain,* Penguin (3rd ed., 1973), p. 138.

4 *Post,* p. 16.

5 On the importance of autonomy see *post,* p. 206.

6 *Per* M. Barrett, *The Opression of Women,* Verso, 1980, p. 199.

7 Published in French in 1976 and translated into English and published by Cambridge U.P., 1979.

8 *Idem,* p. 4.

9 *Idem,* p. 9. The definition is Littré's.

10 A point also made by R. Fletcher, *op. cit.,* note 3.

11 See further L. Berkner, *Journal of Marriage and the Family* 35 (1973), pp. 395–405.

12 *Critical Theory of the Family,* Pluto Press, 1978, p. 167.

13 In French, that is. The entry is attributed to the Chevalier de Jaucourt.

14 *Op. cit.,* note 7, pp. 6–7.

15 *Op. cit.,* note 6, p. 203.

16 See R. Fletcher, *op. cit.,* note 3, p. 100.

17 *Op. cit.,* note 12, p. 196.

18 Cf. Barrett, *op. cit.,* note 6, at p. 203.

19 For example, Eli Zaretsky, *Capitalism, the family and personal Life,* Harper Colophon Books, 1976.

20 See E.P. Thompson, *The Making of the English Working Class,* V. Gollancz, 1963.

21 *Op. cit.,* note 6, p. 165. See also H. Hartmann, 'Capitalism, Patriarchy and Job Segregation by Sex', *Signs I* (1976), pp. 137–70; also in M. Blaxall and B. Reagan (eds), *Women and the Workplace,* 1976.

22 See also Ann Foreman, *Femininity as Alienation,* Pluto Press, 1977.

23 *Op. cit.,* note 19, p. 30.

24 *Haven in a Heartless World,* Basic Books, 1977, p. 6.

25 *Idem.*

26 The phrase was coined by Aileen Kraditor, *Up From the Pedestal: Selected Writings in the History of American Feminism,* Quadrangle, 1968.

27 *At Odds: Women and the Family in America from the Revolution to the Present,* Oxford U.P. 1980. But see now W. Leach, *True Love and Perfect Union: The Feminist Reform of Sex and Society,* Routledge and Kegan Paul, 1981.

28 A.S. Kraditor, *The Ideas of the Women's Suffrage Movement,* Columbia U.P., 1965.

29 Nancy F. Cott, *The Bonds of Womanhood,* Yale U.P., 1977.

30 Pantheon, 1979.

31 *Idem,* p. 221.

32 'Life in the Therapeutic State', *The New York Review of Books,* XXVII, no. 16 (12 June 1980), pp. 24–32, at p. 27.

33 *For Her Own Good,* Pluto Press, 1979.

34 *Op. cit.,* note 32.

35 *Freud: The Mind of a Moralist,* Gollancz, 1960, p. 390.

36 On which see N. Kittrie, *The Right to be Different,* Penguin, Baltimore, 1971.

37 See, for example, the recent article by Muriel Nissel, 'The Family and the Welfare State', *New Society,* 53, no. 925 (7 August 1980), p. 259; cf. R. Fletcher *op. cit.,* note 3, ch. 5.

38 *Op. cit.,* note 24, p. 19.

39 *Idem.*

40 See, further, M.D.A. Freeman, 'The Rights of Children in the International Year of the Child', *Current Legal Problems,* 33 (1980), pp. 1–31.

41 Quoted in Robert M. Mennel, *Thorns and Thistles: Juvenile Delinquents in the United States 1825–1940,* Univ. Press of New England for the University of New Hampshire, 1973, p. 130.

42 *The Home: its Work and Influence,* McClure Phillips, 1903, p. 165.

43 See F. Musgrove, *Family, Education and Society,* Routledge and Kegan Paul, 1966, and as regards the United States, S. Bowles and H. Gintis, *Schooling in Capitalist America,* Routledge and Kegan Paul, 1976.

44 See E. Ryerson, *The Best Laid Plans,* Hill and Wang, 1978.

45 As to which see A. Platt, *The Child Savers,* University of Chicago Press (2nd ed.), 1977.

46 *Op. cit.,* note 30, p. 100.

47 *Idem,* p. 89.

48 *Op. cit.,* note 32, p. 30.

49 The phrase is Philip Rieff's. See *The Triumph of the Therapeutic: Uses of Faith after Freud,* Penguin Books, 1966.

50 *Op. cit.,* note 32, p. 30.

51 'The Welfare State and the Needs of the Dependent Family', in S. Burman (ed.), *Fit Work for Women,* Croom Helm, 1979, pp. 153–72, at p. 154.

52 A myth effectively demolished by Christine Delphy, *The Main Enemy,* Women's Research and Resources Centre Publications, 1977.

53 *Sexual Politics,* Hart Davis, 1969, p. 343.

54 *Per* Barbara A. Brown *et al.,* 'The Equal Rights Amendment: A Constitutional Basis for Equal Rights for Women', *Yale Law Journal,* 80 (1971), pp. 871–985, at p. 873.

55 See, generally, H. Land, 'Social Policies and the Family: Their Effect on Women's Paid Employment in Great Britain', in R.S. Ratner (ed.), *Equal Employment Policy for Women,* Temple University Press, 1980, pp. 366–80.

56 Equal Opportunities Commission, 5th Annual Report, 1980, p. 60 and Figure 2 (p. 61).

57 Department of Employment, *Gazette* 85, no. 6 (June 1977), p. 590.

58 *Idem.*

59 Department of Employment, *Gazette* 86, no. 4 (April 1978), Table 2 (p. 427).

60 *Op. cit.,* note 57.

61 *Social Trends,* no. 9, HMSO, 1979, Table 5.6 (p. 86).

62 *Idem.*

63 Department of Employment, *New Earnings Policy Survey 1975,* 1980, Part E, Table 135.

64 'Women's Work in Nineteenth-Century London: a Study of the Years 1820–50', in J. Mitchell and A. Oakley (eds), *The Rights and Wrongs of Women,* Penguin, 1976, pp. 59–111.

65 See I. Pinchbeck, *Women Workers and the Industrial Revolution 1750–1850,* Cass, 1977. See Appendix on occupations of women in 1841.

66 *Working Life of Women in the Seventeenth Century,* G. Routledge, 1919.
67 See M. Barrett, *op. cit.,* note 5, p. 121.
68 *Op. cit.,* note 6, p. 182.
69 See A. Heitlinger, *Women and State Socialism: Sex Inequality in the Soviet Union and Czechoslovakia,* Macmillan, 1979.
70 See E. Croll, *Feminism and Socialism in China,* Routledge and Kegan Paul, 1978.
71 See A. Hunt, *A Survey of Women's Unemployment* (OPCS), HMSO, 1968.
72 DHSS, *Two Parent Families and their Needs,* HMSO, 1971, p. 14.
73 See A. Hunt, *The Home Help Service in England and Wales* (OPCS), HMSO, 1970, p. 424.
74 The term is M. Young and P. Willmott's. See *The Symmetrical Family,* Routledge and Kegan Paul, 1973.
75 See M. Hillman *et al., Transport Realities and Planning Policy,* PEP, 1976. The survey was conducted in South-East England. In other parts of the country the percentage will be lower.
76 See E. Hope *et al.,* 'Homeworkers in North London', in D.L. Barker and S. Allen (eds), *Dependence and Exploitation in Work and Marriage,* Longman, 1976, pp. 88–108.
77 See M. Brown, *Sweated Labour,* Low Pay Unit, 1974.
78 S. 1(4). Nor is it prohibited by Art. 119 of the Rome Treaty 'unless it is in reality an indirect way of reducing the pay of part-time workers on the ground that that group of workers is composed exclusively or predominantly of women', *per* European Court in *Jenkins v Kingsgate (Clothing Productions) Ltd.* [1981], 2 C.M.L.R. 24, 42.
79 See *Handley v H. Mono Ltd.* [1979], I.C.R. 147 (EAT).
80 *The Guardian* (5 September 1979).
81 See H. Land, 'The Family Wage', *Feminist Review,* 6 (1980), pp. 55–77.
82 See Equal Opportunities Commission, 5th Annual Report 1980, 1981, p. 70 (Table 4.2).
83 *Idem,* Table 4.1.
84 *Idem.*
85 *Idem,* Table 4.5.
86 *Idem,* Table 4.2.
87 [1978] I.C.R. 800(CA). See also M. Snell, 'The Equal Pay and Sex Discrimination Acts: Their Impact in the Workplace', *Feminist Review,* 1 (1979).
88 See *op. cit.,* note 64, Part A, Tables 10 and 11. When overtime is included, women earn 64.8 per cent of men's earnings. This has changed only marginally since the Equal Pay Act. It was 64.3 per cent in 1976.
89 *Post,* p. 34.
90 On female unemployment, see Department of Employment, *Gazette* 89, no. 2 (February 1981), Table 2.7.
91 See L. Mackie and P. Pattullo, *Women at Work,* Tavistock, 1977, ch. 4.
92 Figures in V. Novarra, *Women's Work, Men's Work,* M. Boyars, 1980, p. 93 – based on OECD and Eurostat data.
93 *Idem.*
94 'The Economic Slowdown and Women's Employment Opportunities', *International Labour Review,* 117, no. 1 (Jan–Feb. 1978).
95 'Women as a Reserve Army of Labour: A Note on Recent British Experience', *Feminist Review,* 3 (1979), pp. 12–23, at p. 21.
96 The classic exposition of which is R. Barron and G. Norris, 'Sexual Divisions and the Dual Labour Market', in D.L. Barker and S. Allen (eds), *op. cit.,* note 76, pp. 47–69.
97 *Op. cit.,* note 6, pp. 157–8.
98 'Beyond the Domestic Labour Debate', *New Left Review,* 116 (1979), pp. 3–27, at p. 24.
99 See M. David, *The State, the Family and Education,* Routledge and Kegan Paul, 1980. See also A.M. Wolfe, *Some Processes in Sexist Education,* Women's Research and Resources Centre Publications, 1977.
100 See W. Secombe, 'The Housewife and her Labour Under Capitalism', *New Left Review,* 83 (1974), pp. 3–31.
101 *Op. cit.,* note 6, p. 175.
102 See H. Braverman, Labor and Monopoly Capital, *Monthly Review Press,* 1974; and I. Bruegel, *op. cit.,* note 95.
103 See J. Holloway and S. Picciotto, *State and Capital: A Marxist Debate,* Arnold, 1978.
104 Editorial foreword to J. Eekelaar, *Family Security and Family Breakdown,* Penguin, 1971, p. 7.

105 *Idem,* p. 76.
106 Weidenfeld and Nicolson, 1978, p. xxvii.
107 It does not always do this. See S. Diamond, 'The Rule of Law Versus the Order of Custom', *Social Research,* 38 (1971), pp. 42–72.
108 *Per* K. Klare, 'Law-Making as Praxis', *Telos* (1979), pp. 123–35, at p. 129.
109 See also P. Alcock, 'Ideology in Family Law', Paper at British Sociological Association Annual Conference 1979, Warwick University.
110 *Juristic Socialism,* in Marx and Engels on *Religion.*
111 *Prison Notebooks,* Lawrence and Wishart, 1971.
112 'Ideology and Ideological State Apparatuses', in *Lenin and Philosophy and Other Essays',* NLB, 1971, pp. 123–73.
113 *Whigs and Hunters,* Allen Lane, 1975, particularly pp. 258–69.
114 Particularly 'Property, Authority and the Criminal Law', in D. Hay (ed.), *Albion's Fatal Tree,* Allen Lane, 1975, pp. 17–64.
115 For example, Klare, *op. cit.,* note 108; A. Fraser, 'The Legal Theory We Need Now', *Socialist Review,* 40–41 (1978), pp. 147–187.
116 M.D.A. Freeman, 'Violence Against Women: Does the Legal System Provide Solutions or Itself Constitute the Problem?', *British Journal of Law and Society,* 7 (1980), pp. 215–41.
117 See also R. and R. Dobash, 'Love, Honor and Obey: Institutional Ideologies and the Struggle for Battered Women', *Contemporary Crises,* 1 (1977), pp. 403–15.
118 *Op. cit.,* note 114.
119 *Idem,* p. 49.
120 *Idem,* p. 55.
121 *Idem.* See also S. Burman, 'Symbolic Dimensions of Law Enforcement', *British Journal of Law and Society,* 3 (1976), pp. 204–217.
122 *Idem.*
123 *Idem,* p. 56.
124 Discussed in E. Wolgast, *Equality and the Rights of Women,* Cornell University Press, 1980. See also J. Feinberg, 'Noncomparative Justice', *Philosophical Review,* 83 (1974), pp. 297–338.
125 *Per* K. O'Donovan, 'The Male Appendage – Legal Definitions of Women', in S. Burman (ed.), *Fit Work for Women,* Croom Helm, 1979, pp. 134–52, at p. 135.
126 This may have led Kahn-Freund and Eekelaar to make the comments referred to at notes 104–6.
127 Switzerland is one such example.
128 In 'The Regulation of Marriage: Repressive Benevolence', in G. Littlejohn *et al.* (eds), *Power and the State,* Croom Helm, 1978, pp. 239–66, at p. 242.
129 See *post,* p. 29 and 74.
130 In *Women and the Welfare State,* Tavistock, 1977, p. 153.
131 See *Re L* [1950], 2 All E.R. 784; cf. *Le Marchant v Le Marchant* [1977], 3 All E.R. 610, where Ormrod LJ says he cannot understand why the expression 'loyal, faithful and good wife' has 'crept into the standard form of pleading' (p. 612).
132 See, generally, R. Lister and E. Wilson, *The Unequal Breadwinner,* NCCL, 1976, and E. Wilson, *Women and the Welfare State,* Tavistock, 1977.
133 See Barbara A. Brown *et al.,* 'The Equal Rights Amendment: A Constitutional Basis for Equal Rights for Women', *Yale Law Journal,* 80 (1971), pp. 871–985, at pp. 873–4.
134 See 'Women: Supporters or Supported?', in D.L. Barker and S. Allen (eds), *Sexual Divisions and Society: Process and Change,* Tavistock, 1976, pp. 108–32.
135 An instructive 'case' illustration is reported by Jones, 'What Do You Do if the DHSS says You're Dependent and You Aren't', in *The Guardian* (22 September 1980).
136 'United Kingdom', in S.B. Kamerman and A.J. Kahn (eds), *Family Policy,* Columbia U.P., 1978, pp. 331–66, at p. 342. See also H. Land, 'Who Cares for the Family?', *Journal of Social Policy,* 7 (1978).
137 DHSS, *Two Parent Families and Their Needs,* HMSO, 1971, p. 14.
138 *Wives as Sole and Joint Breadwinners,* Govt. Economic Service Working Paper, no. 15 (1978). See, further, M. McNay and C. Pond, *Low Pay and Family Poverty,* Study Commission on the Family, 1980.
139 *Class, Capital and Social Policy,* Macmillan, 1979, p. 79.

140 See *post,* p. 29 and 74.

141 Supplementary Benefits Commission Annual Report, 1978, Table 12.7.

142 'Continuities and Discontinuities in Marriage and Divorce', in D.L. Barker and S. Allen (eds), *Sexual Divisions and Society: Process and Change,* Tavistock, 1976, pp. 76–89, at p. 81.

143 *Social Insurance and Allied Services,* Cmd 6406, p. 45.

144 *Idem,* p. 50.

145 *Idem.*

146 *Op. cit.,* note 130, p. 151.

147 See A. Snare and T. Stang-Dahl, 'The Coercion of Privacy: A Feminist Perspective', in C. and B. Smart (eds), *Women, Sexuality and Social Control,* Routledge and Kegan Paul, 1978, pp. 8–26, at p. 14.

148 *Op. cit.,* note 139, p. 87.

149 See, for example, R. Lister, *As Man and Wife,* Child Poverty Action Group, 1970.

150 See *ante,* p. 11 note 6.

151 DHSS, *Cohabitation,* HMSO, 1971, para. 14.

152 *Idem,* para. 15.

153 There are some systems of law in the Commonwealth which impose an obligation in such circumstances. For example, the New Zealand Domestic Proceedings Act 1968, s. 53. See, further, Eekelaar, *op. cit.,* note 106, pp. 205–12.

154 See Affiliation Proceedings Act 1957, as amended by Affiliation Proceedings (Amendment) Act 1972 and Domestic Proceedings and Magistrates' Courts Act 1978.

155 See Family Income Supplement Act 1970, a good discussion of which is provided by A. Ogus and E. Barendt, *The Law of Social Security,* Butterworths, 1978, ch. 13.

156 Social Security Statistics 1976, Table 32.10.

157 See Social Security Act 1980, s.7, and P. Healy, 'A Small, Slow Blow against Sexual Discrimination', *The Times* (6 March 1980).

158 Income and Corporation Taxes Act 1970, s.12.

159 *Op. cit.,* note 125, pp. 145–6.

160 See Social Security Act 1975, s.37(3).

161 See Social Security Act 1975, s.36(2).

162 See C. Glendinning, *After Working All These Years,* The Disability Alliance, 1980, p.13.

163 *Social Security Provision for Chronically Sick and Disabled People,* House of Commons Paper 276, HMSO, 1974.

164 See I. Loach and R. Lister, *Second Class Disabled,* Equal Rights for Disabled Women's Campaign, 1978.

165 As to which see J. Edwards and P. Kluck, 'Patriarchy: the Last Universal', *Journal of Family Issues,* 1 (1980), pp. 317–37.

166 'The Myth of Judicial Neutrality: the Male Monopoly Cases', in P. Carlen (ed.), *The Sociology of Law,* Sociological Review Monograph, University of Keele, 1976, pp. 104–33, at p. 107.

167 In *Edwards v Attorney-General for Canada* [1930], A.C. 124, a Privy Council decision, discussed in A. Sachs and J.H. Wilson, *Sexism and the Law,* Martin Robertson, 1978, pp. 38–40.

168 *Op. cit.,* note 166, p. 114.

169 *Sexism and the Law,* Martin Robertson, 1978, p. 225.

170 *Idem,* p. 52. See also A. Sachs, 'The Myth of Male Protectiveness and the Legal Subordination of Women', in C. and B. Smart, *Women, Sexuality and Social Control,* Routledge and Kegan Paul, 1978, pp. 28–34.

171 The 'Manchester Voters' Case' reported at (1868–1869) L.R. 4 C.P. 374.

172 'Barristers and Gentlemen: A Critical Look at Sexism in the Legal Profession', *Modern Law Review,* 43 (1980), pp. 400–14, at p. 401.

173 *Op. cit.,* note 169, p. 6.

174 *Op. cit.,* note 166, p. 108.

175 [1973] Fam. 72.

176 *The Equality of Women,* Eleanor Rathbone Memorial Lecture, Liverpool. Liverpool University Press, 1960, p. 15.

177 As to which see S. Maidment, 'Financial Provision and the One-Third Rule', *Family Law,* 4 (1974), pp. 172–81.

178 *Op. cit.,* note 175, p. 94.

179 Lord Denning, *The Due Process of Law,* Butterworths, 1980.
180 *Whigs and Hunters,* Allen Lane, 1975, p. 268.
181 *Idem,* p. 263.
182 *Per* D.L. Barker, *op. cit.,* note 128. See also C. Smart, *Int. J. of Soc. of Law* 129–147 (1982). (1982).
183 Domestic Proceedings and Magistrates' Courts Act 1978, s.1.
184 The best example of this is *McGuire v McGuire* (1953), 59 N.W. 2d 336. See further, J. Pahl, 'Patterns of Money Management', *Journal of Social Policy,* 9 (1980), pp. 313–35.
185 s.1.
186 *Edward v Cheyne* (No. 2) (1888), 13 App. Cas. 385 and *Re Young* (1913), 29 T.L.R. 319 (where that presumption was rebutted on its facts).
187 L.A. Tilly and J.W. Scott, *Women, Work and Family,* Holt, Linehart and Winston, 1978.
188 'Legal Regulation of Marriage: Tradition and Change', *California Law Rev.,* 62 (1974), pp. 1169–288, at p. 1170.
189 Namely Diana Leonard Barker in *op. cit.,* note 125, at p. 261.
190 For example, D. Oliver, 'The Mistress in Law', *Current Legal Problems,* 31 (1978), pp. 81–107; D. Pearl, 'The Legal Implications of a Relationship Outside Marriage', *Cambridge Law Journal,* 37 (1978), pp. 252–69; and J. Eekelaar, *Family Law and Social Policy, op. cit.,* note 106.
191 'The Coercion of Privacy: a Feminist Perspective', in C. and B. Smart (eds), *Women, Sexuality and Social Control,* Routledge and Kegan Paul, 1978, pp. 8–26.
192 *Op. cit.,* note 166, p. 137.
193 See A. Platt, *The Child Savers,* University of Chicago Press, 1969, for a classic exposition.
194 See J. Mercer, 'A Policy Statement on Assessment Procedures and the Rights of Children', *Harvard Educational Review* (1974) (Reprint Series No. 9), pp. 328–44.
195 *Per* S. Spitzer, 'Toward a Marxian Theory of Deviance', *Social Problems,* 22 (1975), pp. 638–51, at p. 642.
196 Smith, Elder, 1873, p. 286.
197 Quoted in Susan Griffin, 'Rape: the All-American Crime', Ramparts (1971).
198 'Violence and the Social Control of Women', in G. Littlejohn *et al.* (eds), *Power and the State,* Croom Helm, 1978, pp. 217–38, at p. 228.
199 See M. Amir, *Patterns in Forcible Rape,* University of Chicago Press, 1971. cf. L. Clark and D. Lewis, *Rape: The Price of Coercive Sexuality,* Women's Press, Toronto, 1977, p. 71.
200 'Rape: the All-American Crime', Ramparts (1971), reprinted in S. Griffin, *Rape: The Power of Consciousness,* Harper and Row, 1979, ch. 1.
201 For example, by Sally Alexander *op. cit.,* note 64.
202 'The Protection Racket?', *Feminist Review,* 4 (1980), pp. 1–12, at p. 10.
203 *Per* M. McIntosh, 'The State and the Oppression of Women', in A. Kuhn and A.M. Wolfe, *Feminism and Materialism,* Routledge and Kegan Paul, 1978, pp. 254–89, at p. 262.
204 *Per* J. Rubery, 'Structured Labour Markets, Worker Organisation and Low Pay', *Cambridge Journal of Economics,* 2 (1978), pp. 17–36.
205 'The Unhappy Marriage of Marxism and Feminism: Towards a More Progressive Union', *Capital and Class,* 8 (1980), pp. 1–33, at pp. 15–16.
206 'Protective Legislation, the Capitalist State and Working Class Men: The Case of the 1842 Mines Regulation Act', *Feminist Review,* 7 (1981), pp. 1–33.
207 *Op. cit.,* note 206, p. 15.
208 Cf. H. Hartmann and A.R. Markusen, 'Contemporary Marxist Theory and Practice: A Feminist Critique', *Review of Radical Political Economics* 12, (1980).
209 *Op. cit.,* note 206, p. 28.
210 *Op. cit.,* note 206, p. 28.
211 *Ante,* p. 16.
212 198 U.S. 45.
213 208 U.S. 412.
214 *Op. cit.,* note 169, p. 116.
215 Equal Opportunities Commission, *Report on Health and Safety Legislation: Should We Distinguish Between Men and Women,* HMSO 1979, p. 92.
216 *Op. cit.,* note 202, p. 7, quoting A. Coote, 'Equality: A Conflict of Interest', *New Statesman,* 31 August 1979, pp. 8–9.

3 The Path to Cohabitation

Writing in 1971, Margaret Mead described American society as 'terribly overmarried'. Americans had, she thought, 'over-depended on marriage . . . vastly overdone it'.[1] Her comments were apposite and fitted more than just American society. But change was already in the air and now, ten years later, with cohabitation only one of many alternative life-styles firmly established, her remarks take on a new significance. A decade of rapid social change demands, if it rarely gets, appropriate legal responses. The charge has been made that family law in Western society is 'limited to a narrow conceptualisation of monogamous marriage and the nuclear family as the only models for intimacy'.[2] The development of alternative life-styles poses a number of questions. When will the state accept the right of participants to engage in alternatives to marriage free from hindrance and discrimination? What is the form and basis of such a recognition to be? To what extent will recognition of alternative life-styles cause radical restructuring of family law? These are questions we try to answer in this book.

Different approaches to cohabitation

As yet the courts and legislatures have demonstrated no consistent policy in tackling cohabitation. In England, we have been told,[3] no significant amount of legislative time will be devoted to dealing with the legal problems of cohabitation in the near future. We would argue for the adoption of a clear, consistent policy. There is currently, however, no consensus as to what that policy should be. Some argue[4] that it should be rooted in the principle of according cohabitants legal rights and responsibilities equivalent to those possessed by married couples. Others argue for differential treatment.[5] This has the merit of respecting the decision of the parties not to marry.[6] This approach postulates the treatment of parties as if they were individuals who had entered into a business relationship. It invites solutions to their problems, based on contractual,[7] partnership[8] or trust[8] models. It rejects reliance on a status model. Each of the two approaches reflects a particular ideology.[10] Each in its turn may have momentous consequences for the family as a whole. The development of an equivalence approach could herald a renewed public law response to the legal problems of all families, with greater intrusion by the state into the family. The adoption of a differential approach could encourage a move towards contract and autonomy within marriage as well, thus stimulating a private law response.

There is also a view which sets its face against any recognition of the legal position of cohabitants, on the ground that such recognition would undermine the traditional family and lead to the disintegration of society. Riga, for example, doubts whether cohabitation has the 'staying power of the traditional marital and sexual love', which, he says, has 'served mankind well in the past'.[11] Swedish evidence suggests that the move to cohabitation outside marriage is not a temporary phenomenon.[12] Clark argues ostrich-like against the law being concerned in the problems of cohabitants in any way, claiming that a status-based recognition of cohabitation would lead to a blurring of distinctions and confusion as to the defining characteristics of marriage. He bemoans the erosion of the importance of marriage. 'Whatever the social reality', he argues, 'it may still be efficient and not inequitable to retain conventional marriage as the criteria for property rights and duties.'[13] Clark begs more questions than he purports to answer. His argument that the property rights of cohabitants should not be regulated at all is impossible to support. In part Clark's problem is his over-concentration on the issue of the assimilation of marriage and cohabitation with, concomitantly, little detailed consideration of alternative approaches.

The arguments for equivalent and differential treatment of marriage and cohabitation are considered fully in chapters 6 and 7. In the remainder of this chapter we consider why cohabitation has emerged or re-emerged as an alternative to marriage.

The decline of marriage

Part of the importance of marriage in past times has been linked to property. Marriage has always been of greater significance for the propertied classes than for the others.[14] The need for an established body of rules to provide for the orderly and certain transmission of property on death necessitated the creation of a status like the traditional legitimate family.[15] This could be attained only upon marriage. Property considerations intruded in a wider sense as well.

The wife was seen as a valuable piece of property, not just amongst the wealthy. Her value was not limited to her dowry. For the farming and skilled artisan classes her value lay in her productive labour, as well as in producing children and running a household.[16] As Alice Clark states: 'men did not at this time regard marriage as necessarily involving the assumption of a serious economic burden but on the contrary often considered it to be a step which was likely to strengthen them in life's battles'.[17] As indicated in chapter 2, industrialisation profoundly affected family life, particularly the lives of women. Women became dependent on men, and a cult of domesticity was engendered. In this century women's dependence on men, even where it did not accord with social reality, has been an established fact and a mainspring for social policy.

After the Second World War the romantic ideal of marriage was cultivated further. It was part of the 'feminine mystique',[18] nurtured by the media and more particularly by commercial advertising. Theories like Bowlby's on maternal deprivation[19] and writings on child care by 'progressive' authorities such as Winnicott[20] and Spock[21] reinforced the happy family image, 'the cereal packet' norm, with marriage and child-rearing as the ultimate goals and fulfilment for women. Until well into the 1960s marriage and raising a family continued to occupy a central position in women's lives. Indeed, with the introduction in that decade or shortly thereafter of easier divorce,[22] dependence on the husband for economic support was further reinforced by the maintenance provisions attached to the divorce laws.[23] In the 1970s the divorce rate rose dramatically[24] in line with increasingly high expectations of the marriage relationship.[25]

Divorce has proved to have problems barely articulated when the new wave of divorce laws was passed. It has led to 'serial polygamy', which as Glendon has remarked, 'is practised by many people who cannot finance it'.[26] Women, formerly dependent on husbands, find their ex-husbands cannot support them and their children as well as a new wife and any children of that union.[27] They are forced either to fall back on state support or to be responsible for their own welfare. As suggested in an earlier chapter,[28] the incentive to resume dependence, either by remarriage or cohabitation, is great. Marriage then no longer carries at best any guarantee of permanence or at worst any guarantee of economic support after breakdown.

Another factor which has contributed to the decline in marriage from its former position of pre-eminence has been the changing position of women.

The Women's Movement

In part the improving position of women in society has been responsible for the current crisis in marriage. Hacker encapsulates this point well when he says 'the institution we call marriage can't hold two full human beings – it was only designed for one and a half'.[29] The growth of individualism has affected women's views of themselves and fostered the growth of the Women's Movement. The Women's Movement encouraged women to achieve economic, social and sexual independence and to believe in their own separate identity. Feminists have questioned the social roles allocated to women and by doing so have rendered problematic traditional concepts of womanhood, femininity and sexuality. Women's liberation has also been linked, as Elizabeth Wilson has noted, 'with reassessments of sexuality and the meaning for women of their sexual experiences'.[30] Where the state was slow to allow women to capitalise on the advances offered by scientific and technological breakthroughs, the Women's Movement was vocal in its clamour for change. The right to contraception, abortion, to freedom from discrimination and sexual harassment, to equal pay, maternity benefits, and other social security provision, have all figured prominently in Women's Movement campaigns. One effect was that many women, particularly those of marriageable age, no longer saw marriage and the family as the chief focus of their attention or satisfaction.[31]

Some commentators[32] have sought to link the Women's Movement, particularly its stress on employment for women, with the declining success of marriage. Ross and Sawhill[33] in 1975 indicated, in America, that the likelihood of divorce was directly related to the level of the wife's participation in the labour market. Further, the higher a wife's income from employment, the more likely it was that the marriage would fail. This is further borne out by Huber and Spitze's recent study[34] which postulates that husbands' and wives' thinking about divorce increased proportionately with the level of the wife's work experience. Although one interpretation of these studies is that by working the wife puts greater strain on her marriage, and another suggests that she has sought employment in preparation for divorce,[35] the most convincing interpretation is that she wants employment for what it can offer her.

A recent survey, published in the United States, found that a high prestige job, and not marriage or motherhood, correlated most closely with a woman's sense of self-esteem.[36] In two other studies[37] the importance of women's independence and their equality with men have also been strongly emphasised. Both have seen independence 'to be a strong value for women's mental health'.[38] It is also a common assumption that the discovery of female sexuality is in part responsible for increased marital fragility. But changes in sexual behaviour began before the development of women's new consciousness and occurred independently of it. As Sandra Coyner has noted: 'women's liberation has seemed to coincide with a wave of breakups and divorces which probably antedates the movement and may even have contributed to the need for it'.[39] She believes that 'the new relationship established by sexually liberated people'[40] may last longer. What cannot be in doubt, however, is that traditional limits on female sexuality have reinforced monogamy.[41] In this sense, cohabitation, like celibacy,[42] autoeroticism,[43] bisexuality[44] and lesbianism,[45] are in part responses to women's discovery of their own sexuality, a rejection of unequal, male-oriented sexual experience. Women who want sexuality under their own control, who want self-determination, may reject the institution of marriage, which has traditionally been linked with male domination in the sexual sphere, as in others.[46]

The high expectations of marriage

The marriage relationship has been built up steadily in the past century and a half into something which looks almost inevitably doomed to ultimate failure. The problem is that for many the reality is so very different from the ideal portrayed by the media and popular fiction. These also indicate, however, that if these high expectations are not fulfilled, escape through divorce is a legitimate, wise and even an emotionally mature response. This has led to a feeling amongst some that it would be better to avoid marriage in the first place. Such disillusionment is graphically captured in the following:

> Contemporary marriage is a wretched institution. It spells the end of voluntary affection, of love freely given and joyously received. Beautiful romances are transmitted into dull marriages; eventually the relationship becomes constricting, corrosive, grinding and destructive. The beautiful love affair becomes a bitter contract.[47]

Perhaps a more realistic view at the outset of marriage would reduce the level of disillusionment. The advice proffered anonymously to young people some 100 years ago may be apposite even today: 'better to enter the marriage state in the frame of mind of that company of American settlers who in naming their new town called it Dictionary "because", as they said, "that's the only place where peace, prosperity and happiness are always to be found" '.[48]

If the current level of disillusionment with marriage is as high as the rising divorce rates and the trend towards cohabitation seem to suggest, why is it that so many people, having failed once, try again or even again and again? One commentator[49] has in fact urged that remarriage is the more complete institution and, if the statistics are to be believed, a large number of people have a similar faith in such an idea. Certainly, the statistics in both the USA[50] and England[51] reveal a more or less steady fall in first marriages, though this has now halted,[52] and a dramatic increase in the proportion of marriages where one or both has been previously married. In England between 1971 and 1979 the proportion of such marriages increased from 10 to 21 per cent.[53] There has, in addition, been a particularly marked increase in the number of marriages in which both partners have previously been married. In 1979 such remarriages accounted for nearly one in six of all marriages contracted in England and Wales, a slight decline from 1978.[54] Furthermore, the statistics on divorce reveal an increasing proportion of divorces occurring among couples who had been previously married and divorced; in 1979 over 16 per cent of divorces occurred in marriages where one or both partners had been married before.[55]

Some may be depressed by these statistics. Others may wonder why we are so dependent on marriage. Why cannot a large section of the population think of any other way in which to live except in matrimony as couples? The answer probably lies in a compound of economic considerations and romantic dreams, marriage and the family still offering a 'haven in a heartless world'. For women, left with children to look after, the economic incentive to remarry may be high. The statistics for 1978 for England and Wales[56] show that women with children are equally as likely to remarry as women without, more especially if they were under 40 at the time of the divorce, and the youngest child under 10, which may seem surprising, given that the new husband can inherit all sorts of problems. Why are men so willing to shoulder the burdens marriage entails? Jesse Bernard, in discussing this, refers to the 'ball and chain' jokes frequently made by men and comments: 'once men have known marriage they can hardly live without it . . . Indeed it might not be too farfetched to conclude that the verbal assaults on marriage indulged in by men are a kind of compensatory reaction to their dependence on it'.[57] There is considerable force in this argument.

For many people who have once been married, life without marriage is impossible. For other groups, such as young people, the never married the divorced but not remarried, marriage is not the only way in which they can think of living as couples. To what extent has the current disillusionment within marriage fostered the trend towards cohabitation, and has this trend been further encouraged by the ambivalence or even at times neutrality of social and state institutions towards this life-style? It would certainly appear from the statistics[58] that an increasing number of young people are resisting the urge to marry as soon as possible, while at the same time enjoying many of the advantages which such a relationship is supposed to give. In addition, the proposed[59] and actual[60] changes in the law relating to illegitimacy, liberal divorce laws, the extended support apparatus of the welfare state and the consumer nature of the society in which we live, have contributed to the diminution in the importance of marriage. An increasing number of young people have been victims of the present rather painful divorce process,[61] and for many of them the experience of their parents' marriage may be a vital factor affecting their future choice of life-style.[62]

State and social institutions may also influence people's attitudes to new life-styles. In Sweden, for example, it has been argued,[63] the drafters of the social security legislation have effectively discouraged marriage. English and American courts have also, as we show,[64] somewhat haphazardly developed a considerable body of cohabitation law, a development mirrored in many other societies, so that living together may not seem as precarious as it once did. The Church, once powerful enough to exert irresistible pressures to marry, has now in many Western societies lost its position of influence. Religious pressures to marry are, therefore, unlikely to be experienced by many young people; indeed, religious convictions are unlikely to be the reason why the majority who marry in church do so. In fact more than half (51 per cent of marriages in England in 1979) were solemnised with a civil ceremony. In 1966 the corresponding figure was 33 per cent.[65]

With the weakening of legal constraint, and the waning of religious influence, little is left of any social pressure to marry. Indeed, arguably, it is precisely social pressure which has achieved the discarding of religious considerations and the relaxation of the law. What is beyond doubt, however, is that there has been a drift away from marriage. It has declined in importance and popularity.

The reasons for the growth in cohabitation

We have thus far discussed the reasons for the declining status and popularity of marriage which could be characterised as negative factors rather than as factors positively encouraging the trend towards cohabitation.

We must now look more closely at the reasons why people choose to cohabit rather than to marry. No full-scale research has been conducted to answer this question and no definitive answer can, therefore, be given.

The trend can be analysed as the result of a number of responses to a variety of different factors. Thus, it could in part be due to a rejection of the traditional marriage contract which state-regulated marriage seems to impose (the ideological response);[66] or due to some legal impediment to marriage (the 'law avoidance' response);[67] or due to a rejection of the financial responsibilities imposed by state-regulated marriage, or an acceptance of the financial advantages arising from cohabitation (the financial response);[68] or more simply it could in large part be due to a desire to postpone the assumption of the roles, rights and duties incidental to legal marriage (the postponement response).[69] The last response category could probably be further broken down into the 'trial marriage response'[70] and the 'pre-marital experience response'.[71] It would be wrong to see any one of these responses as chiefly contributing to the growth in cohabitation; the likelihood is that the increase is due to the operation of all of them and others as well. These are, in our view, the important ones, to which greater attention should be devoted.

The ideological response

One important factor is promoting the trend towards the more informal life-style would certainly appear to be the rejection of the traditional marriage contract and the assumption of the roles which necessarily seem to go with it. Thus, Weitzman has commented that

> the state imposed marriage contract assumes a limited, sex based traditional family form: the union of a single man and woman who commit themselves to each other for life. The psychological tyranny in this model is that it allows no individual choice in the degree of commitment and involvement in a relationship. Yet in our rapidly changing society not all people want the same degree of intensity in their personal relationships: some want it in individual relationships at specific times but not necessarily in a marriage relationship at all times.[72]

Traditional legal marriage imposes inequalities on the parties, whereas cohabitation is freer, more flexible and more equal.[73] Extra care should therefore be taken by those who urge greater legal recognition for cohabitation that those same inequalities are not similarly imposed upon cohabitants.

We have seen how in the past certain roles have been ascribed to the parties to the marriage contract; thus, in nineteenth and twentieth century capitalist societies the husband as breadwinner has generally exchanged his financial support for his wife's services as housewife, mother and companion. Even in 1962 a court could say in *Rucci v Rucci:*

> A wife has a duty to be a helpmate, to love and care for him in such a role, to afford him her society and her person, to protect and care for him in sickness and to labour faithfully to advance his interests. Likewise she must perform her household and domestic duties without compensation therefor. A husband is entitled to the benefit of his wife's industry and economy.[74]

The wife's household services are now recognised and upon the breakdown of the marriage she will generally receive compensation in respect of them,[75] although some may deplore such a development. Recent cases on cohabitation claims in both the USA and in England have surprisingly revealed a tendency on the part of the courts to ascribe similar roles to cohabitants. This move, which we deplore, may be viewed as an attempt to reinforce women's traditional position of dependence upon men, as well as an infringement of the cohabitant's right to reject any of the usual consequences of legal marriage. The danger in such a development is, as Deech comments, that 'cohabitation will be made as expensive and legalistic as marriage and therefore no more attractive'.[76]

Despite the quite fundamental changes in marriage patterns which have occurred as the result of the economic activity rates of women, there appears to be little chance of any radical restructuring by legislative enactment of the anachronistic view of marriage currently enshrined in the traditional marriage contract. Indeed, quite the opposite view seems to be at work in the policy statements of those in power in both England[77] and the USA.[78] It should come as no surprise that an increasing number of men and women are currently experimenting with periods of cohabitation, since this does not demand conformity by either of the parties to sexual or social stereotypes. Even where cohabitation is essentially a trial marriage, education out of the usual roles can take place without the parties being trapped in the bonds of marriage should the experiment fail. But cohabitants must be warned that danger lurks for them in the courtroom, where those selfsame stereotypes, roles and obligations may be imposed with or without their consent.[79]

Another factor promoting the ideological response is, as Weiss detects,[80] that there seems to be a greater mutual considerateness when a couple are living together than when they are married. The quality of the relationship is improved. Indeed, the reasons why people are living together in the USA seem to have much to do with what Trost terms 'these ideological motives'. As one young American woman, quoted by Thorman put it:

> I have seen so many young couples who were very happy when they were just living together. Then they decided to get married, and after that things really got to be a drag. I don't know why. Maybe it's because when you are just living together it isn't a duty kind of relationship. You feel free to be yourself and you really try harder to keep the relationship a good experience for both of you. I think if Bill and I were married we would take each other for granted.[81]

Trost,[82] studying Swedish society, identifies a variety of such ideological motives influencing the growth in cohabitation: that people want to be free and independent; that those without religious convictions feel no pressure to marry; that people have political reasons for rejecting marriage; that many feel that love is strong enough without marriage; and that the partners in such a cohabiting relationship are more careful to keep the 'syndyasmos'[83] intact than when they are married. That the general quality of the relationship is much better also seems to be the experience of other European couples, as evidenced by a 1975 study conducted in member countries of the European Economic Community.[84] The conclusion to be drawn is surely that cohabitation may be more attractive than marriage because both parties are concerned to make the relationship work. They are apparently prepared to assume responsibilities on a more equal basis than they would do in marriage, where traditional socialised attitudes create the expectations of a certain role-playing.[85] Trost's work certainly seems to support this view,[86] although there are one or two surveys from the USA which suggest that role-playing in cohabitation is taking on a form similar to that in ordinary marriage.[87] Generally speaking, however, the trend to cohabiting relationships does seem to favour a distinctly more open approach.[88]

The law avoidance response

The existence of some legal or legal-religious impediment to marriage is another reason why people cohabit rather than marry. Legal impediments include the fact that one of the partners remains married to another possibly against his or her will; that divorce is impossible or a lengthy delay inevitable. In England, where one of the spouses deserts the other and goes to live with someone else, it could be five years before the deserter could petition for divorce if the deserted spouse refuses to agree to an earlier petition. Similarly in Denmark, Pedersen estimates that a sizeable number of those cohabiting outside marriage are actually awaiting the opportunity which divorce will give them legally to formalise their informal relationship.[89] Other legal impediments may be the strict rules prohibiting marriage between those related by blood or marriage. As debates in the British House of Lords have shown in late 1980 and in 1981, couples barred from marriage by the affinity rules are often desperate to have their relationship legalised by marriage.[90] Interestingly enough, even in Sweden, where cohabitation is as respectable and as accepted as marriage, the King was recently petitioned to give a special dispensation allowing marriage between a half-brother and sister, where they had lived together and had had children of their relationship.[91] There may also be impediments under religious laws which are for the groups concerned just as much a barrier to marriage. In Israel, for example, this would seem to constitute the main reason why people live together outside marriage.[92] In many other countries impediments under religious laws will only concern a very few. Where religion and law overlap very closely and the established religion takes a particular view of marriage, this also may encourage large numbers of informal unions. Thus, in Roman Catholic countries when divorce was impossible, as it still is in some, the number of persons cohabiting was thought to be quite high.[93]

The financial response

Past experience of divorce may encourage people to cohabit, where they discover that the whole process of divorce was not only emotionally destructive but financially draining. Very often emotions run deepest over financial and property arrangements. It is almost as if these proceedings are used to punish the other spouse. Joseph Epstein's *Divorced in America*[94] recounts the feelings of bitterness experienced by many men who find themselves ordered to pay alimony to their wives, and the financial difficulties in which many find themselves if such orders prove to be high. In England, the *Campaign for Justice in Divorce*, a group consisting largely of men, objects vehemently to the awards of maintenance which husbands are ordered to pay in respect of their ex-wives.[95] But, if such considerations have encouraged people to cohabit, rather than to try marriage again, they should be warned that cohabitation may also attract the adjustive jurisdiction of the courts upon 'splitting'. Indeed, Weitzman[96] notes that the Berkeley Co-Operative in California now offers a course in preventive legal care for couples in 'living-together' arrangements, so that they may learn how to avoid the unwanted effects of the present law.

Other financial questions are influential in encouraging the trend towards cohabitation amongst certain segments of the population. Sundberg[97] and Trost[98] point out that in Sweden tax and social security legislation has tended to benefit cohabitants rather than the legally married. In England, too, there are some advantages to be gained by certain people living together without marriage.[99] For those in the USA, however, although the high cost of divorce is probably a major factor encouraging cohabitation, the general trend in the tax and social security system has been to favour marriage and punish more unconventional life-styles.[100]

The postponement response

Financial considerations may also be relevant when considering the postponement of marriage. Thus, cohabitation in the short term as an alternative to marriage may be a better arrangement for young 'dual-career' couples. Rapoport and Rapoport have reached the conclusion that 'young couples contemplating marriage today may decide to live together but not get married until both have established themselves in their chosen occupations',[101] although Kay[102] has argued that there are all sorts of problems posed for the 'dual-career' marriage. While both partners are attempting to establish themselves in their occupations, the more open and less stereotyped character of cohabitation may make it a more attractive proposition, with the option to convert to marriage at a more convenient time, or these selfsame attractive characteristics may encourage cohabitation as a permanent alternative to marriage for the 'dual-career' couple. The opportunity to accumulate the capital assets with which to start a marriage, while not experiencing any external pressures to start a family, may also be a factor encouraging cohabitation and the postponement of marriage. This may be especially the case in England, since it seems that ownership of a home and possession of certain material goods apparently figure very largely in the Englishwoman's conception of what constitutes the basis of a good marriage.[103]

We indicated that this response category could be further broken down into the trial marriage response, which we have discussed, and the pre-marital sexual experience response. Trost[104] identifies the former as one of the most significant of responses in Sweden. Newcomb[105] suggests that many of the studies in the USA show that the majority of cohabitants do not intend to marry and do not eventually marry each other. While it is the case that those surveys of cohabitants which have been carried out, principally in the USA, have for the most part concentrated on college students,[106] they reveal interesting characteristics about people who cohabit.

Macklin states[107] that American cohabitants normally share certain characteristics, although, as she says, the surveys from which such conclusions are drawn are based on college samples whose members frequently come from the middle classes. Thus, cohabitants tend to perceive themselves as more androgynous, to hold more liberal attitudes and to have lower rates of religious affiliation. They are not, however, more likely to come from unhappy or divorced homes, to perform less well academically, to be less interested in eventual marriage or have lower personal adjustment scores.

A small-scale British survey in Reading in the early 1970s, when cohabitation was still thought to be rare, found that cohabitation was largely a social class I and II affair.[108] The French survey of 1977 carried out by the demographic institute INED found that there were a disproportionate number of the wealthier and better educated young adults among cohabiting couples, with Parisians leading the way.[109] Evidence from England[110] and other European countries such as Switzerland[111] and Scandinavia,[112] however, suggests that cohabitation can be found in all social classes.

The trend towards cohabitation cannot be attributed to any particular group, or even to a type of individual and, in relation to any one couple, the motives for adopting the life-style can be a complex mixture of financial, ideological and social factors, and can be adopted as a permanent or a temporary alternative to marriage. What information do we have on the number of people cohabiting? Can we now in the early 1980s detect any trends? Do the statistics show one factor emerging more clearly than any other, and, if so, can this be a guideline for future legal policy?

As far as England is concerned, there are no recorded statistics on the actual number of people cohabiting, chiefly due to the absence of questions which would elicit this information on the present census form.[113] All we can do is attempt to detect the trend towards cohabitation from the random sample surveys conducted by the Office of Population Censuses and Surveys, the slowly but steadily increasing rise in the illegitimacy rate,[114] the sharply rising number of single people in all age groups,[115] the age at first marriage rates,[116] and the rate of remarriage.[117] Leete notes,[118] in his survey of *Family Formation and Dissolution in England and Wales 1964–1976,* that 'at a time of changing social and legal norms real changes may be masked in the statistics, thus an apparent increase in the properties of single people at younger ages might disguise an increased trend towards cohabitation outside marriage'. It would certainly appear from the available statistics and from surveys like the 1976 OPCS *Family Formation Survey* and the 1979 *General*

Household Survey that the number of couples cohabiting before and outside marriage is on the increase. In her *Family Formation Survey,* published in 1976, Dunnell showed that about 10 per cent of the women in her survey who had married for the first time between 1971 and 1975 had lived with their husbands before marriage, compared with roughly 3 per cent who had married for the first time in 1966.[119]

The 1979 *General Household Survey* showed that this number had nearly doubled, so that 19 per cent of women marrying in the late 1970s had lived with their husbands before marriage.[120] In 1979, 3 per cent of the sample of women aged between 18 and 49 indicated that they were cohabiting. Dunnell's statistics also revealed that nearly two-thirds of those who had lived with their husbands prior to marriage had done so for less than a year. The *General Household Survey* produced similar evidence; the length of pre-marital cohabitation was under a year in 62 per cent of cases in the sample. In the case of those with previous experience of marriage, the length of pre-marital cohabitation was greater (56 per cent had cohabited for more than a year before a second or subsequent marriage).[121]

Leete,[122] comparing other countries, notes that there are similarities in trends internationally. He comments that, while these demographic indications appear to be moving in similar directions, they differ in detail from country to country. According to his study, falls in first marriage rates have been detected not only in England but also in the USA, France, Belgium and Germany, with the largest falls of all in Scandinavian countries. In Scandinavia this fall has been accompanied by a substantial increase in cohabitation. In England the 1979 *General Household Survey* showed that 8 per cent of the single women in the sample over the age of eighteen were living with someone as man and wife; 20 per cent of divorced women were cohabiting as were 16 per cent of separated women. As Brown and Kiernan say: 'if the proportion of women cohabiting in each marital condition and age-group in the population of Great Britain were the same as in the survey, this would lead to an estimate for 1979 of about one-third of a million cohabiting women aged under 50'.[123]

Available evidence appears to show that in England the trend towards cohabitation is more one towards the postponement of marriage.[124] Leete comments that 'postponement is an unusual phenomenon in modern demographic history'.[125] Many historians of the family would take issue with him on this.[126] Brown and Kiernan, though, noted a distinction between cohabiting women who so described themselves and those who regarded themselves as married. The latter's period of cohabitation was on average one year; and half of them were also mothers. There were clear social class differences between the 'living together' group and the 'married' group. The former were more highly educated; a higher proportion of the latter were in manual occupations and living in local authority housing. The *General Household Survey* appears to have isolated two distinct categories of single women who were cohabiting: a group which regards itself as married and another which, in Brown and Kiernan's words, 'perhaps' regard their relationship 'as being temporary, or as a stage preceding legal marriage'. 'It is possible,' they continue, 'as the period of cohabitation lengthens that they may come to regard themselves and present themselves as "married".'[127] Leete has noted that 'the recent large rises in cohabitation outside of marriage coupled with the increased ability of couples to control their reproductive destiny suggest that for some couples de facto unions may be a permanent rather than transient way of family life'.[128] It is too early to speculate further on this.

The upsurge in the trend towards cohabitation has also been seen in other European countries. In France, there has been a rapid rise in cohabitation; thus, a 1977 sample survey shows an increase in the proportion of married couples who had lived together prior to marriage from 17 per cent of those who married in 1968–9 to 44 per cent of those who married in 1976–7.[129] The length of such cohabitation was found to be quite short, however, on average just under 18 months, and it was almost invariably childless. In France, cohabitation appears to be a form of trial marriage; thus it is most popular with the 20–24 year olds and the proportion of men and women married by the age of 30 did not change between 1968 and 1975. The 1977 survey results also showed that one-third of those cohabiting planned to marry; another third had not made up their minds; a quarter had not discussed the nature of the relationship and only 7 per cent were ideologically opposed to marriage. Five per cent of women were cohabiting, but 10 per cent of those aged between 20 and 24. Other European countries also have falling marriage rates, and increases in the number of women cohabiting. In Norway, Finland and West Germany the cohabitation rate is between 10 and 15 per cent.[130] Cohabitation is on the increase also in Switzerland,[131] and even in Italy.

It is, however, in Scandinavia that cohabitation is most common. Trost estimated that in Sweden '15 per cent of marriage-like dyads consist of unmarried cohabiting couples'.[132] Among younger couples the trend towards cohabitation is most marked (only 14 per cent in one of Trost's surveys were 34 years or older).[133] Hofsten[134] found that in Sweden 29 per cent of women aged 20–24 were cohabiting in 1975. Leridon's figure for Denmark is 30 per cent.[135] According to Festy,[136] by the mid-1970s more than half the couples lived together before marriage in Denmark and Sweden. The patterns of cohabitation in Sweden and Denmark need to be distinguished from those in other European countries. Childbearing is more common among young cohabiting couples in Sweden. The same to a lesser extent is true of Denmark.[137] In Britain and France, on the other hand, cohabitation is largely a childless period, and most childbearing still occurs within the framework of marriage.[138]

In Australia it is generally believed that there is an increasing trend towards cohabitation, although there is little concrete demographic evidence to confirm this. Information relating to the number of cohabiting couples has been inferred from statistics relating to marriage, divorce, remarriage and illegitimate births. According to Evatt, Watson and McKenzie, there has in the period 1971–9 been a slight decline in the number of persons married at all ages, although more Australians are marrying than ever before, if at a rather later age. They cite the work done by the Australian Family Formation Project, which indicated that an increasing number of persons have favoured 'pre-marital freedom and the chance to mature alone', and which concluded that the tendency to delay marriage may contribute to or be connected with the alleged increase in the number of cohabiting couples. Thus, comment Evatt *et al*, 'more persons may be cohabiting in their early 20s prior to later registered marriage'.[139] After reviewing other trends in divorce and remarriage rates, they indicate that they see cohabitation chiefly in terms of postponement responses in a variety of forms: as an experience prior to marriage; as a preparation for marriage; or as a temporary waiting period prior to remarriage.

US statistics on cohabiting couples are much more accessible. The Census Bureau figures reveal a steady and marked trend towards cohabitation. The latest official figures available from the Bureau, those of March 1978, reveal that the number of couples officially recorded as living together had more than doubled from the 1970 figure of 523,000 to 1,137,000;[140] 2.8 per cent of couples living together in the USA are cohabiting outside marriage. The actual figures are likely to be substantially higher than the official ones. Weyrauch notes that 'informal marriages are not likely to be made public as such and many American marriages assumed to be ceremonial are not so in fact'.[141] If the official statistics are doubled, a more reliable indication of the number of cohabiting couples may be gauged. This would suggest the number of couples cohabiting in the USA may be closer to 2 million. In the USA the most dramatic rise in cohabitation has been among the young. The 1978 census indicates that 42 per cent of people cohabiting were under 25, but there is evidence of an increased number of cohabiting relationships among all age groups. In 1978, 32 per cent of cohabitants were between 25 and 44, 15 per cent between 45 and 64 and 11 per cent were over 65. Perhaps the most significant thing is that cohabitation in the USA has become acceptable for ordinary people.[142] How is the trend towards cohabitation in the USA to be analysed?

Some of the American surveys reveal that financial[143] or ideological[144] motives are among the most important reasons for cohabiting, while others reveal that supposed ideological gains do not actually work out in practice.[145] The trial marriage approach does not appear to be a significant response, at least in the case of many men who see cohabitation as an alternative to marriage.[146] Indeed, one survey found that cohabitation was not a more effective screening device than traditional courtship patterns,[147] thus contradicting, says Newcomb, the commonly held notion that one of the potential positive outcomes of cohabitation is improved mate selection.[148] This would tend to be supported by the absence of any evidence in England to suggest that a preliminary period of cohabitation will make subsequent marriages more durable than those of couples who marry without previously having cohabited.[149] The various American studies do not, however, indicate that the trend towards cohabitation is posing a serious threat to the institution of marriage, at least in the case of the young. Certainly, it seems that the great majority of college cohabitants desire to marry at some time.[150] Newcomb comments, however, that it is conceivable that for previously married and older people cohabitation does present a real alternative to marriage, 'though this may be principally for financial reasons'. He states that 'the former group may be cohabiting due to the experience of failure in marriage while the latter may be cohabiting due to the increased social security benefits for two single people as compared to those for a married couple.'[151] A majority of cohabiting couples in 1975 included at least one divorced partner. Glick and Spanier found that half the men and three-fifths of the women in cohabiting relationships had been previously married.[152] They found that most cohabitants who had never been married were in the youngest age group (85 per cent) but previously married cohabitants were evenly spread over the age categories. That people, including older couples, feel both prepared to live together without marriage and to admit to this indicates the extent to which cohabitation has become a respectable social institution. Newcomb believes that part of the increase in cohabitation is due to 'an increased willingness for people to identify themselves as cohabitants', which may in turn be due to the 'increasingly favourable attitudes expressed towards this once stigmatized behaviour'. Weyrauch[153] also notes that extra-legal marital patterns have gradually become absorbed into American law, and that the contemporary legal status of informal marriage owes much to the creative imagination of practising lawyers.

Conclusion

In this chapter we have looked at the social and economic contexts in which cohabitation is occurring in Western society, and we have considered whether the trend is a temporary phenomenon or whether it is here to stay. Cohabitation may perhaps be seen as a real and permanent alternative to marriage for significant segments of the population only in Scandinavia and the USA. In these countries the trend could perhaps best be described as ideological in character. In relation to Sweden, for example, Sundberg has pointed out that 'socialist ideology in Sweden always took a negative view of bourgeois church marriage, and favoured as a matter of principle free partnership based on conscience and it is an ideology which has found common expression in the actions of the ordinary working man since the early years of this century'.[154] Clearly Sweden and Denmark have the highest cohabitation rates in the Western world: one in eight couples live together outside marriage.[155]

In the USA the number of cohabiting couples could vary from 1,137,000 to twice that number, and it is increasing. Much of the literature claims that the popularity of cohabitation over legal marriage is due to its more open, more democratic, less traditional and less stereotyped character. Many of the cohabitants hold to the view that they will eventually get married: for others cohabitation is a real alternative to marriage. It is not surprising in the United States, where freedom of the individual is an exalted principle, that people should thoroughly embrace the individualist philosophy, feel free to adopt a life-style which allows them to develop their own individual careers and amass various capital assets, and furnishes them with opportunities for sexual gratification, without subjecting them at the same time to the social pressures and legal obligations associated with traditional marriage.

There is little doubt that there is a general trend towards cohabitation in the West. It should not, and, we submit, it cannot yet be shown from the evidence, flimsy though it is, to be, a widespread movement away from marriage. Nowhere in the Western world do cohabiting couples constitute more than one-eighth of couples who live together. Cohabitation remains for most either pre-marital experience with certain tangible bonuses, or pre-marital preparation with not only tangible but also possible intangible gains. For the rest – the elderly, the previously married, and those who choose cohabitation on ideological or political grounds – there is no doubt that it can have many and various benefits.

The arguments for denying cohabitants access to the courts can no longer, however, be justified on the basis that the adoption of this life-style threatens the institution of marriage, and thereby undermines society. Marriage still appears to be the most popular form of family life in the West, and even when previous marriages have failed, people seem to be more than anxious to remarry and try again. Even were marriage still not so popular, and it could be shown that it was being undermined by cohabitation, this could not be a reason for denying cohabitants access to the courts, for, as Deech notes, 'marriage should not be shored up independently of its utility and desirability'.[156] The problem, however, that remains to be answered is upon what basis cohabitants should be treated by the law, bearing in mind the variegated nature of cohabitation.

Notes

1 M. Mead, 'Future Family', *Transaction* (Sept. 1971), pp. 50–3, at p. 52.

2 R. Libby, in R. Libby and R. Whitehurst, *Marriage and Alternatives*, Scott, Foresman & Co., Illinois, 1977, p. 383.

3 S.M. Cretney in 'The Law relating to Unmarried Partners from the Perspective of a Law Reform Agency', in J. Eekelaar and S. Katz (eds), *Marriage and Cohabitation in Contemporary Societies*, Butterworths, Toronto, 1980, hereafter cited as Eekelaar and Katz, p. 366.

4 On the basis that the partner in the weaker bargaining position, usually the woman, should be protected. See D. Oliver, 'The Mistress in Law', *Current Legal Problems*, 81 (1978); D. Pearl, 'The Legal Implications of a Relationship outside Marriage', *C.L.J.* 252 (1978); P. Clayton, *The Cohabitation Guide*, London, Wildwood House, 1981, pp. 153–5.

5 We have argued for this approach in the past; see M.D.A. Freeman and C.M. Lyon, 'Towards a Justification of the Rights of Cohabitees' *N.L.J.*, 130 (1980), p. 228. See also R. Deech, 'The Case against Legal Recognition of Cohabitation', in Eekelaar and Katz, *op. cit.*, note 3.

6 Although some commentators question whether such a decision can be inferred. See *post*, p. 190.

7 See, e.g. in England, *Ward v Byham* [1956], 1 W.L.R. 496; and *Tanner v Tanner* [1975], 3 All E.R. 776; and in the USA, *Levar v Elkins*, 604 P. 2d 602 (1980), Alaska and *Kozlowski v Kozlowski*, 403 A.2d 902 (1979), New Jersey.

8 See in the USA, *Estate of Thornton*, 541 P.2d 1243 (1972).

9 See, e.g. in England, *Cooke v Head* [1972], 2 All E.R. 38; *Eves v Eves* [1975], 3 All E.R. 768; in the USA, see *Omer v Omer*, 523 P.2d 838 (1974); in Canada, see *Becker v Pettkus*, 87 D.L.R. 1011; in Australia, see *Olsen v Olsen and Another* [1977] 1 N.S.W.L.R. 189.

10 The former expressing a paternalist and protectionist philosophy; the latter an individualist philosophy.

11 'The Supreme Court's View of Marriage and the Family: Tradition or Transition, *Journal of Family Law* 18 (1979), pp. 301, 330.

12 See in J. Trost, 'Cohabitation without Marriage in Sweden', in Eekelaar and Katz, *op. cit.*, note 3, p. 16.

13 In 'The New Marriage', 12 Will. LJ 441, 452 (1976).

14 See, for example, J. Bernard, *The Future of Marriage*, Penguin, 1976, p. 289; A. Oakley, *Housewife*, Penguin, 1976, pp. 20–2; M. Anderson, *Approaches to the History of the Western Family*, London, Macmillan, 1980, pp. 53–4.

15 The Church played a considerable part in emphasising the importance of this status and developing a complex body of Canon Law regulating both entry into marriage and its consequences. See M. Anderson, 'Insights from the History of the Family', in M. Anderson (ed.), *Sociology of the Family*, Penguin (2nd ed.), 1980, p. 43; and L. Stone, *The Family, Sex and Marriage in England 1500–1800*, Penguin, 1979, pp. 105–6, 109.

16 See A. Clark, *The Working Life of Women in the Seventeenth Century*, Routledge & Sons, 1919, p. 5; and also Oakley, *op. cit.*, note 14, pp. 14–21.

17 *Op. cit.*, note 16, p. 39.

18 See B. Friedan, *The Feminine Mystique*, Penguin, 1965.

19 Popularised in J. Bowlby, *Child Care and the Growth of Love,* Penguin, 1953. See now M. Rutter, *Maternal Deprivation Re-assessed,* Penguin (2nd ed.), 1981.

20 D. Winnicott, *The Child, the Family and the Outside World,* Penguin, 1964.

21 B. Spock, *Baby and Child Care* (originally published under the title *The Common Sense book of Baby and Child Care),* Duell, Sloan and Pearce, New York, 1945.

22 In England easier divorce was introduced by the Divorce Reform Act 1969: in Scotland by the Divorce (Scotland) Act 1976. In the USA throughout the 1970s states variously enacted reformed divorce laws based wholly or in part on the provisions of the Uniform Marriage and Divorce Act. Although many states now have no-fault divorce, most states retain some fault grounds, e.g. desertion or abandonment (34 states); incurable impotence (19 states); habitual drunkenness (26 states); non-support or neglect (15 states).

23 Examples are sections 23–5 of the Matrimonial Causes Act 1973 (England); Connecticut, Gne. Stats. Ann. ss.46–51–46–52 (USA).

24 See tables showing number of marriages and divorces per 100 marriages for selected countries: United Nations, *Demographic Yearbook,* 30 Issue 1978.

25 See P. Berger and H. Kellner, '**Marriage** and the Construction of Reality', *Diogenes* 46 (1964), pp. 1–24, at p. 23.

26 In 'The New Family and the New Property, *Tul. L. Rev.,* 53 (1979), p. 697, at p. 707.

27 See the findings of the Michigan University panel study of 5,000 American families: Saul Hoffman and John Holmes, 'Husbands, Wives and Divorce', in Duncan and Morgan (eds), *Five Thousand American Families – Patterns of Economic Progress,* Vol. IV, 1975.

28 *Ante,* p. 28.

29 Andrew Hacker, 'The American Family – Future Uncertain', *Time Magazine* (28 December 1970), pp. 34–40, at p. 34.

30 *Only Halfway to Paradise,* Tavistock, London, 1980, p. 82.

31 See J. Epstein, *Divorced in America,* Baltimore, Penguin, 1974, pp. 76, 79.

32 Including J. Epstein, *op. cit.,* note 31, and K. Melville, *Marriage and Family Today,* Random House, New York, 1977, p. 395.

33 H.L. Ross and I.V. Sawhill, *Time of Transition,* The Urban Institute, Washington, DC, 1975.

34 J. Huber and G. Spitze, 'Considering Divorce: An expansion of Becker's Theory of Marital Instability', *Amer. J. Soc.,* Vol. 86 (1980), pp. 75–89.

35 See Melville, *op. cit.,* note 32, p. 395.

36 Progress report by G. Baruch and R. Barnett of the Wellesley Centre for Research team's study on the effects of the Women's Movement (January 1981).

37 The twenty-year follow-up of the Midtown Manhattan Longitudinal Study of Mental Health (1974), conducted by Dr Lee Srole and Anita Kassen Fischer of Columbia University. The second, earlier study was that done by the National Center for Health Statistics (NCHS) in 1971.

38 *Per* Dr Harold Dupuy, director of the NCHS study.

39 'Women's Liberation and Sexual Liberation', in R. Libby and R. Whitehurst (eds), *Marriage and its Alternatives,* Scott Foresman, 1977, pp. 216–28, at p. 226.

40 *Idem,* p. 227. See, more generally, C. Bohmer and R. Lebow, 'Divorce: Comparative Style', *Journal of Divorce,* vol. 2 (1978), pp. 157–73.

41 For feminist analyses of female sexuality, see B. Seaman, *Free and Female,* New York, Coward, McCann and Geoghegan, 1972 and M.J. Sherfey, *The Nature and Evolution of Female Sexuality,* New York, Random House, 1972.

42 'Living Without Them', *Ms Magazine* (October 1975).

43 B. Dodson, *Liberating Masturbation,* New York, Bodysex Designs, 1974.

44 See N. Myron and C. Bunch (eds), *Lesbianism and the Women's Movement,* Baltimore, Diana Press, 1975; and J. Johnson, *Lesbian Nation: the Feminist Solution,* New York, Simon and Schuster, 1973.

45 See M. Duberman, 'The Bisexual Debate', in R. Libby and R. Whitehurst (eds), *op. cit.,* note 39, 241–252.

46 See P. Schwartz, 'Female Sexuality and Monogamy' in R. Libby and R. Whitehurst (eds), *op. cit.,* note 39, pp. 229–40.

47 M. Cadwallader, 'Marriage as a Wretched Institution', *Atlantic,* 218 (1966), pp. 62–6.

48 Anonymous, *'How to be Happy though Married',* London, T. Fisher Unwin, 1885, p. 55.

49 T.C. Halliday, *'Remarriage – The More Compleat Institution?', Amer. J. Soc.,* 86 (1980),

pp. 630–5.

50 Table 117, *'Marriages and Divorces in the US Statistical Abstract of the USA'*, US Department of Commerce – Census Bureau, 1979.

51 Table 2.21, *Annual Abstract of Statistics* (1981 Edition), London, HMSO, p. 31.

52 At least this is what the English figures for 1979 would suggest. See Office of Population Censuses and Surveys, *Monitor, Marriages 1978 & 1979,* Reference FM2 81/1 (24 March 1981) Table 1.

53 *Idem,* Table 2.

54 *Idem,* Table 1 (the decline was 0.4 per cent).

55 OPCS, *Monitor,* FM2 81/2 Divorces 1979 (24 March 1981), Table 2.

56 *Social Trends,* vol. 11 1981, Central Statistical Office, HMSO, p. 34.

57 J. Bernard, *The Future of Marriage,* New York, Bantam, 1974, p. 19. On remarriage generally, see *Journal of Family Issues,* vol. 1, no. 4 (1980) (Special Issue on Remarriage).

58 *Op. cit.,* note 56, p. 32 and Tables 2.10 and 2.12.

59 See *post,* p. **88**.

60 See *post,* pp. 93–95.

61 In England, for example, the total number of children under 16 involved in divorce cases in 1978 was 170,000. See Table 2.14, *op. cit.,* note 56, p. 34.

62 See e.g. D. Whitehouse, 'Youth Views Marriage', in *op. cit.,* note 2, 294–302.

63 J. Sundberg, 'Recent Changes in Swedish Family Law', *Am. Jo. Comp. Law,* 23, p. 38, at p. 49 (1976).

64 *Post,* chs. 4 and 5 *passim.*

65 See Office of Population, Censuses and Surveys, *Monitor, Marriages 1978 and 1979,* FM2 81/1 (24 March 1981).

66 Identified by J. Trost, in 'Married and Unmarried Cohabitation in Sweden', in M. Corbin (ed.), *The Couple,* p. 160; D. Kelly Weisberg, 'Alternative Family Structures and the Law', in *Family Coordinator,* (1975), p. 549, at pp. 550–1.

67 Identified by D. Friedmann in, 'The "Unmarried Wife" in Israeli Law', *Israel Yearbook on Human Rights* (1972), p. 287, but also applicable to those couples prevented by strict divorce laws from remarrying as soon as they would wish. See, for example, those couples who live together in England because one party is having to wait five years before filing a petition for divorce based on ground 1(2)(e) of the Matrimonial Causes Act 1973.

68 Both identified by Trost, *op. cit.,* note 66, at p. 162, and by R. Newcombe, 'Cohabitation in America' *J.F.L.* (1979), p. 597, at p. 598.

69 See J. Trost, in 'Cohabitation without Marriage in Sweden', in J. Eekelaar and S. Katz, *op. cit.,* note 3, p. 16, at p. 20; by Newcomb, *op. cit.,* note 68, at p. 597; and R. Leete, *Changing Patterns of Family Formation and Dissolution in England and Wales 1964–1976,* London, HMSO, 1979, p. 11.

70 This would appear to be in part the character of the response in England. See *post,* p. **55**.

71 Research in the USA postulates that this is more likely to be the character of the response there: see Newcomb, *op. cit.,* note 68, and *post.* See also as regards Sweden *post,* p.55.

72 'To Love, Honor and Obey – Traditional Legal Marriage and Alternative Family Forms', *Family Coordinator,* **24** (1975) pp. 547, 550.

73 See R. Weiss, 'Couple Relationships', in *The Couple, op. cit.,* note 66, p. 142.

74 181 A.2d 125 Supr. Crt. (1962).

75 See, for example, s.25 of Matrimonial Causes Act 1973 (England). In relation to the USA, see the useful discussion in J. Areen, *Family Law: Cases and Materials,* Boston, Little Brown, 1980, p. 635; and also C. Bruch, 'Property Rights of de Facto Spouses', *F.L.Q.* 10, p. 101.

76 Deech, *op. cit.,* note 5, p. 310.

77 See, for example, the statement of Patrick Jenkin, Secretary of State for Social Services, in a BBC 2 Documentary, 'Working Mothers', October 1979.

78 For example, the decisions by the Republican Government that the Equal Rights Amendment will not be pushed, and that there will be a tightening of abortion laws.

79 See, for example, the judgments of Lord Denning MR in *Eves v Eves* [1975], 3 All E.R. 768, and of Tobriner J in *Marvin v Marvin,* Sup. 134 Cal. Rpt. 815.

80 Weiss, *op. cit.,* note 73, p. 142.

81 G. Thorman, 'Cohabitation: A Report on the married–unmarried life style', *The Futurist* (December 1973), pp. 250–3, at p. 251.

82 *Op. cit.*, note 66.
83 *Ante,* p. 2.
84 Commission of the European Communities, *Report on European Men and Women,* 1975, pp. 151–4.
85 See R. Weiss, *op. cit.,* note 73.
86 *Op. cit.*, note 66.
87 Bruch notes that a study of 51 couples in the mid-Western USA, conducted by sociologists at the University of Utah, suggested this conclusion, in C. Bruch, 'Property Rights of de Facto Spouses', *F.L.Q.* 10, p. 101; and see also R.R. Clayton and H.L. Voss, 'Shacking-Up: Cohabitation in the 1970s', *Journal of Marriage and the Family,* 39 pp. 273–83; M.A. Segrest and M.O. Weeks, 'Comparison of the Role Expectations of Married and Cohabiting Subjects', *Int. Jo. Soc. Fam.* 56, pp. 275–81; D. Olday, 'Some consequences of heterosexual cohabitation for Marriage', unpublished doctoral dissertation, Washington State Library (referred to in E.D. Macklin, 'Non-Traditional Family Forms: A decade of Research' *Journal of Marriage and the Family* (1980) p. 905.
88 See Trost, *op. cit.,* note 66; Weiss *op. cit.,* note 73; Bernard *op. cit.,* note 57.
89 I. Pedersen, 'Danish Law Relating to Non-Marital Relationships', *ICLQ,* 28, (1979), p. 117.
90 See H.L. Deb., vol. 427, cols. 783–94, (22 February 1982).
91 Referred to by J. Sundberg, *op. cit.,* note 63. Upon a petition by the couple, the King in Council by Resolution granted a pardon.
92 *Op. cit.,* note 67.
93 See figures quoted in 'Social Trends: The rising popularity of Cohabitation', *New Society* 8 January (1981), p. 57.
94 *Op. cit.,* note 31.
95 See Campaign for Justice in Divorce, *An Even Better Way Out,* and J. Allan and R. Horne, *The Financial Anatomy of The Divorce Man,* both C.J.D., Aylesbury, 1980.
96 *Op. cit.,* note 72 at p. 546.
97 *Op. cit.,* note 63.
98 *Op. cit.,* note 66.
99 *Post,* p. 105.
100 See, generally, Weisberg, *op. cit.,* note 66.
101 R. Rapoport and R. Rapoport, 'Dual Career Families Re-examined', in M. Anderson (ed.), *Sociology of the Family, op. cit.,* note 15, at p. 259.
102 In 'Legal and Social Impediments to Dual Career Marriages', *U.C. D.L.R.,* 12, (1979), pp. 207–23. See also J. Scanzoni, 'Contemporary Marriage Types', *Journal of Family Issues,* vol. 1, (1980) pp. 125–40.
103 See K. Dunnell, *Family Formation 1976,* OCPS Social Survey, HMSO, especially pp.19–27.
104 *Op. cit.,* note 69.
105 *Op. cit.,* note 68.
106 See *ante,* p. 3 and 50.
107 'Nontraditional Family Norms: A Decade of Research', *Journal of Marriage and the Family* (1980) p. 905, at pp. 907–8.
108 *Op. cit.,* note 93.
109 *Idem.* See also R. Nerson, 'Les Couples Non-mariés en France', in J. Eekelaar and S. Katz, *op. cit.,* note 3, at p. 198.
110 See R. Leete, *op. cit.,* note 69; K. Dunnell, *op. cit.,* note 103; and A. Brown and K. Kiernan, 'Cohabitation in Great Britain: Evidence from the General Household Survey', Office of Population Censuses and Surveys, 1981.
111 *Op. cit.,* note 93, and J.M. Grossen, 'Aspects of de facto Marriage under Switzerland's Private Law', in Eekelaar and Katz, *op. cit.,* note 3, at p. 258.
112 See J. Trost, *op. cit.,* note 69, at pp. 16 and 18 for Sweden; I. Pedersen, *op. cit.,* note 89, suggests that cohabitation cuts across all classes.
113 The 1981 Census omitted this question, although such a question was included in the 1979 *General Household Survey.* See *ante,* p. 6.
114 Table 2.24 of CSO, *Annual Abstract of Statistics* (1981 ed.), p. 35.
115 *Idem.*
116 *Op. cit.,* note 56, at p. 32.
117 *Op. cit.,* note 114, at p. 31; and *op. cit.,* note 56, at p. 31.

118 *Op. cit.,* note 60, at p. 8.
119 *Op. cit.,* note 103, at para. 2.4.
120 See A. Brown and K. Kiernan, *op. cit.,* note 110.
121 *Idem.* The median period was 10 months where it was a first marriage for both and 17 months where it was a second or subsequent marriage for one party or both.
122 *Op. cit.,* note 69, p. 7.
123 *Op. cit.,* note 110.
124 There is similar evidence from France: see *op. cit.,* note 93.
125 *Op. cit.,* note 69, p. 8.
126 E.g. L. Stone, *op. cit.,* note 15, at pp. 43–6.
127 *Op. cit.,* note 110.
128 *Idem,* p. 108.
129 See H. Leridon, 'Factors Affecting Fertility in Developed Countries', World Fertility Survey Conference, July 1980.
130 See P. Festy, 'Data and Perspective on the New Context of Marriage in Western Europe', *Population and Development Review* (June 1980).
131 Data from Switzerland (quoted *op. cit.,* note 93) indicates that of those married in Geneva in 1974–5, 60 per cent lived together before their wedding.
132 'Dissolution of Cohabitation and Marriage in Sweden', *Journal of Divorce,* 2 (1977), p. 415, at p. 416.
133 *Op. cit.,* note 69, at p. 18 (Table 1).
134 See E. Hofsten, 'Consensual Unions and Their Recent Increase in Sweden', *Statistisk Tidskrift,* No. 1 (1978).
135 *Op. cit.,* note 129.
136 *Op. cit.,* note 130.
137 See P. Festy, 'Extra-Marital Fertility and its Occurrence in Stable Unions in Western Europe', in M. Niphuis-Nell (ed.), *Demographic Aspects of the Changing Status of Women in Europe,* Martinus Nijhoff, The Hague, 1978.
138 See K.E. Kiernan, 'Patterns of Family Formation and Dissolution in England and Wales in Recent Years', OPCS Occasional Paper 19/2, 1980.
139 'The Legal and Social Aspects of Cohabitation and the Reconstituted Family as a Social Problem', in J. Eekelaar and S. Katz, *op. cit.,* note 3, p. 398, at p. 400.
140 US Bureau of the Census, 'Marital Status and Living Arrangements: March 1978', *Current Population Reports,* series P–20, no. 338 (May 1979), p. 3 (and Table D). See also P. Glick and G. Spanier, 'Married and Unmarried Cohabitation in the United States', *Journal of Marriage and the Family,* vol. 42 (1980), p. 19.
141 'Metamorphoses of Marriage: Formal and Informal Marriages in the United States', J. Eekelaar and S. Katz (ed.), *op. cit.,* note 3, at p. 277, fn 26.
142 See P. Glick and A. Norton, 'Marrying, Divorcing and Living Together in the US Today', *Population Bulletin,* vol. 32, no. 5 (1977), p. 32.
143 I. Arafat and J. Yoburg, 'On Living Together without Marriage', *Journal of Sex Research, 9* (1976), pp. 97–106.
144 See D. Olday, *op. cit.,* note 87.
145 See D. Olday; R.R. Clayton and H.L. Voss; N.A. Segrest and M.O. Weeks, *op. cit.,* note 87.
146 See Arafat and Yoburg, *op. cit.,* note 143.
147 D. Olday, *op. cit.,* note 87.
148 *Op. cit.,* note 68, p. 599.
149 See comments of Leete, *op. cit.,* note 69.
150 *Op. cit.,* note 68, p. 598.
151 *Idem,* p. 597.
152 *Op. cit.,* note 140.
153 *Op. cit.,* note 141, p. 269.
154 *Op. cit.,* note 63, p. 38.
155 12 per cent in Sweden; 13 per cent in Denmark (according to J. Trost, *Unmarried Cohabitation,* International Library, Vasteras, 1979).
156 *Op. cit.,* note 5, at p. 310.

4 Some Responses of English Law to Cohabitation

The twentieth century has seen a dramatic change of attitudes on the part of the courts in their responses to the legal problems arising from a cohabiting relationship. The courts have moved from considering such relationships as flagrantly immoral and threatening to the institution of marriage[1] to the position in which such considerations are deemed to be irrelevant.[2] Apparently, it is 'social reality' which now concerns the courts,[3] especially where that reality discloses that unmarried couples are fulfilling exactly the same functions and performing identical roles to those of their married counterparts.[4] Relationships of a 'casual or intermittent character' may still be excluded from the popular concept of a family unit[5] unless there are other family-type incidents. It is no longer possible to say that it is the ceremony of marriage only which counts, and that rights and obligations begin on marriage and not before.[6]

Developments in the English courts, leaning heavily for their justification on the family-like or quasi-marital behaviour of the cohabiting parties, are mirrored in the various statutory provisions which have emerged in the recent past. Thus, membership of a person's family, legal or de facto, is the criterion for protection under Rent Act legislation,[7] and for protection under the Housing Act 1980,[8] though such membership is more easily established by children than by their unmarried parents. The archetypal quasi-marital phrase 'living together as husband and wife' was to surface many times in statutory provisions from the mid-sixties onwards,[9] while the 'reputed spouse' made two surprise appearances in 1974[10] and 1979.[11] The language of economic dependence, however, formed the basis for provisions for cohabitants from a deceased partner's estate,[12] and for increases to certain state benefits payable to men in respect of women with whom they were living.[13]

Objections to such developments, on the basis that their effect might be such as to undermine marriage, were, surprisingly perhaps, seldom articulated,[14] and when they were, rarely attracted much attention.[15] Such fears as were voiced were mainly heard in Parliament[16] rather than the courts, and when any judge expressed concern as to the possible effects of a decision favourable to cohabitants, he could justify his decision by reference to legislative provisions protecting their position.[17] By 1980, however, at least one Court of Appeal judge[18] felt able to declare that the objects of promoting the support of marriage, and the reduction of illicit unions, were no longer influential or relevant factors when considering the effect of a decision in favour of a cohabitant. He also took comfort from the fact that there were various legislative provisions which now sought to protect such unmarried parties. Another judge of the Court of Appeal[19] had referred to current legislative policy aimed at eliminating differences between legitimate and illegitimate children as justifying a decision the effect of which was to eliminate differences between such children's parents.

Indeed, during the last decade, it has become legislative policy in England,[20] as in many other countries,[21] to reduce differences between legitimate and illegitimate children. The English Law Commission proposed the abolition of the status of illegitimacy altogether in 1979.[22] The proposed changes in the law consequent upon such a reform have met with some unexpected opposition,[23] so that the fate of the Commission's proposal is as yet uncertain. Current legislative policy in respect of illegitimate children has undoubtedly affected the legal position of their parents, both by direct statutory provision[24] and by the more indirect intervention of the courts.[25] Cohabitants with children have certainly fared better[26] than their childless counterparts,[27] being 'rewarded' for fulfilling family-like functions, though where the parties have been able to prove marriage-like behaviour, the absence of children has not necessarily been fatal to their claims.[28]

How far has this equalisation process, if such it may be called, gone? What peculiar incidents still attach to the status of marriage to indicate that it retains a favoured and central position in English law? To what extent is it true to say that living together without the benefit of a marriage licence may mean living together without the benefit of much more?

Income support during the relationship and upon breakdown

In England today either party to a marriage may apply to the courts for an order for financial provision, on the ground that the other party to the marriage has failed to provide reasonable maintenance for the applicant.[29] In the higher courts it must also be proved that one of the grounds for judicial separation exists,[30] but in the magistrates' courts simple failure is sufficient.[31] Nor do the parties to the marriage have to be living apart at the time when such an order is made,[32] although, as far as a magistrates' court order is concerned, that order will cease to have effect if they live together for a continuous period exceeding six months.[33] Since the element of wilfulness which formed part of the old law has now been dispensed with, and, moreover, since the failure can be that of either party, not just the man, it is suggested that little if anything remains of the husband's old common law duty to maintain, at least insofar as financial provision is concerned.[34] Where the marriage relationship breaks down completely and divorce proceedings are begun, either party may apply for the various orders for financial provision set out in sections 22 and 23 of the Matrimonial Causes Act 1973.

The parties to a childless cohabiting relationship have no similar enforceable rights to maintenance either during or upon the breakdown of the relationship. Where there are children of the union, however, the position of the woman may be changed. One Court of Appeal judge[35] has indicated that he reads the amended s.4(2) of the Affiliation Proceedings Act 1957 as empowering the lower courts to make financial provision for the mother within the terms of an affiliation order. An affiliation order under the old law was an order of the court that a man who had been adjudged the father of an illegitimate child should make what the court deemed to be appropriate financial provision for the offspring.[36] Such orders could include sums to meet expenses incidental to the birth,[37] but it now seems that they will in the future possibly include sums to meet the maintenance needs of the mother.[38] The justification for such an approach could doubtless be found in the argument that this also would be a valuable step in eliminating the differences between legitimate and illegitimate children in line with current legislative policy.[39] Even without the aid of the amended section 4 (2), which did not come into force until 1 February 1981,[40] the judiciary had not been slow in coming to the aid of women left with the responsibility of looking after children on the breakdown of the cohabiting relationship.[41] There may have been no legally recognised right to maintenance support for such parties but attempts were made to compensate for such a lack, justification for such actions being sought both inside and outside the law.[42] In *Ward v Byham*[43] and *Tanner v Tanner*[44] attempts were made to infer a legally binding contract from the behaviour of the parties.

In both cases the male and female partners had been making arrangements for the future, to some extent at arm's length, because the cohabiting relationship had broken down. The Court of Appeal in each case was able to impute an intention to create legal relations and, furthermore, some sort of contractual arrangement, even where the consideration relied on was the legal obligation of all mothers of illegitimate children.[45] The shift of emphasis over nearly twenty years is interesting, more especially since Lord Denning gave the lengthier judgment in each case. The emphasis in *Ward v Byham* is much more on the elements of contract, whereas in *Tanner v Tanner* attention is focused rather more on a general discussion of vague rights and duties abstracted out of thin air. Thus, in *Ward v Byham* Denning LJ said: 'in looking after the child the mother is only doing what she is legally bound to do. Even so I think there was sufficient consideration to support the promise'.[46] In *Tanner v Tanner* there is no mention of the mother's legal duty to look after the children but various actions of hers in looking after them, including surrendering the protected tenancy of less roomy accommodation, are taken to be sufficient consideration to support a contractual licence in her favour.[47] Lord Denning declared that the father's legal duty towards the babies extended towards their mother: 'she was looking after them and bringing them up. In order to fulfil his duty towards the babies he was under a duty to provide for the mother too'.[48]

An even more robust attitude to the duty of a father to provide for the mother of his children can be seen in the judgment of Ormrod LJ in *Re Evers's Trust.*[49] He reacted very strongly to the suggestion by counsel for the male partner that the court below, when making an order that the trust for sale of the joint house should be postponed, had failed to take into account the fact that his client was under no legal liability to provide for the mother of his children. As Lord Scarman said, in *Horrocks v Forray,*[50] this whole area concerning the maintenance support of children and their caretakers on the breakdown of a cohabiting relationship is a fertile area for the growth of an inference of a legally binding contract. He thought that there would certainly be nothing contrary to public policy in the parents coming to an agreement, which they intend to be binding in law, for the maintenance of the child *and the mother.* In fact, he considered that in many ways it would be better for the parents in such a situation to regulate their position by contract. It should be noted that Lord Scarman added that it would not follow that because there exists a relationship which can be regulated by contract the proper inference is that the parties in their particular circumstances have so regulated their relationship. Indeed, in the particular case Lord Scarman found that there was no express or inferred contract. It would appear then that if the children's caretaker, usually the mother, can demonstrate a legitimate expectation arising from the partner's words or behaviour that she was to be maintained while looking after the children, then the courts may infer a contract to that effect.

The cohabiting women who is left with children is upon breakdown in a better position than one without children.[51] It is hard to see why maintenance provision by either party under the terms of an express or implied contract should be restricted to those cases where there are children. It should be made clear that we are not advocating any encouragement of the idea of the economic dependence by women on men. We believe that where one of the parties (in nearly all cases the woman) has foregone some career opportunity or sacrificed work position, she should receive some sort of compensation from her cohabitant.[52] Arguably this is the basis of the District Court judge's award of $104,000 by way of rehabilitative maintenance for Michelle Marvin.[53] Indeed, the idea of a short-term high award of maintenance for rehabilitative purposes is not completely alien to the English courts when dealing with married couples.[54] We would argue that this should be the approach in relation to married and unmarried alike, and would encourage the growth of the idea of individual autonomy within all cohabiting relationships.[55] It is, after all, the case that the courts dealing with maintenance claims by married women upon the breakdown of a short marriage have for a long time been averse to the award of anything like a 'meal ticket for life',[56] and in recent years have strongly advocated the 'clean break' principle,[57] even in respect of marriages of longer duration. Yet the courts when dealing with married couples are still bound by statutory guidelines when making financial provision orders on divorce.[58] Thus, the court must seek to place the parties in the position in which they would have been had the marriage not broken down.[59] In our view such a direction is inequitable. The payee, usually the woman, is encouraged to be dependent upon the man, and marriage is portrayed as offering the right to a certain standard of living to continue even after its breakdown.

The reality, of course, is, for many, very far from the aspiration expressed in the guideline, for, what has been called, the 'new property' rarely stretches sufficiently to ensure such a position.[60] But why should it? There is surely something wrong with a system which fosters economic dependence on another for no really good reason.[61] Furthermore, it offers a person lifelong rights in another's job success, when he, or more likely, she has made no sacrifice or contribution to that success. We would suggest, therefore, the concept of sums awarded by way of compensation or rehabilitation on the breakdown of any couple's relationship where such an award would be appropriate. Such an approach would accord with the philosophy of the 'clean break' principle, and encourage a move away from further institutionalising women's economic dependence on men.

Despite the fact that the parties to a cohabiting relationship have no rights to income support, either during the relationship or on breakdown, such a relationship may be taken into account when considering financial awards on a marriage breakdown. Thus, in *Roberts v Roberts,*[62] the man's responsibility to provide for his cohabitant was something that could be taken into account in assessing the amount of maintenance for his wife. Correspondingly, since a cohabitant may be deemed to be a responsibility within the terms of section 25, he or she may also be considered to be a resource, where such a party is providing any form of support.[63] This was seen in *Ette v Ette,*[64] where the husband, who was living in his cohabitant's house, running her business interests and drawing whatever money he required, was held to be a man of substantial income. The court decided that he would not be likely to have to repay the money he had received from her and was therefore deemed to be able to pay out maintenance for his wife. Similarly, in *W v W,*[65] where the wife had, after the divorce, moved into the house of another man, the court held that the house was therefore an asset of hers, which would operate to diminish the amount of her interest in the former matrimonial home. The law stops short of insisting that the other party to the cohabiting relationship should be forced to file an affidavit of his or her means.[66] It is interesting to note the courts' attitude to periods spent living together with a person before marriage when it has to consider awards of financial provision on divorce at some time in the future. In *Campbell v Campbell,*[67] the court refused to have regard to such a period. Four years later, in *Kokosinski v Kokosinski,*[68] the twenty-four years the parties had spent living, working and bringing up their son together before the marriage was taken into account, along with the rather brief period of four months spent living together after the marriage.[69] Rather more curiously, where the parties have lived together after the divorce, such periods have been held to be relevant to any awards under the adjustive jurisdiction.[70]

Support rights in the public law area

The public law obligations of support as between married couples and cohabiting couples present a somewhat more complex picture. Under the provisions of the social security system those parties who are, or have been, married will generally be at a greater advantage than couples who live together. We say 'generally' because there are situations where no distinction is made between the married and the unmarried, though this arises chiefly in the areas of means-tested non-contributory benefits.[71] Under the present provisions of the National Insurance and

Industrial Injuries schemes a husband is able to get a dependant's increase for the wife[72] where they are residing together[73] or where he is contributing to her maintenance at not less than the amount of the increase.[74] So an increase for the wife may be claimed in respect of a large number of benefits.

Where the wife is earning more than the amount of the increase in remunerative employment, then such a dependant's addition is not payable in the case of short-term benefits.[75] In the case of long-term benefits, where she is residing with the husband, an incentive rule applies and income up to a certain level is disregarded. Any income beyond that level reduces the amount of the increase by 50 per cent for income up to £4 and by 100 per cent for any greater excess.[76] Where it is the wife who seeks to claim benefit for herself and a dependant's increase for the husband, then, in his case it must, prior to full implementation of the EEC Directive on Equal Treatment,[77] be proved that he is additionally incapable of self support.[78] When the Social Security Act 1980 is fully brought into force, all the increases which under the rules described are presently payable to a husband will also be payable to wives.[79] Such increases to short-term benefits will be subject to exactly the same earnings rules, but where long-term benefits are concerned, the earnings level of the husband must not exceed £14, a much lower amount than that allowed for wives.[80]

The position with regard to cohabiting parties is considerably less favourable. In no case will an increase be payable for a dependent man, but in certain circumstances where the man is the claimant he will be able to apply for an increase for a woman who has the care of children.[81] The children must be those in respect of whom child benefit is payable to the claimant,[82] but the focus of attention is on the children and not on any relationship between the woman and the man. Indeed, the woman need not be living with the claimant,[83] and can even be paid where the claimant is living with his wife, provided his wife is out at work and does not 'principally look after the children'.[84] The increase is also payable to a female claimant normally in full-time work.[85] This explains the fact that maternity allowance, and unemployment, sickness and industrial injury payments, are short-term benefits for which such an increase may be paid. The long-term benefits for which the addition is payable include industrial disablement pension with unemployability supplement, non-contributory invalidity pension, invalid care allowances, invalidity pensions and Category A and C retirement pensions.[86] Before the claimant can establish entitlement to such an increase, he must prove that the woman is either residing with, being maintained by, or being employed by, him for not less than the amount of the addition.[87] Where the claim arises from the fact that the parties are living together, similar earnings rules apply, as in the case of wives.[88] An additional rule not applicable to wives disqualifies a claim for such an addition to disablement or invalidity pension if the claimant has a wife who is entitled to a Category B or C retirement pension.[89]

These provisions for increases for persons having the care of children have also been amended by the Social Security Act 1980, in order to give effect to the EEC directive, but no date has been given for the implementation of the changes.[90] The amendments mean that the allowance will be paid regardless of the sex of the person providing the child care, but the differential earnings limits are again carried over into this area, so that where the child-minder is female and the claimant is on long-term benefits, the more generous earnings limit applies. Another point worth noting in this area is that at the present time the female partner of a cohabiting couple who cannot herself satisfy the contribution condition is unable to rely on the male partner's contribution for the purposes of claiming maternity grant.[91] A wife, however, is able to rely on her husband's contributions.[92] In practice, where hardship has arisen, a claim by the woman for an urgent needs payment has been met under the provisions of the Supplementary Benefits scheme, but from 1982 such a claim will be unnecessary. It was announced on 19 February 1980 during the Committee Stage of the Social Security Bill that maternity grant would become non-contributory in 1982, and the only condition to be satisfied would be one of residence for six months in Great Britain.[93] Again it is interesting to note that the probable justification for such a move is that of favouring family provision, with the emphasis on children.

Where the relationship, be it marriage or cohabitation, breaks down, then, where there are children who continue to be looked after by the woman, or in due course the man, provision under the contributory scheme is on the same basis. The claimant has only to establish that instead of living with the other person he is maintaining the other party or paying her for looking after the children.[94] Increases will also be payable in respect of the children in the same way.[95] Any shortfall in the partner's resources may be met by the use of the Supplementary Benefit scheme.[96] The cohabiting partner who has no children to look after will have no choice but to resort to that scheme for financial provision.[97]

The equality provisions found in the private law area governing maintenance as between husbands and wives have existed for some time in the public law area, at least insofar as Supplementary Benefit is concerned. Thus, s.17(1) of the 1976 Act provides that (a) a man shall be liable to maintain his wife and children and (b) a woman shall be liable to maintain her husband and children. There is no similar liability imposed on unmarried couples. During the relationship the married and unmarried couple will be treated in exactly the same way,[98] and the definition of an unmarried couple in the Act is two people 'living together as husband and wife'.[99] Such an approach may seem distinctly equivocal as regards marriage, but the policy justification advanced for this treatment is that it ensures that cohabitants are not placed in a better position than their married counterparts.[100] Thus, if the requirements and resources of an unmarried couple were not aggregated in the same way as those of a married couple, in order to calculate benefit, the unmarried couple could receive two single non-householder rates with the appropriate shared housing expenses addition, instead of the considerably lower rate for a couple. All couples are treated alike for the purposes of calculating the award of benefit, but it is laid down in the 1976 Act that in the case of an unmarried couple a period of adjustment may be allowed before they are treated as a unit for assessment purposes.[101] During this period benefit will continue to be paid for an individual or for both parties in their own right, together with any relevant dependant's additions. The circumstances in which such a period may run are where the unit is likely to suffer an abrupt reduction in income, and thus needs time to adjust, in which case the period may run for a maximum of ten weeks. Despite the definition provided in the Act,[102] no further attempt is made in the Act or the Regulations to indicate the criteria which should be used to decide whether the parties are 'living together as husband and wife'. Guidance is, however, provided in the *Supplementary Benefits Handbook,*[103] and it is worth noting that the guidelines given there form the basis for ascertaining a couple's position throughout the field of Social Security law, and are strikingly similar to those used by the courts when interpreting the issue of whether a couple's relationship could be said to be family-like.[104] The main criteria are membership of the same household, stability of the relationship, financial arrangements, the existence of a sexual relationship, the presence of children, and the degree of public acknowledgement. If all those criteria are satisfied in the opinion of the benefit officer, then the couple will be treated as living together as husband and wife.[105]

Before the implementation of regulations giving effect to the new equality provisions, only the male partner of a couple can claim benefit,[106] which can cause difficulties if he proves reluctant to hand over money to the woman. The same sort of problems arise upon the breakdown of the relationship, and marital status is relevant. Where the parties are married, the 1976 Act provides that they are under a duty to maintain each other.[107] Furthermore, the Act provides that where a party to the marriage so fails to maintain the other party that she has to resort to benefit, the Secretary of State can take steps to recover the amount of benefit originally paid out for the other party.[108] This is done by laying a complaint before the magistrates for the recovery of that amount, and if one spouse continues to fail to maintain the other, he can be made the subject of criminal proceedings.[109] Additionally, where the marriage relationship has broken down and one spouse has obtained a court order for maintenance,[110] should the partner fail to pay such maintenance and his spouse be forced to resort to benefit, the Secretary of State can use similar procedures to recover that benefit and ensure future compliance with the court order.[111]

As far as cohabitants are concerned, however, benefit is paid out to the male claimant, but there seems to be no obvious method of enforcing his liability to use it or pay it over for his partner's benefit. The woman is unable to claim more benefit in her own right, since she is deemed to be living with the man, and her only recourse may be to the provisions relating to payments in urgent cases under s.4 of the Act.[112] By virtue of regulation 22 of the Supplementary Benefit Urgent Cases Regulations 1981,[113] if by default or otherwise the man is not maintaining the women, a payment may be made to her, and furthermore the DHSS is not debarred from attempting to recover it in the way outlined above by anything in Regulation 25. It can, therefore, be argued that there is a back door method of enforcing the man's responsibility to maintain someone for whom he is claiming an allowance, but only where she applies for an urgent needs payment. Where the cohabiting relationship has come to an end, however, there is no continuing duty on either party to support the other, and each party will once again have to claim benefits in their own right.

Under the Family Income Supplement scheme there is the same test for an unmarried couple.[114] There must be at least one child before resort can be made to this scheme.[115] The unit for assessment has to be a 'proper' family; once again the presence of children is all-important. Where the family income falls below prescribed levels for a family of that size, then half the difference between the prescribed level and the actual income will be paid to meet the family's needs.[116]

The other area in the state non-contributory scheme where unmarried parties are in a similar position to their married counterparts in relation to income support is when the female partner applies for 'housewives non-contributory invalidity pension'. Under the provisions of the relevant Acts[117] a woman either married or living as a wife with a man to whom she is not married is entitled to a non-contributory invalidity pension where she is 'incapable of performing normal household duties'. Since, as Pearl points out,[118] the regulations relating to qualification for this benefit are extremely restrictive, it is to be hoped that the cohabiting claimant is not further handicapped by the fact that her situation does not call for the same household duties as those owed by a wife to a husband.

Pensions

This is a field of considerable interest, because, while the position now seems clear as regards public sector pensions, it is much less so in respect of those in the private sector. Moreover, there have been some surprising shifts in direction over the course of years.

In the state scheme, where both parties to a marriage have worked, then each is entitled to Category A pension plus the additional Category B component based on their respective contributions and earnings where they have not opted for an occupational pension scheme.[119] Where the woman has had time out of work looking after children or a relative, the home responsibilities provision applies, and provided such time amounts to no more than twenty years, she can still potentially achieve the same rate of pension as would a woman who had had no time out.[120] Where there is any shortfall in the basic component because of a deficiency in her contribution record, this can be made good by reference to the husband's contributions.[121] The additional component is, however, payable only by reference to her contributions. For cohabitants who are both working the same provisions apply, except that the woman could not rely on the man's contributions to make up any shortfall in her record for the basic pension.

If the woman is not employed, or has not paid voluntary contributions, she will have a claim to a Category B retirement pension when she and her husband reach retirement, provided he has met the contribution conditions.[122] This amounts to 60 per cent of the basic Category A pension, and the same benefit is available to the husband as an increase to his pension if he has reached retirement age and retired but the wife has not, and she is dependent on him. Where the wife is employed but paying reduced rate contributions, then the position is exactly the same. There is no such pension for cohabiting couples except insofar as the man can claim an increase to the Category A pension where the woman has the care of his children.[123] Where such a woman is living with a man who is in receipt of a pension, then, if she is over pensionable age, she will have to apply under the Supplementary Benefit scheme for a supplementary pension.[124] The 'cohabitation rule' applies, so that the couple's requirements and resources are aggregated, and pension for the woman calculated accordingly.

Upon the breakdown of the relationship spouses are again in an advantageous position as compared to cohabitants. Upon divorce, the wife loses direct and indirect claims to the Category B pension unless the divorce occurs after she is 60,[125] but her claim to a Category A pension may be based on the husband's contribution record during the years of marriage and the spouses' qualifying years before and after marriage.[126] The position of a divorced husband is similar. He may rely on his wife's contribution record in exactly the same way.[127] Where the cohabiting relationship breaks down, the parties have no right to a pension by reason of the other party's contributions, although the man may still claim an increase to his pension where the woman is looking after children, provided he is still entitled to child benefit in respect of them.[128] Again, the cohabitants will have to resort to supplementary pensions where insufficient contributions have failed to secure to them a pension in their own right.[129] The importance of the loss of pension rights upon breakdown is acknowledged in relation to married couples in the statutory guidelines for the assessment of maintenance laid down in the Matrimonial Causes Act 1973. Thus, s.25(1)(g) specifically refers to the effect of the loss of any benefit, such as pension, which would be occasioned by the dissolution or annulment of the marriage. The loss of such support may even be the basis for refusing a divorce based on five years' separation and the absence of the respondent's consent, where the party can prove that grave financial hardship would ensue and that it is contrary to the interests of justice to grant a divorce.[130] So far no such defence has been raised in relation to 'state' pension rights, presumably because of the special provisions relating to divorces occurring after the wife has reached the age of 60,[131] and also because differences in the rates of ordinary and supplementary pensions would in the past have been quite small.[132] Cohabitants are thus in a far worse position than married parties, being unable to rely on their partner's contribution records, or to take any action to protect themselves.

Under private occupational schemes cohabitants may fare slightly better, and certainly under the servicemen's war pension schemes they once occupied a much more secure position than, curiously, they do now.[133] Such military pensions are today more correctly characterised as part of the social security system, being analogous to the benefits provided under the industrial injuries scheme.[134] but this was not always so. Indeed, for a considerable period after the Second World War these pension schemes were similar to occupational schemes. They included in their eligibility provisions a person known as an 'unmarried dependant living as a wife' who was entitled to all spousal-type benefits, including receipt of a pension.[135] Female spouses and cohabitants were treated similarly, except the amount of benefit payable to a wife was usually higher. Under some schemes even separated wives took priority in any disputes.

Thus, as Rosettenstein comments: 'these military schemes were prepared to recognise plural forms of domestic relationships and the member's right to make his own choice in regard thereto, while indicating in quantum a preference for legal marriage'.[136] The system was changed, however, in 1964 by administrative direction, so that these war pension schemes thenceforth only recognised the position of the cohabitant where she was looking after the claimant's dependent child.[137] The schemes were thereby aligned with the state schemes and the woman effectively turned into a child-minder on behalf of the state.

Currently, many occupational pension schemes in England do allow a member to nominate part of his pension in favour of a spouse or dependant, the amount of such nomination being up to one half, but generally limited to one third.[138] Most partners will not pretend to be spouses, so that entitlement to a pension will depend upon proof of dependence. A finding of such dependence is subject to the exercise of administrative discretion, as is the general question of the acceptance of the individual as a beneficiary under the scheme. In any event, as far as cohabitants are concerned, they can only be nominated when the member is about to retire, unlike a spouse, who may qualify immediately upon the partner joining the scheme.[139] In addition a cohabitant's claim may be defeated by a prior or subsequent allocation of the portion, or alternatively by the partner's later marriage.[140] The cohabitant, unlike the spouse, has no recourse to any adjustive procedure whereby compensation could be made for such a loss.[141] Where the member spouse has made no provision by nomination, then any payments will be solely at the discretion of the officials operating the scheme, and if a cohabitant is given nothing, resort must be made to other measures.[142]

Support after the partner's death

While recognition of a dependent cohabitant is entirely discretionary under the nomination provisions of private pension schemes, Parliament has acknowledged that cohabitants may in certain circumstances make a claim against a deceased partner's estate where no or inadequate provision has been made for that partner. The Inheritance (Provision for Family and Dependants) Act 1975 allows an application to be made by a de facto spouse for reasonable maintenance out of the deceased's estate, where that person died on or after 1 April 1976.[143] The Act gives the court power to overturn the express wishes of the testator in any way it thinks fit. The deceased's lawfully married spouse can also apply under this procedure where the spouse died testate but without making any provision in the will for such spouse, though it must be noted that a spouse's claim is not restricted to 'reasonable' provision.[144] Where the deceased died intestate, a lawful spouse but not a cohabitant is protected by the Administration of Estates Act 1925.[145]

Considerable controversy surrounded the introduction of the 1975 Act. It was argued that the provisions protecting de facto spouses would cause trouble amongst families and would become a 'Mistresses'

Charter'.[146] Despite such predictions the Act seems to have worked well.

The 1975 Act provides in s.1(3) that an application can be made by a de facto spouse as a 'dependant' for reasonable financial provision, provided that immediately before death he or she was being wholly or partly maintained by the deceased. Such maintenance by the deceased had to be otherwise than for full valuable consideration and by way of a substantial contribution in money or money's worth towards the other party's reasonable needs. A surviving spouse does not have to satisfy any such test, even where the marriage was actually void, nor indeed does the deceased's former spouse where he or she has not remarried, and such spouses are not limited to provision by way of maintenance. It will be apparent from the terms of the section that the Act is not unduly generous to unmarried partners: thus, it might be difficult for a man to prove the necessary degree of dependence;[147] where the survivor has been the breadwinner there can be no claim against the partner's estate;[148] and where there are surviving legitimate family members, the unmarried partner's claim may be postponed to any of their interests.[149] An interesting gloss has been put on the interpretation of s.1(1)e by virtue of s.3(1) and (3). S.3(3) directs the court to look at the basis upon which the deceased had assumed responsibility for any maintenance; s.3(1) provides a list of guidelines to form the basis for the exercise of the court's powers to award provision, including 'any other matter including the conduct of the applicant or any other person, which in the circumstances of the case the court may consider relevant'. Out of these two provisions the courts have managed to construct a concept of the morality of the parties' respective positions.

Thus, in *Re Coventry*,[150] the Court of Appeal said that whether the deceased was under some moral duty to maintain an applicant could be relevant in assessing whether reasonable provision had been made. A similar stance has been adopted in *C.A. v C.C.*[151] In this case a comparatively young female cohabitant was awarded reasonable financial provision of £5,000 out of the estate, which the deceased partner had left by will to his legitimate son. The parties' own child was held to be entitled to an equal share in the estate with his legitimate half-brother. Counsel for the legitimate son argued that the woman had merely acted as a housekeeper for the deceased. The court did not agree with this contention and found that the woman had been much more than an employee. She and the deceased were described by the court as having had a stable family relationship; she had been a loyal de facto wife, she had given birth to a son by him, and she had been fully maintained by him up to his death. The deceased had, said Sir George Baker, the President of the Family Division, 'a moral obligation to make reasonable financial provision for her'. To what extent such a moral obligation arose from the existence of a child of the union is a matter of speculation. Whatever the reason, the moral obligation was legally recognised.

The problems faced by parties without children was demonstrated by two cases reported in 1980. *Re Beaumont*[152] concerned a claim by a male survivor of a relationship which had begun in 1940. The parties had more or less shared household expenditure and duties along traditional lines, though the woman had throughout the relationship made it clear that the bungalow was hers and had even paid the man for decorating work he had done. On the female partner's death, the man applied for provision under the 1975 Act, but his claim was rejected by the court. The Vice-Chancellor, Sir Robert Megarry, found that not only had the applicant failed to prove that the deceased had ever in fact assumed responsibility for his maintenance, but, even if this were the case, such a pooling of joint resources as they had practised constituted full valuable consideration for such maintenance and would thus also have barred the claim.

The case of *H v G and D*[153] also indicates a tougher line where the parties have clearly been economically self-supporting while pooling their resources in order to share living expenses. The decision also seems to be one with moral overtones, since it comes out firmly in favour of legitimate dependants. The parties had lived together for only two years. The court found that there had been very full consideration from both, and held, following *Re Beaumont,* that making equal contributions to each other's needs by sharing expenses amounted to full valuable consideration under the provisions of the Act. Looking at all the circumstances, Reeve J considered that the application was an impertinent one which should never have been made, particularly since this and similar applications could work considerable injustice towards beneficiaries under small estates. Furthermore, he thought the interest of legitimate dependants, in this case a son and daughter, had to be protected. A distinct moral reaction against cohabitants and in favour of legitimate family members can be detected here.

Where a claim is made by a dependant or a cohabitant, how does the court calculate reasonable financial provision? In *CA v CC* it was almost as though a figure was plucked out of the air, but in *Malone v Harrison*[154] the calculation was tackled in a rather surprising way. This case was made even more interesting by the presence of one wife, one de facto wife, and one 'mistress' in the old sense of that term. The deceased was a successful businessman who had separated from his wife, lived with another woman and her son for some years, and later met and established a relationship with the plaintiff which largely accorded with the man and mistress arrangement common in previous centuries. Until his death in 1977 he had provided quite generously for the plaintiff. The court ruled that she was a dependant of his, that a lump sum was the appropriate method of compensation, and that this should be calculated by a capitalisation of the plaintiff's future needs. This quite remarkable innovation contrasts sharply with the divorce courts' practice of awarding a lump sum 'by way of recognition of a spouse's previous contributions to the welfare of a marriage'.[155] The actual method used to quantify those needs was the multiplier, a device used by lawyers in calculating damages for personal injuries. From actual annual needs were deducted present annual resources, the resultant figure then being multiplied by the number of years left before retirement age. This sum was added to the figure produced by multiplying the sum of her annual needs by five to provide a capital sum for the period after her working life. Finally, from the combined totals, free capital and capital assets were deducted, leaving the appropriate figure for the lump sum. Bryan[156] quite justifiably comments that, in view of the poor press which the multiplier has received from tort lawyers, it is surprising to find the Family Division 'experimenting with this dangerous toy'. The combination of the 1975 Act and what has been called the 'Mistresses' Multiplier' suggests that a surviving cohabitant, or even a dependent mistress, would be better off where the partner dies rather than deserts, at least so far as rights to maintenance are concerned.[156a] It may also be noted that the term 'wife' has been held to be effective to pass a gift to a de facto spouse even where a lawful wife is living at the date of disposition, and even where they could never have contracted a marriage because they were within the prohibited degrees of relationship.[157]

Under the Fatal Accidents Act 1976, however, although a lawful spouse can claim, as can any child (legitimate or otherwise), to be within the class of 'dependants' who can claim in respect of the deceased tort victim's death, this provision does not extend to cohabitants.[158] So, in *K v J.M.P. Co.,*[159] the Court of Appeal rejected the argument that a mother as housekeeper and guardian of children suffers financial loss as a result of being deprived of the deceased's support, which loss should be reflected in the damages for the dependent children. The cohabitant's only remedy is to resort to the provisions of the 1975 Act[160] or, if appropriate, the Industrial Injuries Death Benefit scheme.[161]

The position of the cohabitant within the social security scheme on the partner's death could scarcely be less attractive. The lawful spouse is entitled to a death grant and, if a woman, to a widow's allowance[162] and, depending on the circumstances, to various other allowances.[163] A male spouse is entitled on his wife's death to an invalidity pension,[164] and to pensions in exactly the same way as a widow.[165] A cohabitant is not entitled to any of these benefits, even the meagre death grant.[166] The only two provisions of social security system which benefit cohabitants are in the Industrial Injuries and Diseases area. If death occurs as a result of industrial injuries, a female cohabitant may claim an allowance of £1 a week.[167] A male cohabitant may not.

The most generous treatment of cohabitants in the state schemes is provided by the Pneumoconiosis Act 1979. This provides for compensation for those who suffer ill-health through lung diseases, namely pneumoconiosis, byssinosis and diffuse mesotheliema. Where a person so suffering dies, the categories of people entitled to claim compensation under s.3 include 'any reputed spouse living with him or her'. There is no condition as to proof of dependence or maintenance, as there is under the Inheritance (Provision for Family and Dependants) Act 1975. In the 1979 statute the lawfully married spouse and the reputed spouse are put on an equal footing. Parliament has not, however, specified what is meant by 'reputed spouse'. The concept is, war-time experience and the Consumer Credit Act 1974[168] apart, a new one in English law. Whatever the reason for its presence, the concept has found a place within the social security system, and, in the generous treatment it affords to cohabitants, stands in stark contrast to the other generally punitive cohabitation provisions. It could be a potential source of embarrassment, and perhaps even a threat, to the broad principles of preferential treatment for married persons which in general characterises the whole English social security system.

Income support for the child

(i) While both parents are alive

Recent legislative policy in England, as in a number of other countries, has clearly favoured moves towards the elimination of differences between the legitimate and illegitimate child. The illegitimate child continues, however, to experience some discrimination within the legal system. Whereas responsibility for the maintenance of a legitimate child rests equally with both parents,[169] that of the illegitimate child falls on the mother alone.[170] During marriage either spouse can obtain an order for financial provision for the child against the other, where that other has failed to provide reasonable maintenance for the child.[171] Such an order can be made even though the parties are living together.[172] Where a married couple is in receipt of supplementary benefit, and one party fails to maintain the child, then the DHSS can threaten and take proceedings against a culpable parent.[173] Failure by a cohabitant parent to maintain the child while the parents live together can only result in proceedings where the culpable party is the father, since the mother can use affiliation proceedings.[174] Where the offending party is the woman, the man has no recourse to the law whatsoever.

Upon the breakdown of his parents' marriage the legitimate child can be provided for in proceedings alleging failure to maintain.[175] Where his parents divorce, a whole range of financial provision and property adjustment orders is available.[176] The maintenance of such children is the equal responsibility of each parent. Special guidelines are laid down [177] to assist the court to determine the amount and type of order. These include the standard of living enjoyed by the child before breakdown, the manner and type of his education, and his financial needs and resources. The children of divorcing parents are given further limited protection by a statutory condition preventing the final dissolution of the parents' marriage unless the court is satisfied that the arrangements for their future are satisfactory, or the best that can be devised in the circumstances.[178] No such mantle of protection is thrown around the children of cohabiting parents whose relationship breaks down. Mothers of such children are forced to rely on the Affiliation Proceedings Act to obtain a court order declaring the man to be the father of the children and ordering him to pay maintenance for them.[179] The orders which can be made by the magistrates in such proceedings resemble the orders which those courts can make for legitimate children.[180] Periodical payments and lump-sum orders are now available regardless of status. Further, the guidelines provided for the magistrates when exercising their discretion in making orders for children are now very similar.[181] In the past the amount of affiliation orders has been low and there have been notorious difficulties relating to enforcement.[182]

Action has to be taken under the Affiliation Acts by the mother either within the first three years of the date of the child's birth, within twelve months of the father's return to the country if he left during that three-year period, or at any time where the mother can prove that the father has been maintaining the child during the last three years.[183] Proceedings may be undertaken while the parties are cohabiting. In addition to the drawbacks already mentioned, such proceedings are limited to applications by the mother alone,[184] so that where the woman has been the breadwinner, the man will be forced to resort to the supplementary benefit scheme. Where circumstances warrant the payment of benefit for the children, then it is possible that the DHSS at least could take action against the woman as the liable relative.[185] It is not at all surprising that no provision has been made for men in such a situation, given previous social mores. The affiliation procedure seems unsuitable for use by men, since it was designed specifically for use against them. It was devised to meet a very different problem from that posed by cohabiting parents whose relationship breaks down. It is supposed to provide some small measure of support for children whose fathers had more than likely had only a very casual relationship with the mother, and who would probably have preferred to ignore the results of such brief encounters altogether. An affiliation order could almost be characterised as a punishment inflicted on a man for the 'crime' of casual sexual intercourse resulting in the birth of a child outside marriage. In a sense it is a fine and compensation order rolled into one.

Proposals for reforming the provisions relating to the maintenance of children born out of wedlock have been made by the Law Commission's Working Party in its paper on *Illegitimacy*. In addition to proposing the abolition of the status of illegitimacy,[186] it proposes that maintenance procedures be reformed and that jurisdiction to make maintenance orders conferred on the courts under the Guardianship of Minors Act 1971 be extended to all children.[187] It further proposes that fathers and mothers should equally be able to apply for maintenance orders; there would be no time limit on the bringing of such proceedings, and there should be powers to make secured periodical payments and even property adjustment orders in such proceedings.[188] Until such reforms are enacted, the position of children born of a cohabiting relationship is very weak in comparison with those born in lawful wedlock.

State income support for children through the contributory and non-contributory schemes generally makes no distinction between the legitimate and illegitimate child. Thus, increases can be obtained to all state benefits in respect of dependent children,[189] and, on breakdown of the parents' relationship, be it marriage or cohabitation, the partner who is actually contributing to the child's maintenance can claim the child's increase to the contributory benefits,[190] although child benefit will be payable usually to the party actually living with the child.[191] Similarly, under the supplementary benefit scheme, the child's increase is payable in respect of the assessment unit of which he forms a member,[192] as is Family Income Supplement.[193] The parent who is left looking after the child, whether legitimate or not, is also entitled to the child benefit increase for the first child in a lone parent family[194] and at present to the benefit of the reduced rate of hours qualifying as a full week's work for Family Income Supplement purposes.[195]

(ii) On the death of one of the child's parents

Where the relationship of the child's parents is ended by the death of one of them, there are now fewer differences between the respective positions of the illegitimate and legitimate child. If the deceased parent has left property in a will to his or her 'child', such reference now includes legitimate and illegitimate offspring.[196] Where a parent excludes an illegitimate child from his will, such a child has a right under the Inheritance Act 1975 to claim provision, and does not, unlike the surviving unmarried parent, have to prove dependence.[197] Indeed, in *C.A. v C.C.*[198] the legal representative was more than willing to acknowledge at once the right of the illegitimate child to an equal share in the father's estate with his half-brother. On the intestacy of a deceased parent an illegitimate child is entitled to claim provision, under the Administration of Estates Act 1925 as amended, in the same way as the legitimate child,[199] and similarly on the child's death intestate the parents are equally entitled. But the illegitimate child cannot inherit on the intestacy of any of his other relatives nor they on his, although the Law Commission has further proposed that this rule should be removed so as to equalise the inheritance provisions for children and their relatives regardless of status.[200] Under the Fatal Accidents Act 1976 a child, whether or not legitimate, may make a claim; so may the father or mother of any child.[201]

As far as state benefits are concerned, awards under the Industrial Injuries Death benefit scheme[202] and the Pneumoconiosis Act 1979[203] are payable in respect of dependent children with no condition as to status. Where the legitimate child's father has died and the parents have been divorced, then, although the mother will have lost the right to widowed mother's allowance, she will in certain circumstances be able to rely on the ex-husband's contributions to claim child's special allowance, which is at a higher rate than the ordinary dependent child's increase to her benefit.[204] The mother of an illegitimate child whose ex-partner has died cannot make such a claim and is forced to rely on ordinary dependent child increases.[205] The only situation in which a surviving cohabitant could claim extra provision for the child under the state scheme is where the survivor is not a parent, or the other parent cannot be found, or is also dead, or is in prison. Such a person is rewarded for undertaking the task of child-minding on behalf of the State and may claim Guardian's Allowance.[206]

Other parental rights and duties in respect of children

The Children Act 1975 provides in s.85(1) that parental rights and duties encompass all the rights and duties which by law the mother and father have in relation to a legitimate child and his property, and include a right of access and any other element included in a right or duty. It is interesting to note that parental rights and duties are defined by reference to the legitimate child, whose parents indeed share such rights equally,[207] whereas they are possessed only by the mother in the case of an illegitimate child.[208] While one of the parental rights includes the right to agree to a child's adoption,[209] it is interesting to note that couples may adopt a child only where lawfully married.[210] The unmarried couple is excluded by statute,[211] although it may be possible to argue that this provision breaches the European Convention on Human Rights by denying the individual's right to family life.[212]

Disputes as to the legitimate child's upbringing or custody can be readily resolved by resort to a variety of procedures. Disagreements between the cohabitant parents can be resolved by unilateral action on the mother's part, since she has sole rights, and if the father desires to have some control, he has first to make an application for custody under the Guardianship of Minors Act 1971.[213] The same procedure has to be used upon breakdown of the relationship should the father want custody of his illegitimate children,[214] access to them,[215] or even the right to be consulted as to their future upbringing.[216] Once this process is set in motion, the court can make orders similar to those available in respect of legitimate children.[217] Where one of the partners is not a parent but has treated the child as 'a child of the family', his only recourse will be to wardship proceedings. The parents of a legitimate child face no such procedural hurdles before they can apply for orders in respect of their children. Stepfathers upon breakdown of a relationship are also in a better position than putative fathers. As a party to a marriage the stepfather may, if he has treated the children as 'children of the family',[218] be awarded custody of them, or access,[219] though conversely he may also be ordered to pay maintenance in respect of them.[220] A stepfather is not, however, a parent for the purposes of the Guardianship legislation[221] and, therefore, where any dispute arises during the relationship, the procedure under the 1971 Act cannot be used, with the result that the mother has the final power to make a decision in any dispute between them.

Where one of the parents of the illegitimate child is not given custody or some of the parental rights, then the other parent is put in a much stronger position than the ex-spouse, whose every move may be disputed and referred to the court.[222] Whereas both the legitimate parents must always give their agreement and be consulted no matter what the order in divorce proceedings,[223] where the non-custodial cohabitant is a man, he only has a right to be consulted where he is paying maintenance and has no right to withhold his agreement to an adoption.[224] Where the non-custodial parent is the mother, she retains the power to withhold agreement.[225] Clearly, then, without a custody order in his favour the illegitimate father may experience difficulties. It has not been unknown, however, for the father of an illegitimate child, hearing of an adoption proposal to intervene, to bring custody proceedings and apply for liberty to adopt the child himself.[226] Such situations are rare and those where the court grants such a request even more so, but they may occur with greater frequency in the future.[226a] It is clear that the present procedure is cumbersome and unduly discriminatory against the fathers of illegitimate children. The proposals in the Law Commission Working Paper would undoubtedly improve their position. Thus, consequent upon the abolition of the status of illegitimacy, the parents of an illegitimate child would henceforth have equal parental rights and duties.[227]

This would entail the granting of many new rights to the illegitimate father, even when he is not awarded custody. He would thenceforth as a parent claim the right *inter alia* to agree to adoption, to the child's marriage, to the change of the child's surname, and would have the power to appoint testamentary guardians.[228] Although these proposals and the others which have been referred to are in line with recent legislative policy, they have met with considerable opposition, with the result that the Commission is finding it difficult to translate its proposals into an acceptable legislative formula. The crux of the proposals, the complete abolition of the status of illegitimacy, must, if enacted, mark an unprecedented blow against the weakening armour of legislative protection surrounding the institution of marriage. It is partly because of the legal disadvantages and the resultant stigma attaching to the status of illegitimacy that many cohabitants still marry upon, or in anticipation of, the birth of a child.[229] If the legal disadvantages were to be removed, the social stigma attaching to illegitimacy would in due course diminish, and one of the few remaining and pressing reasons for marriage might decrease in importance.

Rights of the parties in the home

There is no special property regime for married persons, though the courts have made allowances for the marriage relationship when settling any property disputes.[230] Such allowances are not necessarily made for those couples who live together;[231] some judges, however, have increasingly demonstrated an alarming willingness to make them,[232] and only a few have held out against doing so.[233]

Marriage enables its participants to use provisions and procedures specifically intended to aid the resolution of property problems arising during, or on the breakdown of, the marriage relationship. The Married Women's Property Act 1882 established the principle of separate property as between husband and wife, and by s.17 provided a means by which any disputes over property could be referred to, and determined by, the courts. Later statutes were, however, to make inroads into this principle of separate property, which even at the time of its passage was more of a sop to middle-class ideals than working-class practice. The Married Women's Property Act 1964 provided by section 1 that where the wife had met any expenses on the home, purchased any property, or made any savings, from money derived from a housekeeping allowance paid by the husband, then any interests arising therefrom belonged to the couple jointly. Where either of the spouses contributes in money or money's worth to the improvement of real or personal property in which, or in the proceeds of sale of which, either or both of them has or have a beneficial interest, then that party shall, if the contribution is of a substantial nature and subject to any express or implied agreement to the contrary, be treated as having acquired a share or enlarged share in that beneficial interest.[234] Finally, once property rights as between the married couple have been determined in accordance with these statutory provisions, the court has the power on divorce, nullity or judicial separation, or thereafter, to vary or even extinguish the interests of one party in favour of the other.[235]

In exercising its powers the court is restricted in the same way as it is in making orders under s.23. Thus s.25 of the 1973 Act declares that it is the duty of the court to have regard to all the circumstances of the case and the guidelines therein laid down. The court has to consider many factors, such as the income, resources and responsibilities of the parties, their respective ages, their health, the duration of the marriage, and the contributions of either to looking after the family and the home. It may also look to the conduct of each of the parties to the marriage, though it rarely does so.[236] In just the same way as these guidelines seemed to influence the courts when dealing with problems of income support as between cohabitants, and as regards their children, they have also exerted considerable influence upon decisions regarding property rights. Obviously, most judges[237] make no conscious reference to the guidelines when looking at the rights of the unmarried couple, but if the decisions are analysed, a large number reveal a consideration of some or all of those factors to which the divorce court judge must have regard.[238] The very construction of what is now s.25 was influenced by factors not only deemed relevant as between spouses, but which had prior to the 1970s been found to be of importance in justifying the conferring of property interests on cohabitants.[239] Yet again it was to be the fulfilment of family type or quasi-marital roles which was to determine the nature and extent of the rights of the cohabiting couple.

Crucial differences remain in the means used to determine property rights between married and unmarried couples, even if the results achieved may be indistinguishable. In creating rights to interests in property for the unmarried, an increasing number of courts have derived support from considerations used to vary established legal rights in the case of married couples.[240] As so often in the past in relation to married couples, so now the justification for varying property interests between unmarried couples is what is said to be the morality of the situation, the need to do justice in the case.[241] But what is the nature of that morality, and what ends does that justice achieve?

Where the legal interests of the parties in the home appear on the face of the deed, one would anticipate few problems. For married couples where the house is in joint names, the adjustive mechanism of s.24 can come into play upon breakdown and vary or even extinguish one spouse's interest, or perhaps more likely postpone the exercise of the trust for sale where there are children,[242] and allot each party a fixed interest in the proceeds of sale at some future date. Provided legal interests are clearly expressed, the parties to a cohabiting relationship should be entitled to such share as is indicated without reference to any other issues. The cases of *Crisp v Mullings*[243] and *Lawrence v McFarlane*[244] are straightforward applications of these principles. The facts were very similar in that both partners had joined in the mortgage and title deeds, with the men in each case later assuming responsibility for the actual mortgage payments and the woman paying all other household expenses. Both men later sought to say that the women were mere nominees holding the legal interest on resulting trust for them. The men's claims were rejected; the courts found that the beneficial interest should be shared equally, subject to certain adjustments for deposit monies, improvements, and mortgage repayments after separation. In each case the courts relied on the indirect contribution principle, described in *Gissing v Gissing*[245] as of particular relevance in cases involving husbands and wives, and adopted in many subsequent cases.[246] That it could be of relevance to married couples was undisputed. There was no need to imply, however, that its extension to unmarried couples had to be by way of analogy. Thus, in *Crisp v Mullings,* Russell LJ felt compelled to describe the couple as having held 'typical man and wife discussions' in relation to their financial arrangements, which he thought were 'highly probable between parties in their situation'. These statements were quoted with approval in *Lawrence v McFarlane.* There seems no reason why such considerations should have crept into the decisions. Applying ordinary principles of law and equity without any reference to marital-like behaviour would have enabled the courts to have achieved exactly the same result.

The cases of *Re Evers's Trust*[247] and *Dennis v McDonald*[248] further demonstrate the courts' felt need to justify decisions affecting cohabitants' property rights by reference to what can be done for the legally married family. In each case premises had been purchased in joint names as a house for the couple and the children of the family. In each case the parents' relationship had broken down and one of the partners had applied for an order for sale under s.30 of the Law of Property Act 1925, which application the other party opposed. In *Re Evers* the Court of Appeal held that in exercising its discretion, the court had to consider both the primary purposes of the trust, i.e. that of sale, and its underlying purpose, i.e. that of providing a home not only for the parents but also for the children. It clearly had no power to adjust the property rights of the parties under s.24 of the 1973 Act, since they were not married, but nevertheless in determining the underlying purpose of a trust in a case under s.30 it held it had to consider the interests of the children both legitimate and illegitimate. Indeed, Ormrod LJ declared that the exercise of the discretion given by s.30 in family cases would bring it as far as possible into line with the exercise of discretion given by s.24 of the 1973 Act.[249] The court accordingly found that the underlying purpose of the trust was to provide a family home for the indefinite future and dismissed the male partner's application, leaving him with liberty to apply at a future date should circumstances change. In *Dennis v McDonald* Purchas J refused the woman's application for an order for sale, citing *Re Evers* as authority for the proposition that an immediate order for sale could not be proper, since the purpose of the trust had been to provide a family home, and the premises were still being used as such, though for only half the family. The woman in this case had left the family home some years before the application with the two younger children, but the man had remained, looking after the three elder children. In the circumstances, however, the judge did order that the man should pay occupational rent to the woman by virtue of the fact that she was a co-owner who had been excluded and prevented from exercising her right to occupy the property. The courts in both cases, though, made explicit reference to, and analogies with, powers under s.24 of the 1973 Act. This, we argue, is totally unnecessary, given that the alleged basis of the decision, the underlying purpose of the trust for sale, was a consideration of which they could legitimately take account.

Where the legal interests are clear on the face of the title deeds, both parties' signatures are required on any documents affecting title to or enjoyment of the property, regardless of the parties' marital status. Similarly on death, if a couple married or unmarried have been legal joint tenants, the deceased's share will accrue to the survivor, although difficulties may arise where the deceased cohabitant was married to someone else or had other legal dependants.

Where a couple has not made their legal position clear on the title deeds, there are likely to be serious problems. Since most disputes arise upon breakdown of the relationship, married persons can generally, though not always, rely on the adjustive mechanism of s.24 of the 1973 Act to achieve 'justice' in their particular case, but cohabitants will have to establish an interest before the courts can consider giving them anything. Thus, cohabitants have in several cases sought to establish a beneficial interest in property by means of implied, resulting[250] or constructive trusts.[251] The courts have consequently had to investigate in detail the factual situations alleged to give rise to such trusts, and in many instances have had to infer that the relevant intention was to create a trust. Making such inferences is not something which the courts for the most part seem to find difficult.

The first case concerning cohabitants in which a resulting trust was raised was that of *Diwell v Farnes*[252] in 1959. The facts disclosed that the parties had shared expenses, with the man for the most part paying rental and later mortgage payments, and the woman paying occasional accommodation expenses but for the most part being responsible for household expenses. On the death of the male cohabitant, his widow claimed to be entitled exclusively to the premises. The Court of Appeal, however, held that the defendant cohabitant did not have an equitable interest in the proceeds of sale in proportion to her contributions to the mortgage. The cases relating to husbands and wives were inapplicable, said the court, and the majority could not find or infer evidence of a joint enterprise sufficient to justify the award of the half share which she had claimed.

By 1972, however, the Court of Appeal felt able to adopt a rather different view. In *Cooke v Head*[253] the parties, who originally intended to marry, built a bungalow together on land purchased by the man, although the woman did much heavy work in respect of the construction. On the breakdown of the relationship, the property was sold and the woman claimed a half share in the proceeds of sale. The court assessed her interest by way of resulting or constructive trust to be a third share, with Lord Denning MR and Karminski LJ agreeing that the method of assessing that interest should be similar to that applied in the case of married and engaged couples and other relationships. Thus, account could be taken not only of monetary contributions but also of such other factors in a relationship as the differences between their respective earnings, the pooling of resources to meet the joint household expenses, the amount of work each did in building the house and their understanding of mutual rights.

Such a quasi-marital approach did not entirely commend itself to Walton J in *Richards v Dove*,[254] where the parties had shared expenses, with the man making rental payments and then mortgage instalments and the woman being at all times responsible for household expenses. She had contributed £150 by way of loan only towards the deposit. The judge, in rejecting her claim for a half share in the proceeds of sale, found that although the woman had provided and cooked food, she had in return received free housing. Further, the £150 had been expressed to be by way of a loan and as such was inconsistent with any joint intention that she should thereby acquire any interest in the property. Walton J referred to the principles laid down in *Cooke v Head*, saying that he had no difficulty in accepting them subject to some qualification. He continued:

> . . . it by no means follows that the application of the same principles will produce identical results in the wife and mistress, because it is impossible to leave out of the picture the fact that as between the husband and the wife the husband has certain legal duties in relation to maintaining his wife, whereas between man and mistress the whole relationship is consensual — if you like contractual with no legal obligation superimposed.

Other courts have not, however, been so reluctant to recognise some sort of obligation on the man's part when considering the amount of the equitable interest to be awarded to the female partner. The parties in *Eves v Eves*[255] had lived together for four and a half years, the woman always believing that they would eventually marry. There were two children of the union. During the relationship the man had purchased a house in his name, though he said this was for technical reasons only and the house was actually for them both. The plaintiff had had no money to contribute to the purchase but she had done a lot of physical work in improving the house and getting it into a habitable condition. On the breakdown of the relationship the plaintiff sought a declaration as to her interest, and the Court of Appeal awarded her a quarter share by way of constructive trust. In Lord Denning's view such a trust had arisen in favour of the plaintiff by virtue of a common intention of the parties to join efforts in acquiring, maintaining and improving the property for their joint use, and that the woman's share should be such as would be fair in view of all that she had done for the defendant and the children.

It is significant that the courts have not only examined the parties' contributions to looking after the house and family but have also been prepared to examine the conduct of the parties. Thus, in *Eves v Eves* the man's assurance that the house was for both of them was found to be relevant, whereas in *Hodges v Hodges*[256] the man's insistence that the woman was to be his 'mistress' only was decisive in influencing the court's refusal of the woman's claim to a one-third interest in the house in which the parties had lived. In that case the property was in the man's name alone, the judge could find no evidence of a joint enterprise, and there were no children; accordingly the woman only received £500 by way of repayment for her contribution towards the purchase of a new motor car.

Conduct is of increasing relevance in the cases, particularly when it affects the 'weaker sex'. Indeed, it is crucial where the doctrine of equitable estoppel is raised. Thus, in *Pascoe v Turner*[257] the court found that the woman, relying on the man's assertion that the house would be hers, had expended much of her meagre capital on quite minor improvements to the property. In attempting to determine the minimum equity necessary to do justice, the court referred to the parties' conduct, their comparative financial position and the man's moral obligations, even though the woman had refused marriage. Simply granting the woman a life interest in the property (which was all she had requested) was not, said the court, sufficient. Equity could only be satisfied by compelling the man to give effect to his promise and her expectations. He had, said Cumming-Bruce LJ, so acted that he must now perfect the gift. Had the parties been married, the same result would no doubt have been achieved under s.24 of the 1973 Act, but to see equitable estoppel being used in this manner is all the more interesting because no reference was made to quasi-marital behaviour. Provided the principles are equally applied as between men and women, little objection may be taken to such an approach. Estoppel was again relied on in the case of *Greasley v Cooke.*[258] Here assurances were given not only by the cohabitant's deceased partner but also by his father and brother. The woman had been told by them all that she would have a home in their house for the rest of her life. Her conduct in living with one brother, looking after the others until they left and caring for their mentally ill sister until her death, demonstrated her reliance on such assertions. An equity had therefore been raised in her favour such that she was allowed to remain in the house rent-free for the rest of her life.

Conduct generally, and evidence of a joint intention in particular, have not only invited solutions to property problems on equitable principles, but have also raised the question of the inference of a contract in certain circumstances. Although the inference of a contract may be easier where the parties are married, the courts have not been loath to employ it in the context of cohabitation.

The contractual licence was the device relied upon by Lord Denning MR in *Tanner v Tanner*[259] in order to ensure that the woman received some form of compensation for the loss of her interest in a house bought by the man for her and their twin babies. The woman had moved with the children from her rent-controlled flat to the house at the defendant's invitation, although they never actually lived there together. The Court of Appeal held that the woman had an implied and irrevocable contractual licence to reside in the house as long as the children were of school age, that she had given consideration for the licence by giving up her own tenancy, and that the appropriate level of compensation for the loss of the tenancy was £2,000. Although such compensation may seem quite generous, it should be noted that he had originally offered £4,000 for her to surrender her interest. Further, if the parties had been married, the level of compensation would have been much higher.

The case of *Chandler v Kerley*[260] again saw the raising of a contractual licence in the woman's favour, although on this occasion it sufficed only to give her twelve months' occupation of the premises while she sought alternative accommodation. The facts were a little unusual in that the woman and her children had remained in her former matrimonial home, which was subsequently purchased at a reduced price from herself and her husband by her lover. Not only did the woman accept a lesser price for the house but she took a reduced share in the proceeds on the basis that she would remain in the home. The relationship broke down only six weeks after the purchase. The court's decision seems unduly harsh in the light of her reduced share, since she should have received some compensation to reflect her financial sacrifice and his gain. Even on principles of unjust enrichment such an award could have been justified. One other point of note (especially given the somewhat vitriolic comments of Lord Scarman) is the absence in this case of any children of the parties.

It is apparent, moreover, that the parties' common intention, express or implied, can be overridden by other more legitimate considerations. Thus, in *Horrocks v Forray,*[261] where the court was faced with the conflicting claims to the deceased's property of a wife and a mistress with a child, it came out in favour of the wife. The mistress had alleged that she had a contractual licence to remain in a house which the deceased had purchased in his name as a house for her and for their child. The deceased had throughout his life lavishly provided for the child and the woman, and indeed it was this conduct which had contributed to the diminution in the remaining residue of the estate. Unless the property was sold, the estate would have been insolvent. The Court of Appeal rejected the woman's contention that she had a contractual licence to remain in the house. She was given nothing from the estate. Megaw LJ after reciting the criteria necessary before a contract can be inferred, concluded that as the deceased had gone no further than contemplating future provision for the woman, and had never taken any steps in relation to the property, such criteria had not been satisfied and no licence could thus be established. The court distinguished the case from *Tanner v Tanner,* although if anything the deceased's conduct in this case pointed more clearly to continuing provision than did the plaintiff's conduct in *Tanner.* The crucial factors in *Horrocks v Forray* were certainly the deceased's extravagant provision in his lifetime for the mistress and child, and the presence of an impoverished widow, whose situation would have been considerably worsened by any finding in favour of the illegitimate family.

Absence of clear and express provision for the mistress and child was thus fatal in the circumstances of that case, but even where unmarried couples try to make express arrangements protecting the position of the survivor upon the death of one of them, the attempt may not always succeed. The position on the death of a cohabitant must, therefore, be examined in more detail.

Where the property is held in joint names, the doctrine of survivorship applies, and where one dies, his half share accrues to the other, who is then solely entitled to it. Spouses and cohabitants are thus treated equally. However, where any claims are made for family provision out of the accrued half-share, a spouse is in a stronger position to resist them than the cohabitant.[262] Similarly, an application to set aside a transaction of the property made six years before the party's death is much more likely to succeed where the applicant is a spouse.[263]

Where the house is in the sole name of the survivor, the partner's death should not generally entail different consequences as between married couples and cohabitants. A problem may arise, however, in relation to cohabitants where the deceased partner provided the whole or the major part of the purchase money.[264] The survivor could be deemed to hold the interest in the house on resulting trust for the estate, since the presumption of advancement does not apply between cohabitants as it may apply between man and wife.[265] What this may mean is that the surviving cohabitant may face a claim for family provision brought by legitimate family members under the avoidance provisions of s.10 of the 1975 Act.[266]

Where the house is in the deceased's sole name but has been left by will to the surviving partner, a lawful spouse is probably in a better position to make and to resist claims for family provision than the cohabitant.[267] If the deceased dies intestate and the cohabitant partner seeks to allege an interest in their home by way of resulting or constructive trust, estoppel or contractual licence, the position will be rather complicated.[268] There is the problem of the right to remain in occupation for the time being, as well as the question of the future position. A dead partner's interest passes to his executors or administrators, who become sole trustees under a trust for sale. The cohabitant should therefore at the same time as making a claim also apply for the appointment of a second trustee.[269] Where the trustees agree a sale may be postponed, but where the deceased's personal representatives and the newly appointed trustee disagree as, for example, where the latter is pressing for the cohabitant to remain in occupation, an application will have to be made to the court under s.30 of the Law of Property Act 1925. An order for sale under this section is in the court's discretion and, by analogy with *Re Evers* and *Dennis v McDonald,* would be unlikely to be ordered where some underlying purpose of the trust still remains. It is more than likely that if the cohabitant establishes a beneficial interest and is still living in the house with children of the union, the court will probably postpone sale until there is some appreciable change in circumstances on either side. The cohabitant could, apart from seeking the appointment of the new trustee, protect the right to occupation arising from the beneficial interest by registration of a charge (or, in the case of registered land, putting a notice or caution on the title)[270] and would in any event be protected by being in actual occupation of the home.[271] Any purchaser from the personal representatives would take subject to an overriding interest, and the existence of an equitable interest protected in this way by actual occupation would constitute such an interest.

Where the cohabitant alleges an interest arising by estoppel, the court makes a full investigation of the circumstances and, if it is proved that the cohabitant relied on assurances made by the deceased, an equity may be raised in the cohabitant's favour. This could result in an outright transfer of interest, analogous to *Pascoe v Turner*. Where there are claims by legitimate family members to be considered, it may result in the award of a life interest, as happened in *Greasley v Cooke.*

The position resulting from a claim to be entitled to the benefit of a contractual licence on the death of the partner has been considered in the case of *Horrocks v Forray.* The actual decision of the court in that case supposedly rested, however, on the lack of evidence of a clear intention to grant a contractual licence, so that, if such a clear intention could be found, the surviving cohabitant could claim protection under the terms of such a licence. Death would not operate to terminate the licence any more than the ending of the relationship did in *Chandler v Kerley,* and the licence would remain enforceable against the deceased's successors in title by means of injunction, provided there was no evidence as to the withdrawal before death of such a licence. This contractual licence would not, however, bind a purchaser for value without notice.

What emerges very clearly from the foregoing discussion is that, unless the parties have made express provision as to their respective interests in the home, the surviving cohabitant may be placed in a very difficult and vulnerable position. The cohabitant would probably be in a much stronger position where the parties had been living in rented property, although this follows from the very nature of such property.

Rights in relation to rented property on death

Where the tenant of property protected by the Rent Acts dies, a surviving spouse who was living with the deceased at the date of death has an immediate right to succeed to the tenancy.[272] Any other person who wishes to inherit, what is termed the 'statutory tenancy', must prove that he or she is a member of the deceased tenant's 'family', who resided with the deceased for the six months before his death.[273] The second condition is a question of fact, but the issue of membership of the tenant's 'family' has been controversial, especially in relation to cohabitation.

An early case concerning the meaning of the phrase 'member of the tenant's family' is *Brock v Wollams*[274] where the court held that an unofficially adopted daughter of the tenant could be a member of his family. The test applied was whether an ordinary man would have thought the parties were all members of the same family. However, in *Gammans v Ekins*[275] the Court of Appeal refused to accept that the male survivor of an unmarried couple who had lived together for twenty years was a member of the deceased partner's family. The court said that the word 'family' was used in its ordinary popular sense and it was impossible to say that the man was a member within that meaning. Asquith LJ put his objections to the man's claim thus: 'to say of two people masquerading as these two were as husband and wife, there being no children to complicate the picture, that they were members of the same family seems to me an abuse of the English language'.

In both *Jones v Trueman*[276] and *Hawes v Evenden*[277] there were children, and in each case the woman's claim on the death of her male partner to be considered a member of his family was accepted. In *Hawes v Evenden* the Court of Appeal was able to find this family relationship even though the woman had never taken the man's name. It was made clear, however, in *Ross v Collins*,[278] and approved in *Carega Properties v Sharratt*,[279] that simple membership of the same household by itself can never justify the finding of a family relationship. The first case concerned a claim by a housekeeper to be entitled to the statutory tenancy by succession. The court held that she was not a 'member of the tenant's family'. There had not been the kind of 'family relationship' exemplified by the case of *Hawes v Evenden*. *Carega Properties v Sharratt* confirmed this approach. A young man's claim to be considered a member of the deceased's widow's family was rejected. The House of Lords stated that the term 'family' had its ordinary meaning and could never mean 'household'. Furthermore, although 'family' was not limited to cases of a familial nexus in the strict legal sense, it still required a broadly recognisable familial nexus, and two adults living together in a platonic relationship, as had happened in this case, was insufficient to establish it.

Although the presence of children had meant that the strict test laid down in *Gammans v Ekins* could be by-passed, the question remained as to whether a childless couple would constitute a family for the purposes of gaining Rent Act protection. In *Dyson Holdings v Fox*[280] the Court of Appeal held that a woman who had lived with the deceased tenant for forty years, twenty-one of which were spent living on the premises in question, was entitled to succeed to the tenancy as a member of his family. James LJ emphasised that the question was to be decided on the basis of what the ordinary man understood by the use of the word 'family'. Referring to *Gammans v Ekins*, he said that 'the popular meaning given to family is not fixed once and for all time. It has changed with the passing of years and seems to include de facto as well as de jure relationships'.

Clearly, though, the male partner could still experience difficulties. In *Helby v Rafferty*[281] the Court of Appeal held that the male survivor of a cohabiting couple whose relationship had lasted for five years could not be deemed to be a member of the tenant's family. The relationship did not bear the typical incidents of marriage, since she had not taken his surname, there were separate bank accounts, and they never pretended to be married. This case seems to reject the ordinary man's test. Stamp LJ decided to look at the actual circumstances of the case, and, finding that the woman had at all times wished to retain her independence, decided that this was inconsistent with any sort of family relationship.

The 'ordinary man' test sprang to life again in *Watson v Lucas*[282] to protect male partners. The facts of the case disclosed that the man and woman had lived together for twenty years, throughout which the man had remained married to someone else. The parties had no children, they used their own surnames except when they visited his club, but the man refused offers of reconciliation with his wife, indicating a clear intention to remain with the cohabitant. On the female partner's death he sought to argue that as a member of her family he was entitled to Rent Act protection. The Court of Appeal unanimously found that the fact of the man's remaining married did not prevent him being 'a member of the woman's family'. The court further found, Oliver LJ dissenting, that the assumption by one party of the other's name and the holding out of being married were merely indications in favour of a family relationship, so that the reverse, i.e. retention of their own names and no pretence of marriage, did not necessarily indicate that the relationship was not a family one. The parties' relationship had the stability and permanence sufficient to qualify as a family relationship, and the man was thus entitled to succeed to the statutory tenancy.

While disputed cases arising in private-sector tenancies centre on whether the word 'family' can extend to cohabitation, in the public sector the governing statute puts the matter more or less beyond doubt. The Housing Act 1980 provides that a local authority tenancy can pass on the tenant's death to a spouse residing with him at the time of death.[283] Where no spouse fulfils this condition, it may pass to any other member of the tenant's family who had lived with him for twelve months prior to death.[284] S.50 (3) goes on to provide that a person is a member of another's family if they 'live together as husband and wife'. There would thus seem to be a measure of consistency in public law statutes and it is quite possible that if anyone is called upon to decide whether a couple falls into this category, the authorities could well adopt criteria similar to the guidelines provided in the *Supplementary Benefit Handbook*.[285]

These guidelines to aid determination of whether a couple are living together as husband and wife are not as rigorous as the test applied when the issue has related to private-sector tenancies. The handbook indicates that the relationship does not have to have endured for any very lengthy period and, although the Housing Act requires a period of twelve months' cohabitation, the courts have required much more for Rent Act protection. The handbook also does not, and never has, viewed the retention of separate names and financial arrangements as being inconsistent with living together as husband and wife.

Where the relationship between a couple breaks down and one of the parties leaves, then a spouse is in a much stronger position than a cohabitant. Various cases have established that where a wife has been deserted by a husband who was the protected tenant under the Rent Act legislation, the landlord is not able to obtain an order for possession, and the same would probably hold good for husbands in similar circumstances.[286] There is in addition a statutory right of occupation under section 1 of the Matrimonial Homes Act 1967. Where the married couple proceed to a divorce, the court may make an order transferring the Rent Act tenancy to the non-tenant spouse under section 7 of the Matrimonial Homes Act 1967.

No such protection extends to an unmarried couple, and the private landlord could, on the desertion of the tenant spouse, obtain a possession order, as happened in *Colin Smith Music Ltd. v Ridge*.[287] The parties had lived together for five years in a flat with their two children and the woman's two children by her marriage. He left her with no intention of returning and executed a deed of surrender in the landlord's favour. The Court of Appeal found that he had ceased to be a statutory tenant, and that the position of a cohabitant was not analogous to that of a wife. She could not be occupying premises on his behalf, was accordingly a mere licensee, and as such could not claim the protection of the Rent Acts.

Where the marriage relationship breaks down, and one party leaves, the court has had since 1980 the power to order that the local authority tenancy can be transferred to the other spouse.[288] Depending on the circumstances, however, the local authority could find itself in difficulty in interpreting its duties under the Housing (Homeless Persons) Act 1977 towards a spouse who is thereby made homeless. There is no such power in the courts in relation to unmarried couples, and where one of the cohabitants leaves, it will be up to the authority whether to accept the remaining one as a tenant. If it refuses and the cohabitant becomes a homeless person, it becomes bound to exercise certain duties in respect of such a person.[289] The local authority would not be in such difficulty in respect of the cohabitant or spouse who by violence drives the partner out of the premises and who is then excluded by court order, since in those circumstances he or she would be deemed to have become intentionally homeless.[290] The reality of the situation as regards local authority tenancies is that married couples and cohabitants will be treated similarly,[291] although the basis for such treatment arises from different statutes.

Rights of occupation of the home

A spouse's rights of occupation of the matrimonial home are governed by the Matrimonial Homes Act 1967, which protects spouses who have no legal or equitable interest in the property. This right of occupation arises solely from the marriage relationship, and can be protected against prospective purchasers and mortgagees by registration of a Class F Land Charge or by the entry of a notice or caution on the register,[292] although such action is ineffective against trustees in bankruptcy.[293] Where the spouse has an equitable interest and is in actual occupation, there is no need to take such steps, although in most cases it would be a wise precaution.

Cohabitants who have an equitable interest in the property converted by occupation into an overriding interest should also be safe from prospective purchasers and mortgagees,[294] but where the cohabitant has no interest whatsoever, then he or she will be in a very vulnerable position. It seems that the only situation where they can successfully claim the court's intervention is where they have been victims of their partner's violence, and they invoke the assistance of the court under the provisions of the Domestic Violence and Matrimonial Proceedings Act 1976. Violence is widely construed. Indeed, the legislation is often used merely to regulate accommodation. The remedies available under the Act are also granted to spouses in addition to their existing rights of occupation. Thus, under the 1976 Act the power to make an injunction restraining a party from molesting her partner, or excluding one of them from the matrimonial home, covers not only the parties to a marriage but expressly includes those situations where a man and a woman are living with each other in the same household as husband and wife.[295] In this respect it has been declared by the House of Lords in *Davis v Johnson*[296] that the Act plainly gives the unmarried person the same rights as the married person. Where one of the parties has had to leave and seeks to obtain an injunction to gain occupation, there is clearly power to make an injunction, though this was initially disputed. Violence is not required to persuade the court to make an order excluding one partner from the matrimonial home. Indeed, in *Spindlow v Spindlow*[297] there had been no serious violence or adverse conduct on the part of the man towards his cohabitant. An injunction was nevertheless granted. The Court of Appeal stated that it would apply similar principles to unmarried and married couples. In both situations a primary concern is the welfare of the children and the provision of a home for them.

The concept of applying similar principles to married and unmarried couples has been further extended in *Adeoso v Adeoso.*[298] In this case the parties had been living together for three years, the last two as joint tenants of a council flat. The relationship broke down, however, and they formed entirely separate households within the flat and communicated only by notes. The woman applied for an injunction restraining the man from molesting her and ordering him out of the home. The County Court judge refused this because in the circumstances the parties were not living together as husband and wife. The Court of Appeal, however, held that an injunction could be granted since on an objective view the parties were living in the flat as if they were husband and wife, their relationship being comparable to a marriage in the last stages of breakdown. Moreover, the severance of their living arrangements did not mean that they were living in different households, since, having regard to the shared facilities and the size of the flat, the parties were living in the same household for the purposes of the Act.

Rights in personal property

The provisions of the Married Women's Property Act 1964 have already been discussed. It is worth considering what the results would be where a housekeeping allowance was paid by one cohabitant to another. It is not so easy to impute an intention to share everything in a cohabiting relationship as it is in marriage. Were the man to give the woman partner a housekeeping allowance, and the woman made savings, or purchased property from money derived from the allowance, then it could be argued that as donee she merely held the balance saved or property purchased on resulting trust for him. It has been held that no presumption of gift operates where a man gives a woman personal property,[299] but this would not prevent evidence being given of clear intention to make a gift. Thus, an allowance given and expressed to be for the other party's personal use may be sufficient to make a gift of the allowance, whomsoever is the recipient, male or female. Where the allowance is given only for housekeeping purposes, but the recipient with the donor's knowledge saves money and buys items in her own name for the home, which they jointly use, then by analogy with the philosophy behind the 1964 Act it could be argued that the parties would have a joint beneficial interest in such items, the donee being duly rewarded for thrift by the award of an equal interest. It is the donor's money which is used to purchase the item, but it is the donee's saving which has made the expenditure possible at all. Such a construction of a joint interest may be easier where it is the woman who has made the saving, since thrift is assumed to be a female quality.

In relation to other household goods bought by the parties, the general rule for married couples is that, on divorce, orders can be made transferring rights from one party to the other,[300] although sometimes such action may be too late. One of the parties may have already disposed of the more valuable items. Thus, the Law Commission has proposed that special procedures be made available whereby the offending party could be restrained from so acting, or made liable to pay compensation where such items have been sold.[301] There are no proposals that such a remedy be available to cohabitants, who must, as now, rely on the ordinary processes of the law where a dispute arises as to property, and expect to achieve results accordingly. The last resort of course would be to invoke the criminal law.[302]

Where the couple have had joint funds in bank accounts or building societies, then, if the account was in joint names, the balance on the death of one accrues to the survivor, and this applies whether the couple were married or cohabiting. Similarly, upon breakdown the fund would be split between the parties. If the parties both contribute to a fund held in one partner's name, the doctrine of express trusts may be useful, more especially where some other dependant is laying claim to the fund. Thus, in *Paul v Constance*[303] the cohabiting couple had paid money, chiefly a large sum by way of damages for personal injury received by the man, into a bank account in his name. Evidence was given that both parties regarded the money as equally theirs, that they had discussed the matter with the bank manager, informed him that they were living together and sought his advice as to the type of account they should open. He had advised that the account be in the man's name, with the woman being able to draw on the account with his authority. The parties later paid into the account their joint winnings from Bingo, and withdrew from it for luxuries. He repeatedly told her it was as much her money as his. He died and his widow claimed the sum as hers. The cohabitant sought a declaration that she was entitled to half the sum saved by reason of the express trust created in her favour by his words. The Court of Appeal upheld her claim, finding that there had been a sufficiently clear declaration of trust to establish an express trust of the money in her favour.

Unlike married couples,[304] cohabitants have no right to be considered for compensation for loss of the possibility of acquiring some future benefit, or for the loss of continuing benefits. So, where the cohabitant works in her partner's business without remuneration, she is unlikely to receive anything by way of reward for work done, or compensation for future loss of benefits.[305] On the other hand, if the cohabitant should later marry her partner, the possibility of receiving compensation will be much greater, even if the marriage only lasts a short time.[306]

Other financial considerations

(i) The taxation system

Whereas the income of a married couple living together will normally be aggregated for taxation purposes, there is no aggregation for unmarried couples, nor do they have any choice, as do married couples, to elect whether to be separately or jointly taxed. Cohabitants will always be separately taxed. In the case of a married couple under the present aggregation rules the husband is responsible for returning and paying tax on their joint income even if there has been an election for separate taxation.[307] Where an election is made for separate assessment, the wife has responsibility for completing her return and for paying the tax.[308] Even where no separate assessment election has been made, recent administrative changes have generally improved the woman's position in respect of dealings with the Inland Revenue.[309] For example, there is now provision for correspondence to be addressed to her and for repayments to be made to her.[310]

Where a married couple are both working, the man can claim an allowance of £2,445 and his wife £1,565, whereas the cohabiting couple can only claim £1,565 each.[311] If one of the couple does not work, the breadwinner is entitled to £2,445 where they are married, but the unmarried breadwinner is still only entitled to £1,565,[312] despite the fact that each will probably be supporting partners at home. In certain, probably very rare, circumstances where the working cohabitant was previously married and the spouse had died, then a claim could possibly be made for the £100 housekeeper relief under s.12 of the Income and Corporation Taxes Act 1970, as amended. Where the cohabiting couple have children, the earning cohabitant could claim the additional personal allowance under s.14 of the same Act. This will be paid where the working cohabitant has a child resident with him or her, and is not entitled to the higher personal relief given to married persons. The relief currently stands at £880, so that, provided the cohabiting couple has at least one child, their position is the same as a married couple.[313] This apart, the only situation in which married and cohabiting couples are treated the same is where they have sufficient earned income to be taxed at the higher rates.

Occasionally, under the English fiscal system, it may even be beneficial to live together. Thus, where the woman has unearned income and the couple's total taxable income exceeds £11,250, it is financially advantageous to live together, since, if married, the wife's unearned income is aggregated for both higher rate tax and additional rate tax.[314] In addition, where the couple own more than one property subject to a mortgage, the cohabiting couple who are both working could each claim mortgage relief on one property.[315] The income tax position of the older cohabiting couple, i.e. where one is over pensionable age, may also be more advantageous than that of the married couple, where they have substantial amounts of unearned income. Where both partners are over 65, the cohabiting couple may be better off, since the age allowance for a single person is £2,070, whereas that of a married couple is £3,295.[316] There are special favourable tax provisions relating to maintenance payments between separated and former spouses.[317] These do not apply to unmarried partners whose relationship breaks down.

Considerable criticism has been made of the present system.[318] It is said to discriminate over-generously in favour of the two-earner married couple. Any changes, however, would be more likely to eliminate this discrimination than positively to improve the plight of the childless cohabiting couple where only one goes to work.

As far as Capital Gains Tax is concerned, the liabilities of a married couple are generally calculated separately, although the husband is liable for his wife's tax as well as his own unless one of them makes an application for separate assessment, in which case she will be liable for her own tax.[319] One exception to the separate calculation rule allows that any loss by one of them can be set against any gains of the other.[320] There is no such rule in relation to unmarried people. Another advantage attaching to marriage is that where an asset is transferred from one spouse to the other, no tax is payable, no matter how much is paid,[321] whereas the unmarried couple may in such circumstances attract liability to tax. In two cases it may be more advantageous for the parties to live together for Capital Gains Tax purposes: thus, the married couple is allocated only one annual exemption of up to £5,000, whereas the unmarried couple may get two individual exemptions; in addition, the husband and wife are allowed only one exemption in respect of their home, whereas the unmarried couple with two properties could each get one exemption. Under the provisions relating to Capital Transfer Tax a couple with an estate worth over £50,000 in total would be better off married than simply cohabiting, since transfers *inter vivos* or on death between husband and wife are exempt from Capital Transfer Tax.[322] Between cohabiting couples the normal threshold limit of £50,000 applies.[323]

(ii) Provisions relating to bankruptcy

When a spouse is adjudged bankrupt, certain debts owed to the other spouse are postponed to the claims of other creditors,[324] and the trustee in bankruptcy may have power to force an order for sale of the matrimonial home.[325] Where the parties are living together, there is no rule postponing the partner's debts, but it is doubtful whether a cohabitant would be more successful than a spouse in defeating the rights of the trustee in bankruptcy.[326] In addition, any conveyance or transfer by the bankrupt of an interest in the home to the other party may be set aside at any time if made with intent to defraud creditors, irrespective of whether the couple are married or cohabiting.[327] Further, any transfer or settlement of property may be avoided by the trustee in bankruptcy for a period of up to ten years from transfer or date of settlement without any need to show a fraudulent intention.[328] There is, however, a special exemption applicable only to married parties: where the settlement is a 'marriage settlement' or one made 'in contemplation of marriage', such settlements are exempt, except in cases of fraud. A settlement can for these purposes include an insurance policy effected on the spouse's life. Any such policy effected by a cohabitant would not be so protected, and would be subject to the ordinary rules.

(iii) Insurance

A spouse has an unlimited insurable interest in the other's life.[329] The provisions of s.11 of the Married Women's Property Act 1882, whereby binding trusts arise if a policy is expressed to be for the benefit of a spouse, do not apply to cohabitants. A cohabitant could benefit under the policy only where there is an express trust. Where the parties are living together on premises in respect of which one is responsible for insurance for personal property, the cohabiting couple should be warned to include the cohabitant's name on the insurance form. If this is not done, insurance companies have been known to be difficult about claims made by cohabitants.

Position under the criminal law

The doctrine of the unity of the husband and wife still remains in the field of the criminal law,[330] but no such doctrine attaches to parties who live together. It is this doctrine which justifies the approach that a spouse is never to be compelled to give evidence against the other.[331]

Indeed, in many cases, the spouse is not even a competent witness in respect of many criminal offences committed by the partner during the course of marriage.[332] A cohabitant, on the other hand, is both competent and compellable. In addition, a married woman may be able to raise the defence known as 'marital coercion' where she commits an offence in the presence of her husband.[333] The unmarried woman would only be able to rely on the defence of duress, which is not as wide as the defence of marital coercion.

Statute and common law have provided that a husband and wife cannot conspire together, which approach is again based on the doctrine of unity, whereas cohabitants can be convicted in identical circumstances of conspiracy. Although a husband or wife can be convicted of stealing the other's property, neither a spouse nor a third person may institute proceedings against anyone for any offence of stealing or doing unlawful damage to property which at the time belongs to his or her spouse, without the consent of the Director of Public Prosecutions. No such restriction applies as to offences against the property of cohabitants.

A husband cannot be charged with rape of his wife, although there are limited exceptions to this.[334] A cohabitant is able to allege rape by her partner, though whether a prosecution is likely to succeed is another matter. The incapacity of a wife to allege rape arises from the alleged implied consent to sexual intercourse which is said to be an incident of marriage. The husband's immunity is now under challenge in many countries and may not long survive in England.

Where one of the spouses or cohabitants is prosecuted for an offence of violence against the other, then, provided the parties are not still living together at the time of the claim and the injury is one for which compensation of not less than £500 would be awarded, the victim can apply for compensation from the Criminal Injuries Compensation Board.[335] However, where a cohabitant has died as a result of criminal injuries inflicted by another person, his or her partner cannot make a claim under the scheme, though a spouse in similar circumstances can.

Concluding comments

We have attempted in the foregoing discussion to indicate the way in which English law is, and has been, responding to the phenomenon of cohabitation, and to indicate the remaining differences between marriage and cohabitation. Such differences are being, and have been, constantly eroded. We are not concerned with any threat which such an erosion may present to the institution of marriage, but rather more with the effects the current process may have upon cohabitation. It is becoming increasingly apparent just how difficult it is to escape from marriage by cohabiting. Accordingly, we have indicated the extent to which the legislature and many of the judges in England have adopted a status-based approach to the legal problems of cohabitants. Family models and marriage-like behaviour have frequently formed the basis for statutes and decisions affording provision and protection to unmarried couples and their children. Simply by adopting the model of the nuclear, monogamous-like family type, cohabitants have possibly laid a trap for themselves, and made the task of the judiciary and the legislature much easier. It has become possible to categorise people as 'actually husband and wife' or 'living together as husband and wife', and thus simply to adopt an existing body of law as and when desirable. This equivalent treatment approach then simply necessitates tinkering around with the present family law machinery. The differential approach would entail much more, demanding, as it does, the resolution of the unmarried couple's legal problems from a totally different perspective.[336] As to which is preferable, this can only be assessed by examination of the alternative models developed in other countries and of the arguments advanced in those other countries as well as in England for the equivalent or differential treatment of the unmarried couple.

Notes

1 See the judgments in *Upfill v Wright* [1911], 1 K.B. 506, and *Gammans v Ekins* [1950], 2 K.B. 328.

2 See the judgment of Stephenson LJ in *Watson v Lucas* [1980], 3 All E.R. 647, at 652.

3 See the judgment of James LJ in *Dyson Holdings v Fox* [1975], 3 All E.R., 1030 at 1035; and Ormrod LJ in *Re Evers's Trust* [1980], 3 All E.R. 401.

4 See for example, Lord Denning MR in *Eves v Eves* [1975], 3 All E.R., 768 at 770; and Wood J in *Kokosinski v Kokosinski* [1980], 1 All E.R., 1106 at 1117.

5 One of the exceptions referred to in James LJ's definition of family relationships in *Dyson Holdings v Fox, op. cit.*, note 3.

6 An assertion made by Sir George Baker P in *Campbell v Campbell* [1977], 1 All E.R., 1 at 6.

7 See Rent Act 1977, Schedule 1, as interpreted in cases such as *Watson v Lucas, op. cit.*, note 2.

8 S.50(3).

9 See, for example, Family Income Supplement Act 1970, s.1(1)(b); Housing Finance Act 1972, Schedule 2, para. 2; Social Security Act 1980, Schedule 1, para. 3 (1), however, refers to a 'married' or 'unmarried' couple, the definition of the latter being a 'man and a woman who are not married to each other but are living together as husband and wife' (s.34(1)).

10 Consumer Credit Act 1974, s.184(5).

11 Pneumoconiosis (Workmen's Compensation etc.) Act 1979, s.3(1)(c).

12 Inheritance (Provision for Family and Dependants) Act 1975, s.1(1)(e).

13 For a detailed explanation see A. Ogus and E. Barendt, *Law of Social Security*, Butterworths, 1978, pp. 404–9 and pp. 383–9.

14 There was, for example, no debate on the cohabitation rule when it was first introduced into supplementary benefit legislation in 1966. But the idea was not new: its origins may be

traced to the Widows', Orphans' and Old Age Contributory Pensions Act 1925, s.21(1).

15 See *post*, p. 184.

16 There was considerable debate during the Inheritance (Provision for Family and Dependants) Act 1975. See *post*, pp. 184–5.

17 See, for example, the judgment of Wood J in *Kokosinski v Kokosinski, op. cit.*, note 4.

18 Stephenson LJ in *Watson v Lucas, op. cit.*, note 2.

19 Ormrod LJ in *Re Evers's Trust, op. cit.*, note 3.

20 Expressed in such measures as the Family Law Reform Act 1969 and the Domestic Proceedings and Magistrates' Courts Act 1978.

21 For an interesting discussion of European developments see M.-J. Meulders-Klein, 'Cohabitation and Children in Europe', *Am. Jo. Comp. Law*, 29 (1981), p. 359, at pp. 359–63.

22 Law Commission Working Paper no. 74, *Illegitimacy*, HMSO, 1979, pp.27–32.

23 Especially from women's groups opposed to men automatically acquiring parental rights.

24 E.g., the new s.4(2) of Affiliation Proceedings Act 1957, as substituted by Domestic Proceedings and Magistrates' Courts Act 1978, s.50. But see, on the other hand, British Nationality Act 1981, one of the many discriminations of which is against the illegitimate child.

25 E.g., the decision in *Eves v Eves, op. cit.*, note 4; *Re Evers's Trust, op. cit.*, note 3; and *Dennis v McDonald* [1981], 2 All E.R. 632.

26 E.g., *Hawes v Evenden* [1953], 2 All E.R. 737.

27 E.g., *Gammans v Ekins, op. cit.*, note 1.

28 E.g., *Watson v Lucas, op. cit.*, note 2, though note *Helby v Rafferty* (1978), 3 All E.R. 1016.

29 s.27 of Matrimonial Causes Act 1973 (hereafter referred to as M.C.A. 1973) and s.1(a) of Domestic Proceedings and Magistrates' Courts Act 1978 (hereafter D.P.M.C.A. 1978).

30 M.C.A. 1973, s.27(2).

31 M.C.A. 1973, s.1(a).

32 Note, however, the provisions of s.2 of M.C.A. 1973.

33 S.25 of D.P.M.C.A. 1978.

34 See S. Cretney, *Principles of Family Law*, (3rd ed.), Sweet & Maxwell, 1979, pp.271–3.

35 Ormrod LJ in *Re Evers's Trust, op. cit.*, note 3, at 404.

36 S.4(2) of Affiliation Proceedings Act 1957 (hereafter referred to as A.P.A. 1957).

37 S.4(2)(b) of A.P.A. 1957, and see *Foy v Brooks* [1977], 1 All E.R. 113.

38 According to Ormrod LJ, *op. cit.*, note 19, and see also *Haroutunian v Jennings* (1980), 1 F.L.R. 62.

39 See Ormrod LJ in *Re Evers's Trust, op. cit.*, note 19.

40 When the D.P.M.C.A. 1978 came into operation.

41 E.g., *Haroutunian v Jennings, op. cit.*, note 38; *Eves v Eves, op. cit.*, note 4.

42 See, especially, the comments of Lord Denning MR in *Tanner v Tanner* [1975], 3 All E.R. 776 at 778, and Ormrod LJ in *Re Evers's Trust, op. cit.*, note 3, at 404.

43 [1956], 1 W.L.R. 496.

44 *Op. cit.*, note 42.

45 Referred to by Denning LJ, *op. cit.*, note 43, at 497.

46 *Idem.*

47 *Op. cit.*, note 42, at 780.

48 *Idem.*

49 *Op. cit.*, note 3, at 404.

50 [1976], 1 All E.R. 737 at 745.

51 Whether provision is sought under the A.P.A. 1957, as amended, or by reference to an agreement.

52 Similar to that received by the wife in *Khan v Khan* [1980], 1 All E.R. 497; see also for USA *Beard v Beard*, 262 So.2d. 269 (Fla. App. 1972).

53 B.N.A. *Family Law Reporter*, 5, 3077.

54 E.g., *Khan v Khan, op. cit.*, note 52.

55 Cf. the position in Sweden *post*, p. 173.

56 See the comments of Sir George Baker P in *Brady v Brady, The Times* (28 February 1973).

57 See the leading case of *Minton v Minton* [1979], A.C. 593.

58 See M.C.A. 1973, s.25.

59 *Idem,* (s.25(1)).

60 See C. Reich, Yale L.J. 73, 733–87 (1974) and M.A. Glendon, *The New Family and the New Property,* Butterworths, 1981.

61 This is not to suggest that the courts should be deliberately blind to the fact that women's traditional role in marriage can be economically debilitating. Accordingly, we do not urge that the courts should impose the obligations of equality on women before equality of the sexes has in fact been achieved. See, further, *post,* p. 193.

62 [1970] P.1.

63 See s.25(1)(a) and (b).

64 [1965], 1 All E.R. 341.

65 [1975], 3 W.L.R. 752.

66 *Wynne v Wynne* [1981], 1 W.L.R. 69; and also stops short of allowing the maintenance payments for the wife to be paid out of the mistress's resources, see *Brown v Brown; Macey v Macey, The Times* (14 July 1981).

67 *Op. cit.,* note 6.

68 *Op. cit.,* note 4.

69 In *Foley v Foley* [1981], 2 All E.R. 857, it was emphasised (p.861) that periods of cohabitation and marriage were not the same, though a period of cohabitation was a circumstance which could be taken into consideration under s.25 of M.C.A. 1973. In *Hayes v Hayes,* 11 Fam Law 208 (1981), on the other hand, Balcombe J held that a period of six years' 'on-off' cohabitation which had preceded a very short marriage (7 weeks) could have no relevance when assessing financial provision for the wife.

70 *Chaterjee v Chaterjee* [1976], Fam. 199.

71 For example, Family Income Supplement and Supplementary Benefit.

72 See ss.44(1)(a), 45(2) and 66(1)(a) of Social Security Act 1975; S.I. 1975/1058, Reg. 9; S.I. 1976/409, Reg. 13(2).

73 See A. Ogus and E. Barendt, *op. cit.,* note 13, at pp. 390–3.

74 See ss.44(1)(a), 45(2) and 66(1)(a) of S.S.A. 1975.

75 See s.44(1)(b) of S.S.A. 1975; S.I. 1977/343 Reg.8(1).

76 This incentive rule was introduced by s.4 of National Insurance Act 1971; the pro rata reductions are to be found in ss.45(3), (4), and 66 (4)(5) of S.S.A. 1975.

77 This is discussed by S. Atkins, 'Social Security Act 1980 and the E.E.C. Directive on Equal Treatment in Social Security Benefits', *J.S.W.L.* (1981), p. 16 at p. 20. It is operative in Nov. 1983.

78 Ss.44(3)(a), 46(1)(a) and 66(1)(b) of S.S.A. 1975.

79 See Social Security Act 1980, schedule 1, paras. 1–7.

80 See Atkins *op. cit.,* note 77, at p. 18.

81 Such a claim could be made under ss.44(3)(c); 46; 66(1)(d) of S.S.A. 1975 in respect of a female person having care of the children, but Social Security Act 1980 schedule 1, para 4, amends the provision so that a claim can be made regardless of the sex of the person having the care of the child.

82 S.I. 1977/343, Reg. 10(2)(a).

83 CS 726/49.

84 R(S) 20/54.

85 Ss.44(2)(3) and 66(1)(d) of S.S.A. 1975.

86 *Idem,* ss.46(1) and 66(1)(d); S.I. 1977/343 Reg.1(3).

87 *Idem,* reg. 10(2)(b).

88 *Ante,* and *op. cit.,* note 76.

89 S.46(3) of S.S.A. 1975.

90 *Op. cit.,* note 77.

91 See the decision in CG 3/49.

92 See S.S.A. 1975, Schedule 3, para. 2 and S.I. 1975/553, Reg. 3.

93 See the amendments made to the Social Security Act 1975 by s.5 of Social Security Act 1980 and Social Security Act 1981. For a very useful discussion of the recent changes in this area of the law see R. Upex and A. Morris, *I.L.J.,* (1981), p. 218–238.

94 Ss.44(1), 45(2), 47(1) and 66(1) of S.S.A. 1975; S.I. 1975/373, Reg.10(2).

95 Ss.43(1)(2) and 65(1)(2) of S.S.A. 1975.

96 Supplementary Benefit Act 1976, s.1.

97 *Idem.*

98 Their requirements and resources will be aggregated. See S.B.A.1976, Schedule 1, Table 3(1) as amended.
99 *Idem,* (s.34).
100 *Living together as husband and wife,* para. 19, DHSS/SBC, HMSO, 1976.
101 As amended. The regulations made pursuant to the 1980 Act refer to the couple as being separately assessed for a period of adjustment, which initially runs for 4 weeks but which can be extended for a further period of 6 weeks (S.I. 1980/982, reg. 6(1) and (2)).
102 *Op. cit.,* note 99.
103 DHSS, *Supplementary Benefits Handbook,* HMSO, 1980, para. 2.12 a–f.
104 See *post,* pp. 148–153.
105 Nor will the courts be inclined to disturb such findings if they are confirmed by tribunals, and are deemed to be reasonable. It would appear that a prima facie case would be sufficient. See *R v North West Kent Supplementary Benefit Appeal Tribunal, ex. p. Waterman,* Q.B.D., 8 May 1981; and *Campbell v Leicester S.B.A.T.,* Q.B.D., 1 May 1981 (unreported decisions).
106 S.B.A. 1976, Schedule 1, para. 311, as amended by S.S.A. 1980.
107 S.17(1)(a) and (b) of S.B.A. 1976.
108 *Idem* (s.18).
109 *Idem* (s.25).
110 Though not after a divorce decree, since there is no liability then to maintain a former spouse.
111 *Op. cit.,* notes 108 and 109.
112 S.B.A. 1976.
113 S.I. 1981/1529.
114 S.1(1)(b) of F.I.S.A. 1970.
115 *Idem,* s.1(1)(c).
116 *Idem,* s.3.
117 S.36(2) of S.S.A. 1975, as amended by Social Security (Miscellaneous Provisions) Act 1977, s.22(2).
118 'Cohabitation in English Social Security Legislation', in J. Eekelaar and S. Katz, *Marriage and Cohabitation in Contemporary Societies,* Butterworths, 1980, p.335, at p.340.
119 See ss.26–29 of S.S.A. 1975 and Schedule 3, as amended by Social Security Pensions Act 1975.
120 S.20 of S.S.P.A. 1975.
121 S.10 of S.S.P.A. 1975.
122 S.29(2) of S.S.A. 1975.
123 See *ante,* p. 73.
124 S.1(1)(a) of S.B.A. 1976, as amended.
125 S.29(a) of S.S.A. 1975.
126 S.20(1) of S.S.P.A. 1975; S.I. 1979/642, reg.8, as amended by S.I. 1980/1299 and Social Security Act 1979, Schedule 1, para. 5.
127 *Idem.*
128 See *ante,* p. 73.
129 *Op. cit.,* note 124.
130 As in *Julian v Julian* (1972), 116 Sol. Jo. 763.
131 *Op. cit.,* note 122.
132 I.e., before the introduction of Category B pensions.
133 See the examples cited by D.S. Rosettenstein, 'Cohabitation and English Public Sector Occupational Pension Schemes: Problems and Policy in Pursuit of the New Property', in J. Eekelaar and S. Katz, *op. cit.,* note 118, p. 323, especially at notes 35–7.
134 A. Ogus and E. Barendt, *op. cit.,* note 13, at pp. 16, 354.
135 *Op. cit.,* note 133, at p. 326.
136 *Idem.*
137 A. Ogus and E. Barendt, *op. cit.,* note 13, at pp. 353, 354.
138 *Op. cit.,* note 133, at p. 325.
139 For example, reg. E4 of Local Government Superannuation Regulations 1974; S.I. 1974, S.I. 1974/520.
140 For example, reg.24 of Fireman's Pension Scheme Order, 1966, S.I. 1966/1045.
141 Cf. the position of the spouse under s.25 of M.C.A. 1973.

142 E.g., s.1(1)(e) of Inheritance (Provision for Family and Dependants Act) 1975 (hereafter I (P.F.D.) A 1975.
143 *Idem.*
144 *Idem,* s.1(1)(a).
145 By s.46. A cohabitant can now make a claim under the provisions of the 1975 Act.
146 See *post,* pp. 184–5.
147 See, e.g., *Re Beaumont (deceased)* [1980], Ch.444.
148 Because of the terms of s.1(3).
149 As in *H v G and D* (1980), 10 Fam. Law 98.
150 [1979], 3 All E.R. 815.
151 *C.A. v C.C., The Times* (17 November 1978). See also 9 *Fam. Law* 26 (1979).
152 *Op. cit.,* note 147.
153 *Op. cit.,* note 149.
154 [1979], 1 W.L.R. 135.
155 See *O'Donnell v O'Donnell* [1976], Fam.83; *P v P,* [1978], 1 W.L.R. 483.
156 'The Mistress and the Multiplier', *L.Q.R.*, 96 (1980) p. 165, at p. 167.
156a See, further, *Jellεy v Iliffe* [1981], 2 All E.R. 29, and *Kourkey v Lusher, The Times* (9 December 1981).
157 As in *Re Lynch* [1943], 1 All E.R. 168.
158 See s.3 of Fatal Accidents Act 1976.
159 [1975], 1 All E.R. 1130.
160 S.1(1)(e) of I.(P.F.D.) A. 1975.
161 Provided she has the care of children of the deceased (s.73(1) of S.S.A. 1975), although the rate of benefit (£1 per week) is scarcely generous.
162 S.25 of S.S.A. 1975.
163 E.g., widow's pension (s.26 of S.S.A. 1975); widow's invalidity pension, if she is incapable of work (s.15 of S.S.P.A. 1975).
164 Where he is incapable of work (s.16 of S.S.P.A. 1975 and S.S.A. 1979, Schedule 1, para. 18).
165 Ss.8 and 9 of S.S.P.A. 1975.
166 Unless he or she happens to be the deceased's personal representative. See National Insurance Act 1957 s.7, as amended.
167 *Op. cit.,* note 161.
168 S.184(5) of C.C.A. 1974.
169 S.17(a) and (b) of S.B.A. 1976.
170 *Idem,* s.17 (2)(b).
171 S.1(1)(b) of D.P.M.C.A. 1978.
172 S.25(2), *ibid.*
173 S.18 of S.B.A. 1976. If an affiliation order has been made, the DHSS proceeds against an offending father.
174 S.1 of A.P.A. 1957.
175 S.27 of M.C.A. 1973.
176 Ss. 23, 24 of M.C.A. 1973.
177 In s.25(2) of M.C.A. 1973.
178 S.41(1) of M.C.A. 1973.
179 S.4 of A.P.A. 1957.
180 Under the provisions of s.4, as amended by s.50 of D.P.M.C.A. 1978.
181 Cf. the new s.4(3) of A.P.A. 1957 and s.3 of D.P.M.C.A. 1978.
182 See, generally, D. Marsden, *Mothers Alone,* Penguin, 1971; and O. McGregor, L. Blom-Cooper and C. Gibson, *Separated Spouses,* Duckworth, 1970.
183 S.2 of A.P.A. 1957, as amended.
184 By s.1.
185 Under s.18 of S.B.A. 1976.
186 *Op. cit.,* note 22, para. 3.14–3.22.
187 *Idem,* part IV.
188 *Idem,* para. 4.43.
189 Ss.41(2) and 64(1) of S.S.A. 1975 and S.I. 1977/343, reg. 1(3).
190 *Idem,* reg. 6(2).
191 Child Benefit Act 1975, Schedule 2, para. 2.

192 S.B.A. 1976, Schedule 1, para. 3(2), as amended.
193 S.1(1)(c) of F.I.S.A. 1970.
194 S.I. 1977/1328, reg. 2.
195 See *ante*, 76.
196 S.15 of Family Law Reform Act 1969.
197 S.1(1)(c) and s.25.
198 *Op. cit.*, note 151.
199 S.14 of F.L.R.A. 1969.
200 *Op. cit.*, note 22, para. 5.6–5.8.
201 S.3.
202 S.70(1) and (4) of S.S.A. 1975.
203 S.3.
204 S.31 of S.S.A. 1975, as amended.
205 Usually increases to supplementary benefit.
206 S.38 of S.S.A. 1975 as amended. See also S.I. 1975/515.
207 S.1(1) of Guardianship Act 1973.
208 *Idem*, s.1(7).
209 S.18 of Adoption Act 1976.
210 *Idem*, s.16.
211 By inference from s.16 and s.17 A.A. 1976.
212 Article 8.
213 Under ss.9 and 14.
214 *Re C(A)* [1970], 1 All E.R. 309.
215 *R v Oxford City Magistrates ex parte H.* [1975], Q.B. 1.
216 *Re S* [1975], 1 All E.R. 109.
217 S.45–48 of D.P.M.C.A. 1978, amending the relevant provisions of the G.M.A. 1971 and G.A. 1973.
218 S.52(1) of M.C.A. 1973.
219 *Idem*, s.42.
220 Under s.23(1)(d), (e), (f), although the court will have regard to the provisions of s.25(3).
221 Nor generally for the purposes of any other legislation: see *Re N* [1974], 1 All E.R. 126.
222 By reopening proceedings under s.42 of M.C.A. 1973.
223 See, for example, the recent controversy in the English courts surrounding the changing of a child's surname by the custodial parent: reviewed in *W v A* [1981], 1 All E.R. 100.
224 Adoption (County Court) Rules 1976, S.I. 1976/1644 r.4(2)(e).
225 Since she is a parent: a man in the same position is not.
226 *Re C(M.A.)* [1966], 1 All E.R. 838.
226a But *Re C(M.A.)* is unlikely to be followed, particularly after *J v C* [1970], A.C. 668.
227 *Op. cit.*, note 22, paras 4.8–4.9.
228 *Idem*, paras 6.5–6.13 and paras 4.8–4.9.
229 See *ante*, pp. 86–8 and *post*, p. 196.
230 *Per* Lord Upjohn in *Pettitt v Pettitt* [1970], A.C. 777 at 813.
231 See the comments of Walton J in *Richards v Dove* [1974], 1 All E.R. 888.
232 See Ormrod LJ in *Re Evers's Trust, op. cit.*, note 3; Lord Denning MR in *Eves v Eves, op. cit.*, note 4; and *Tanner v Tanner, op. cit.*, note 42.
233 Walton J in *Richards v Dove, op. cit.*, note 231, and Oliver LJ in *Watson v Lucas, op. cit.*, note 2.
234 S.37 of Matrimonial Proceedings and Property Act 1970.
235 S.24 of M.C.A. 1973.
236 Because since *Wachtel v Wachtel* [1973], Fam. 72, it has been thought that conduct must be 'obvious and gross' and only rarely has conduct been found to be of this standard. See *West v West* [1978], Fam. 1; *Cuzner v Underdown* [1974], 1 W.L.R. 641; *Bateman v Bateman* [1979], Fam. 25; *Armstrong v Armstrong* (1974), 118 S.J. 579. But *Wachtel* itself must be treated with caution (*Robinson v Robinson* (1981), 2 F.L.R. 1, and *Evans v Evans* (1981), 2 F.L.R. 34).
237 Although see Ormrod LJ in *Re Evers's Trust, op. cit.*, note 3 at 404.
238 *Post*, pp. 151–3.

239 *I.e.,* wife-like behaviour, the presence of children.
240 The guidelines laid down in s.25 of M.C.A. 1973.
241 *E.g., Pascoe v Turner* [1979] 2 All E.R. 945 and *Greasley v Cooke* [1980] 3 All E.R. 710.
242 *Williams v Williams* [1976] Ch. 278.
243 *The Times,* July 4, 1975.
244 *The Times,* May 19, 1976.
245 [1971] A.C. 886.
246 *E.g., Davis v Vale* [1971] 2 All E.R. 1021; *Hargrave v Newton* [1971] 3 All E.R. 866; *Hazell v Hazell* [1972] 1 All E.R. 923.
247 *Op. cit.,* note 3.
248 [1981] 2 All E.R. 632 (upheld by C.A. [1982] 2 W.L.R. 275). See also *Cousins v Dzosens, The Times,* December 12, 1981.
249 *Op. cit.,* note 3, at 403.
250 *E.g.. Diwell v Farnes* [1959] 1 W.L.R. 624.
251 *E.g., Cooke v Head* [1972] 2 All E.R. 38.
252 *Op. cit.,* note 250.
253 *Op. cit.,* note 251.
254 *Op. cit.,* 231.
255 *Op. cit.,* note 4.
256 Current Law (October 1980).
257 *Op. cit.,* note 241.
258 *Op. cit.,* note 241.
259 *Op. cit.,* note 42.
260 [1978] 2 All E.R. 942.
261 [1976] 1 All E.R. 737.
262 See the circumstances in *Horrocks v Forray.*
263 See comments of C. Cadwallader (1979) Conveyancer 33, 37.
264 See *e.g.,* the difficulties faced by cohabitants in *Horrocks v Forray* and *C.A. v C.C.*
265 *Soar v Foster* (1858) 4 K and J. 152.
266 I (P.F.D.) A. 1975 s.10(7).
267 Given that the courts are disposed to favour legitimate spouses: see *e.g., Horrocks v Forray.*
268 See S. Poulter, 'The Death of a Lover' 126 N.L.J. 417 at 419.
269 Under s.41 of Trustee Act 1925.
270 S.54(1) and s.101(3) of Land Registration Act 1925.
271 S.70(1)(g) of Land Registration Act 1925 and *Hodgson v Marks* [1970] Ch. 892 and see *Williams & Glyn's Bank Ltd. v Boland* [1981] A.C. 487.
272 Rent Act 1977, Schedule 1, para. 2.
273 *Idem,* para. 3.
274 [1949] 2 K.B. 388.
275 *Op. cit.,* note 1.
276 (1949) C.L.Y.B. s.3385.
277 [1953] 1 W.L.R. 1169.
278 [1964] 1 All E.R. 861.
279 [1979] 2 All E.R. 1084.
280 *Op. cit.,* note 3.
281 *Op. cit.,* note 3.
282 *Op. cit.,* note 2.
283 S.30(2)(a).
284 S.30(2)(b).
285 *Op. cit.,* note 103.
286 *Middleton v Baldock* [1950] 1 All E.R. 708.
287 [1975] 1 All E.R. 290.
288 Although if an assignment is made by the tenant pursuant to an order of the court under s.24 M.C.A. 1973, s.37(1)(a) of Housing Act 1980 provides that this is a valid assignment.
289 Under s.4 of H. (H.P.)A. 1977.
290 See s.17 of the H. (H.P.) A. 1977.
291 Unless the court makes an order under s.24 of M.C.A. 1973.
292 S.2(6), (7) of M.H.A. 1967.
293 See s.2(5) of M.H.A. 1967.

294 See *Hodgson v Marks, op. cit.,* note 271 and *Williams & Glyn's Bank Ltd. v Boland, op. cit.,* note 271.

295 Ss.1(1), (2) of D.V.M.P.A. 1976.

296 [1979] A.C. 264.

297 [1979] 1 All E.R. 169.

298 [1981] 1 All E.R. 107.

299 *Op. cit.,* note 265.

300 Under s.24 of M.C.A. 1973.

301 Law Commission, *Third Report on Family Property: The Matrimonial Home (Co-ownership and Occupation Rights) and Household Goods,* Law Com. no. 86, para. 3. 104.

302 The provisions of the Theft Act 1968 ss.2(5), 30(1).

303 [1977] 1 W.L.R. 527.

304 Under s.25(1)(g) of M.C.A. 1973.

305 Though she could perhaps base a claim to a share on a constructive or resulting trust. Spouses have succeeded on similar grounds in *Nixon v Nixon* [1969] 3 All E.R. 1133; *Re Cummins* [1971] 3 All E.R. 782 and *Muetzel v Muetzel* [1970] 1 All E.R. 443.

306 See *Kokosinski v Kokosinski, op. cit.,* note 4.

307 *The Taxation of Husband and Wife,* para. 21. Cmnd. 8093 H.M.S.O., 1980 and see s.23 Finance Act 1971.

308 S.38(1), (3), (4) of Income and Corporation Taxes Act 1970.

309 *Op. cit.,* note 307, paras. 22–26.

310 *Idem,* para. 25.

311 S.8(1) of I.C.T.A. 1970 and s.22(1) of Finance Act 1980.

312 *Idem.*

313 S.14 of I.C.T.A. as amended by s.22(2) and 24(6) of F.A. 1980.

314 S.37 of I.C.T.A. 1970 as amended by s.36(2) of Finance Act 1976.

315 Unlike the married couple.

316 *Op. cit.,* note 307, at p. 60.

317 See Inland Revenue Leaflet No. 30, *Income Tax: Separation and Divorce,* October 1978.

318 See *op. cit.,* note 307, ch. 3.

319 *Op. cit.,* note 307, at p. 61.

320 *Idem.*

321 S.44 of Capital Gains Tax Act 1979.

322 Finance Act 1975, Schedule 6, para. 1, as amended by s.94 of F.A. 1976.

323 See tables in s.37(3) of F.A. 1975 and s.85(1)–(3) of F.A. 1980, Schedule 14.

324 S.36 Bankruptcy Act 1914: the rules differ slightly as between a husband's and a wife's bankruptcy.

325 Under s.30 of Law of Property Act 1925.

326 Spouses have not been particularly successful in such circumstances; see *e.g., Re Bailey* [1977] 1 W.L.R. 278.

327 S.172 of L.P.A. 1925.

328 S.42 of Bankruptcy Act 1914.

329 *Griffiths v Fleming* [1909] 1 K.B. 805.

330 *E.g.,* a husband and wife cannot conspire together. See Criminal Act 1977 s.2(2)(a) and *Mawji v R* [1957] A.C. 126. *Cf.* the tort of conspiracy: *Midland Bank Trust Co. Ltd. v Green (No. 3),* [1981] 3 All E.R. 744.

331 *Hoskyn v Metropolitan Police Commissioner* [1979] A.C. 474.

332 See Criminal Evidence Act 1898, s.4(1), as amended.

333 See J. Edwards, 'Compulsion, Coercion and Criminal Responsibility' (1951) 14 M.L.R. 297 and Law Commission, Law Com. no. 83 (1977), Part III.

334 Those being where there is a decree nisi of divorce (*R v O'Brien* [1974] 3 All E.R. 663) or an undertaking not to molest (*R v Steele* [1976] 65 Cr. App. Rep. 22), and by

analogy a personal protection order under the D.P.M.C.A. 1978 ss.16–18. See further, M.D.A. Freeman, 'But if you can't rape your wife, Who(m) can you Rape?: The Marital Rape Exemption Re-examined' (1981) 15 Fam. L.Q. 1.

335 Amendments to the scheme, which formerly prevented claims in such circumstances, were introduced in October 1979. See M.D.A. Freeman, 'The Criminal Inquiries Compensation Scheme and The Family' (1980) 10 Fam. Law 37.

336 See *post,* pp. 189–93 and ch. 8 *passim.*

5 Other Legal Systems and Their Responses to Cohabitation

This chapter investigates the ways in which legal systems outside England have responded to the phenomenon of cohabitation. It is primarily descriptive and analytical rather than critical. Comparative law[1] has many pitfalls: taking legal doctrine out of its institutional structure and its social context can be at best a foolhardy and at worst a dangerous exercise. But in a book of this nature it is impossible to do more than sketch briefly the cultural and historical context providing the backdrop to a social phenomenon and legal responses to it. The selection of systems to analyse was not easy, but there had to be a selection if this chapter was not to become an arid catalogue. It is important, we believe, to see both how countries with similar cultural traditions to our own and those with very different ones respond to the problems created by people living together outside marriage. It is important also to compare the responses of countries with different ideologies. In many countries, as in England, cohabitation outside marriage has only emerged as a problem in the recent past, but some countries, where the tradition of marriage is not as strong, have had longer to test out approaches and solutions to non-marital unions. Our survey takes these matters into account.

We accordingly begin by looking at the ways in which other common law countries – Australia, Canada, New Zealand and the United States – have faced up to cohabitation. Then we turn our attention to France and examine the ways the French legal system, with its very different legal–historical heritage and juridical methodology, approaches *l'union libre.* Thirdly, we examine the responses of the Swedish legal system and, to a lesser extent, other Scandinavian countries. Sweden's approach to marriage and cohabitation is generally thought to be more radical than most, though a leading commentator has described Swedish legislation as on 'a journey without a destination'.[2] Fourthly, we take a look at the way cohabitation outside marriage is regarded in some Latin American and South American states, where the practice of living together outside marriage is no new phenomenon. Finally, we examine the responses of a 'socialist' legal system, the Yugoslav. The chapter ends with a coda, a synthesis of the responses surveyed and some comparisons.

Common law responses

References are made in other chapters to judicial and legislative responses in the common law world. Here we draw these together rather more systematically.

The common law tradition[3] which unites the legal systems of this country to the Commonwealth, and which permeates the legal systems of much of the United States as well, is essentially a pragmatic one. Rather than laying down general solutions in legislative codes, common law countries have tended to rely on their judges to find solutions to real problems when conflict occurs. The common law has accordingly grown on a case-by-case approach. Its principles have emerged inductively and incrementally. Legislation has been the 'stitch in time' rather than the fabric of the law. Without codes, without a Roman law tradition, the legal systems in common law countries have relied on *stare decisis* as the cement to bind the systems together. With the judiciary occupying centre stage, precedent has been the life-blood of the legal systems. Like England, Australia, Canada and New Zealand have a single court at the apex of the system and this sets precedents which bind courts below. The United States Supreme Court, on the other hand, does not have this power, and, though some of its opinions on constitutional questions have had an impact on family law (*Roe v Wade*[4] is perhaps the best known example and numerous pronouncements on illegitimacy[5] are particularly germane to our subject), there is little federal common law, and as a result divergencies in doctrine between the different states are common. Further, English precedents are still brought to the attention of the Commonwealth courts, as are Commonwealth decisions to the English courts, and there is a tendency to respect each other's case law. As a result, differences in cohabitation law are more the product of legislative action than divergence of judicial responses.

Some of the earliest judicial developments in the Commonwealth countries under consideration followed the lead of the English Court of Appeal. Cases such as *Cooke v Head*[6] and *Eves v Eves*[7] were soon to influence Commonwealth jurisdictions. Lord Denning's pronouncements on the doctrines of implied, resulting and constructive trusts were adopted in all three of the Commonwealth jurisdictions under consideration. In *Rathwell v Rathwell,*[8] Dickson J of the Canadian Supreme Court was rightly critical of the sloppy way in which the concepts of implied, resulting and constructive trusts were used 'with little apparent effort to distinguish the several types', but he and other judges in Canada,[9] as well as those in Australia[10] and New Zealand,[11] applied trust doctrines to spouses and cohabitants with little difficulty. As in England, where some judges repudiated the idea that courts could impose an intention that was not there,[12] so also in Australia, in *Allen v Snyder,* the New South Wales Court of Appeal refused to 'accept the proposition that a trust of the matrimonial home [might] be based upon a common intention, which does not actually exist, but which is ascribed to the parties by operation of law'.[13] It did, however, accept that courts could infer an agreement from the conduct of the parties. One New South Wales judge (Helsham J), writing extra-curially, questioned whether the implied-in-fact intent approved in *Allen v Snyder* could really be distinguished from imputed intent, of which the court disapproved. In language reminiscent of Lord Denning, Helsham J commented: 'the imputed trust . . . can be used to do justice between parties to a *de facto* relationship. The one is no more to be looked at askance legally than the other socially'.[14] Controversy still surrounds a number of matters: which theories to use, which circumstances allow the inference or imputation of an intention, the effect of non-monetary contributions. All the signs, however, suggest a convergence of approaches, with cohabitation law becoming assimilated to that of marriage. Lord Denning has used a second approach (the licence).[15] His lead here has not been taken up in Commonwealth jurisdictions.

Judicial responses in the USA exemplify a much more varied use of common law doctrines. With more developed notions of unjust enrichment,[16] the American judiciary conscience has not been troubled when using constructive trust doctrines, as some Commonwealth and English judges have. This point was remarked upon by Dickson J in *Rathwell v Rathwell* in the Canadian Supreme Court: 'in the United States', he noted, 'where the concept of unjust enrichment enjoys a much greater acceptance than in England, the constructive trust, regarded as remedial, appears to have afforded a more flexible and satisfactory doctrinal base than the classical English institutional approach'.[17] There are American decisions based on a number of other theories as well: contract (express, implied in fact, implied in law), including implied partnership and pooling agreements; resulting (that is implied in fact) trusts as well as constructive (implied in law) trusts; even tort.[18] Courts increasingly recognise domestic services as a basis for unjust enrichment, as they did in the most famous of American cohabitation cases (*Marvin v Marvin*)[19] and as a form of consideration for contract. Public policy defences, though successful in some cases (these are referred to in Chapter 7),[20] are rarely allowed to bar claims in USA courts today. Justice Hill, dissenting in *Rehak v Mathis,* spoke for many when, in response to the public policy defence, which the majority upheld, he said: 'courts normally do not deny judicial relief to sinners. If that were the rule, the caseload in all courts would be drastically reduced'.[21]

There is ample evidence that in the United States, as in England and the Commonwealth, the law is treating cohabitation as a shadow institution reflecting the legal model of marriage. Glendon[22] believes that this movement has been accelerated in states, such as California, which have marital communal property systems, since such systems are based on notions of sharing in intimate relationships, and the extension of such principles to intimate relationships outside marriage is not difficult to contemplate. *Marvin v Marvin* may have surprised commentators outside California but was to be expected in that state.[23] Indeed, the experience of unravelling marital property regimes should give its judges the confidence to handle problems of cohabitants post-*Marvin.* Lest it be thought that the influence of marriage law on cohabitation is only felt in marital community of property systems, a look at the law of New York is instructive. In that state only ten years ago a court was refusing to impose a constructive trust to assist a divorcing wife to share in property in her husband's name which he had bought with his salary while hers had supported the family.[24] This ruling was reversed by statute in 1980, when a provision similar to the English Matrimonial Causes Act 1973, sections 24 and 25, was passed. Almost as soon as the equitable distribution of marital assets on divorce became a reality, the New York Court of Appeals, in *Morone v Morone,*[25] recognised express property agreements between cohabitants. The decision effected a result comparable to one which a court distributing marital assets could have imposed, and is, arguably, yet another example of courts treating cohabitation as a shadow institution of marriage.

As already indicated, in the common law world it is in the main the judges who are left to adapt the law to fit changing social conditions. This is the case with cohabitation, though a number of innovatory statutory provisions have been passed. One of the most remarkable is South Australia's Family Relationships Act of 1975. This creates the legal status of putative spouse and thus entitles parties to a non-marital relationship to the same rights and benefits as spouses. To qualify for 'putative spouse' status, five years' continuous cohabitation or the birth of a child to the parties is required. The Act does not specify legal consequences:

it merely creates the status. A judicial declaration is required before rights may be granted on the basis of status as a 'putative spouse'.[26] The Act is a prelude to reform in substantive areas: at present the only areas in which the status of 'putative spouse' has legal consequences are inheritance and succession, where a surviving putative spouse has the same rights as a surviving spouse as regards family provision, estate duty, intestacy, superannuation and claims for compensation for loss arising from the negligent killing of the other party to the relationship. One interesting consequence of the 1975 Act is that where on intestacy there is both a surviving spouse and a 'putative spouse' (a declaration of status having been obtained), the two share equally in the estate. In both testate cases and those of intestacy, courts are empowered to make an award to 'putative spouse' survivors who are left without 'adequate provisions' for their 'maintenance, education or advancement in life'.

No other Australian state has gone as far as this to treat cohabitation like marriage. Also worthy of note, though, is an 1837 Tasmanian statute, a relic of pioneer days, which allows a woman to claim support from a man with whom she has cohabited for at least twelve months if he has wrongfully abandoned her or committed other specified acts of misconduct.[27] It has been proposed[28] that this statute be liberalised so as to permit support in special circumstances where the cohabitation has lasted for less than a year.

In Canada there has been rather more legislative activity. In 1978 Ontario[29] and Prince Edward Island[30] enacted Family Reform Acts which allow cohabitants to enter into contracts in the same way as prospective spouses and married couples may enter into ante-nuptial and marriage contracts. Such contracts must be made in writing, and be witnessed: they may deal with property ownership, support obligations and such issues of child-rearing as relate to 'education and moral training' but not rights to custody or access. These provisions may be taken to be additional to the equitable trust doctrines developed by English courts and, as noted already, adopted by Canadian ones. In Ontario also there are succession laws comparable to the English Inheritance (Provision for Family and Dependants) Act 1975. The Ontario Succession Law Reform Act of 1977 allows a claim against the estate of the deceased by a survivor who cohabited continuously with the deceased for five years immediately preceding his death or who had been cohabiting for a lesser period immediately preceding the death in a 'relationship of some permanence where there is a child born of whom they are the natural parents'.[31] This applies on intestacy as well, thus going further than the English provision. The court is authorised to make 'such provisions as it considers adequate' for the 'proper support' of the claimant.

Three Canadian provinces have legislation granting support rights to some former cohabitants. The Ontario Family Reform Act of 1978[32] provides for support after separation where (i) there is a written support agreement; (ii) a support agreement has been set aside because it is 'unconscionable' or there has been a default in the payment called for by the agreement; (iii) if a couple has cohabited continuously for not less than five years or in a relationship of some 'permanence' where there is a child of whom they are the natural parents and the action is brought within one year of the parties' separation. In computing the five-year period, a brief separation which was no more than a period of reflection has been held not to constitute withdrawal from the relationship.[33] In assessing the meaning of 'permanence' a relationship of eleven months has been held sufficient.[34] The legislation of Prince Edward Island recognises the first two of these grounds for support, but not the third.[35] In British Columbia the Family Relations Act of 1978 defines 'spouse' for the purposes of support to include those who have 'lived together as husband and wife' for at least two years: the application for support must be made within a year of separation.[36]

New Zealand's legislation in this area is limited in scope and tends to be rather restrictive.[37] For example, the succession rights of a former cohabitant are more limited than those which operate in England, Ontario or Western Australia. The Family Protection Act permits a mother's needs to be taken into account if a non-marital child makes a claim, but a former cohabitant herself may not apply for support from her deceased partner's estate.[38] There were proposals in the mid-1970s to extend property sharing principles to cohabitants who had lived together for at least two years, rather along the lines of the South Australian legislation, but these proposals did not materialise.[39]

In the United States also there has been little legislation. American state legislatures are not known for their forward-looking approach towards law reform, and an activist judiciary has commonly taken the lead.[40] Thus, even where there were suggestions in California, in the wake of *Marvin*, to formulate legislation to clarify the *Marvin* ruling, the response was to leave it to the judiciary who, it was assumed, could be left to refashion the law in the light of experience. Outside California there have been attempts, all of them unsuccessful, to impose a written requirement for property and support agreements between cohabitants in Illinois, Connecticut, Kansas, Virginia and New Mexico.[41] If enacted, these statutes would have cut down the willingness of the judges to enforce agreements not expressed in writing, including, of course, implied agreements. In Oregon legislation was introduced in 1979 which would have authorised petitions for a division of property, for support and for custody of children based upon cohabitation for more than one year or any cohabitation which resulted in the birth of a child.[42] This legislation, comparable to a number of Commonwealth provisions, did not obtain the necessary support. One of the few significant statutory provisions in the USA is the law passed in New Hampshire in 1968,[43] which provides that someone who cohabited with another for at least three years immediately preceding the partner's death in a relationship in which they held themselves out to be husband and wife is to be treated as a surviving spouse for all purposes. The 'holding out' requirement makes this statutory provision much more limited than equivalent Commonwealth enactments. The language used, reminiscent of the notions of 'common law marriage',[44] limits the value of the provision if for no other reason than that very few cohabitants today hold out themselves as married.

What this admittedly sketchy survey indicates is that the general trend in common law countries is towards the retention of marriage as the ideal state, with a halting willingness to allow cohabitation to tag on behind as some sort of shadow institution. But generalisations are difficult to sustain. In truth it is difficult to detect in any of the jurisdictions discussed a general approach. What we are witnessing is a piecemeal extension of rights and obligations of cohabitants in the direction of those already held by married partners. In some systems this has gone further than in others. The survey also emphasises the central position occupied by the judiciary in the common law world. It is in part the result of leaving matters to judges and the incremental way case law works that it is difficult to detect any general philosophy behind developments in any of the common law jurisdictions discussed in this section.

France: freedom in chains?

Glendon prefaces her chapter[45] on 'Marriage-like Institutions' with an old French proverb: *Boire, manger, coucher ensemble est mariage, ce me semble.* To what extent does French law embody this sentiment? An examination of French law is particularly pertinent, as marriage entails more legal consequences in France[46] than it does in common law countries or, for example, in Sweden. There is, it may therefore be thought, more to 'escape from' in France than elsewhere.

The Civil Code of 1804, the foundation of French law still today, barely recognises the notion of cohabitation. It is only referred to in those articles which deal with the relations between the parties and their children. The Code leaves cohabitation, in the words of one French authority, as a *terrain vague.*[47] Though a 'venerable institution'[48] and very prevalent in the divorceless Second Empire,[49] there are few real analyses of the concept in French writing. The terms *l'union libre* and *le concubinage* tend to be used interchangeably. Certainly nothing hinges on the distinction. By the 1930s so many legal consequences attached to *les couples non-mariés* that commentators such as Josserand[50] and Esmein[51] began to describe non-marital unions as a new legal status. Legal writers were almost uniformly critical of this development. They saw cohabitation as undermining the institution of marriage. This *doctrine*, a source of law in France, had its effect, for a series of cases of the *Cour de Cassation*, the highest court in France, heralded a 'moralistic reaction'.[52] Only in the 1970s did cohabitation make a legal comeback in France. Before looking at these recent developments, which date from 1972, it is important for us to analyse the legal consequences of cohabitation in France in order to see in what ways it is distinguished from marriage.

All the French authors stress (Glendon goes along with them) that, to quote Malaurie, *le propre de l'union libre est d'être libre.*[53] Unlike marriage, neither the entry into, nor the exit from, cohabitation is controlled by the state. This truism, though universally the position, seems to be more important in France, where *liberté* is such a central ideal than elsewhere. Of course with marriage easy and divorce relatively painless the difference is formal rather than substantial.

Unlike the majority of common law systems, the French operates a matrimonial property regime. Divorce brings this to an end. A balance sheet is then drawn up showing the couple's acquests, and the spouses participate equally in the division of the assets and the liabilities of the community. 'All property . . . is deemed to be an acquest of the community, if it is not proved to be separate property of one of the spouses by virtue of a provision of the law.'[54] The division pays no regard either to fault or the needs of the parties. Since this may cause former wives left to bring up children considerable financial hardship (there is in most cases no duty to support between the spouses after a marriage is dissolved), it is also provided by a revised article of the Code that one of the spouses may be required to make a 'compensatory payment' to the other to make up for the disparity which the divorce creates in the conditions of their respective lives.[55] The judge is instructed to take into account needs and resources of the spouses at the time of the divorce and in the foreseeable future.[56] In addition, the new law passed in 1975 preserves in a revised article of the Code that where a divorce has been granted because of the fault of one spouse, an action for damages may be instituted by the legally innocent spouse against the legally guilty one for 'material and moral prejudice' suffered by reason of the dissolution of the marriage.[57] 'Material and moral prejudice' has been held to include loss of esteem, loss of social position by one accustomed to a high standard of living, and loneliness.[58] Where, however, the divorce is based on the ground of 'rupture of the life in common', the spouse who has taken the initiative in the divorce remains entirely bound by the duty of support.[59] In addition to the remedies provided by family law, an action in delict (tort) may be brought under article 1382 of the Civil

Code for damage caused by one spouse to the other: an example was a case where the husband had squandered community property on a 'mistress', much of which property had been contributed by the wife.[60]

Marriage thus entails considerable consequences for property, as does the dissolution of marriage. The French judiciary has responded by creating remedies for cohabitants that are not so very different from those the Code provides for spouses who divorce. They have established a kind of 'matrimonial' property system implied in law (*embryon de régime matrimonial*)[61] to deal with cases where partners have accumulated and shared property during their life in common. The judges' concern, according to Malaurie, has been *la protection de la femme.*[62] The judges have resorted to two techniques.[63] First, they have used the concept of *société de fait* (*de facto* partnership). Property acquired during cohabitation for common life is divided as if there had been a *de facto* partnership. A *société de fait* is not automatic. In the absence of a written agreement, it must be established by demonstrating contributions and the intention to share in acquests. The principal difference between this 'pseudo régime matrimonial'[64] and a legal matrimonial property regime of community of acquests is that the latter 'comes into being upon the occasion of the marriage itself unless some other regime is chosen by contract'; the *société de fait* must be proved. But in both situations, as Glendon notes, 'a partner who does not work outside the home can participate in the acquests made by the other partner'.[65] Judges also use the principle of *l'enrichissement sans cause* (unjust enrichment) to enable a partner who has worked for the other gratuitously to acquire compensation for services rendered.[66]

There are a number of other measures used by French judges to make cohabitation as much like marriage as possible. For example, they have awarded damages to an abandoned female cohabitant. The breaking-off of a *union libre* is not itself wrongful, but, the courts have reasoned, the circumstances under which it occurs or even those which induced the woman to enter the relationship may be.[67] The conceptual basis for such a remedy is difficult to grasp, and French commentators content themselves with references to 'natural obligation' and 'duty of conscience'.[68] This comes into operation apparently, and always it seems to provide a remedy to the female partner, 'to repair damage caused by the couples' irregular life' or merely as a debt of gratitude for attending to the male partner's needs.[69] Courts are also prepared to enforce agreements between cohabitants for child custody to take effect upon the termination of their relationship in much the same way as they take cognisance of similar arrangements between married couples.[70] Further, article 220 of the Civil Code has been interpreted to allow a cohabitant to bind the credit of the other just as a spouse can.[71] Statutory provisions relating to social security matters, pensions, and leases, also put the cohabitant or former cohabitant into a similar position to the wife or widow. The statutes tend to be oblique. They use euphemisms[72] (*personne à charge, compagne*) but their intention is clear. For example, legislation provides benefits to female consorts (*compagnes*) of those killed fighting for France. *Compagne* is defined as someone who had lived with the deceased person for three years or less.[73] Indeed, in interpreting eligibility for family allowances and payments under social insurance schemes for death, a female cohabitant has been preferred to a wife separated from her husband.[74] As elsewhere, says Glendon, quoting Saint-Cyr, it seems that in France, 'the more a particular free union resembles marriage in stability and in the way the partners conduct themselves toward each other and the community at large, the more willing the courts have been, in one way or another, to give the union the effect of legal marriage'.[75]

This trend towards the recognition of the effects of cohabitation was accelerated by a number of changes in 1972. Glendon points to three developments in that year. First, a law was passed establishing substantial equality between legitimate and illegitimate children. Though moderate by comparison with many countries, this reform was thought by many to undermine the institution of marriage. Secondly, the *Cour de Cassation* overturned a *jurisprudence constante* going back 35 years, and allowed a married woman damages in the action she brought for the wrongful death of the man with whom she had been living for 36 years.[76] Previously, though courts had allowed 'wrongful death' actions to cohabitants, they had never allowed one to be brought successfully by a woman living in adultery. Adultery was still then a crime in France (it ceased to be in 1975). The third development grew out of a request for an increase in alimony by a woman against her former husband. He was an entertainer whose earnings had gone up considerably. The woman in question was living with another man as his wife. The court not only refused to increase her alimony but permanently terminated it. It noted that she was 'in a situation equivalent to that of a woman who has remarried'.[77] The implication was that the court was treating cohabitation like marriage, certainly insofar as the duty of support was concerned. This case has provoked a lot of critical attention in France. Some commentators (for example, Chabois)[78] have denounced the decision, others (such as Saint-Cyr)[79] have welcomed it. The latter called it the 'crowning' of the evolution of the *union libre*.

French commentators write about developments in cohabitation law rather as do those in England and the United States. Thus, Malaurie has written (in 1975) that *en droit le statut juridique du concubinage singe la mariage.*[80] Even the metaphor used is similar: cohabitation is 'aping' or 'mimicking' marriage. Huet-Weiller notes in a recent article that *l'union libre imite assurément le modèle du mariage*[81] though at the same time she points to islands of resistance and even of, what she calls, legal indifference to the status. She quotes a reply from the Minister of Justice in 1980 to a question about *certificats de concubinage* and *attestations d'union libre,* which a number of social and administrative organisations in France are apparently demanding, to the effect that such certificates have no legal value and only constitute a source of information. She is critical of this ministerial attitude, but surely the Minister of Justice was right to set his face against putting into a straitjacket *une situation qui repose, par definition, sur la liberté des intéressés.*[82] This is an ideological position to which we would give our support. In general the position in France is not so very different from England. Glendon quotes Scapel to the effect that what has happened is that the state has 'imposed the matrimonial model on those who have declined to marry. No longer bothering to look down on its adversaries, [the legitimate family] has transformed them in its own image'.[83] Cohabitation daily grows to look more like marriage. France today is very far from the position a 100 years ago when Bizet, with some poetic licence, has Carmen sing of *l'amour n'a jamais, jamais connu de lois.*[84]

Sweden and 'Neutrality'

If cohabitation as a recognised social status has arrived anywhere, it is in Sweden. Marriage is on the decline (there were 37,300 in 1979 compared to 51,200 in 1956); illegitimacy, though few consequences attach to it, has increased so that the percentage of children born out of wedlock was 37.5 per cent in 1979 compared to 10.2 per cent in 1956. In the great majority of cases mother, father and child are living together as a stable unit. The number of divorces is going down (1,449 in 1974; 1,127 in 1979), though divorce is easier to obtain in Sweden than almost anywhere else. The reason for this is not hard to find: people are living together without getting married, so that the pool of potential divorcees, particularly in the early years of marriage, has diminished.[85] How many people live together outside marriage in Sweden is not known.[86] Reliable estimates in 1978 put the proportion of unmarried couples in the total number of cohabiting couples as 15 per cent.[87] Commentators think it has almost certainly risen since then. Many cohabiting couples do subsequently marry, but in Sweden there is already a tendency for some never to do so.

The Swedish response to this phenomenon has been compared to (and contrasted with) that taken in Bolshevik Russia. 'In the brave new directives of the Socialist Swedish Government there lurks a Roman–Russian approach', Sundberg has argued.[88] It is easy to see why the comparison is made, though care must be taken over such facile generalisations. The policy in Soviet Russia between 1926 and 1944,[89] where '*de facto* marriages' were recognised as valid and could be formally registered at a later date upon the request of one of the parties, had the effect of treating those who cohabited as if they had married,[90] thus denying them autonomy. The Swedish response, by contrast, is summed up in its famous 'neutrality principle'. This was formulated in the terms of reference for Family Law Experts appointed to prepare new legislation by the Department of Justice in 1969. The Minister of Justice wrote in his Protocol: 'in my opinion, a new legislation ought as far as possible to be neutral in relation to the different forms of living together and different moral views. Marriage has and ought to have a central position in the family law, but one should try to see that the family law legislation does not contain any provisions which create unnecessary hardships or inconveniences for those who have children and build families without marrying'.[91] The Protocol also stressed that 'provisions concerning married individuals should generally be given such form that the spouse can retain a large measure of independence during marriage'. The Swedish Protocol does not explain the origin or rationale of the idea of neutrality: it is simply a given. The experts, however, recognised that the implementation of full neutrality would end marriage as a special legal institution.

They recognised that there were two different interpretations of the neutrality principle. First, it could mean that individuals should be given the freedom to choose what norms were to apply to their cohabitation. The legislator, in other words, should not impose uniform rules on cohabitants. A second interpretation of neutrality is that the same rules ought to apply to the cohabitation of men and women whether or not they are married. The two interpretations are, on the face of it, incompatible. The experts thought a balance ought to be struck between them. Swedish law, as Agell recognises, has proceeded to apply both conceptions of neutrality, 'one in the field of marriage law, the other in social and tax law as well as in other legal areas which do not concern the mutual relations of the cohabitants'.[92] Legislation in 1973 embodied the Protocol philosophy. But the contradictions and ambiguities in that make it difficult to describe the present attitude of Swedish law towards cohabitation. Agell attributes this difficulty not only to these contradictions but also to the fact that 'practical needs in individual cases must ultimately determine whether recourse is had to legislation'.[93]

There is surprisingly little case law. As is to be expected, agreements between cohabiting couples governing their economic relations are considered valid: a court in normal circumstances would not refuse to uphold a contract on the ground of the immorality of the parties' relationship. As Agell indicates, 'a contrary view would clearly be quite incompatible with the legislatively accepted neutrality ideology and with the series of legal effects which have been attached to non-marital cohabitation in different parts of the legislation'.[94] There are a number of matters upon which Swedish law is still silent: for example, can one of the parties agree to take on a duty to contribute to the maintenance of the other party during their cohabitation or after a possible separation?

Swedish law does, however, provide answers to many of the questions raised and answered in some of the other systems we have considered. Although there is no legislation as to what happens to property upon the break-up of cohabitation or on the death of one of the cohabitants, a special Act in 1973, extending legislation dating from 1959 which applied only to married couples, permits a lease to be retained by the person who 'needs the dwelling the most, provided that it is reasonable considering the circumstances', irrespective of who is the tenant. It is reasonable where there are children or, for example, the woman is pregnant or the cohabitation has lasted a long time.[95] Agell notes that this is the 'first example' of legislation on cohabitation which makes reference to 'a special social requirement'.[96] This apart, there is no legislation on the economic consequences of cohabitation. So it is 'somewhat uncertain' whether one partner can acquire an interest in property that the other has bought during the cohabitation. Swedish marital property law[97] is an amalgam of separation and deferred community: that is, each spouse is the sole owner of property possessed at the time of marrying as well as that acquired during the marriage, in addition to being responsible for his own debts, but the value of property (after deduction of debts) must be divided equally between the spouses in the event of divorce or death. In the case of death a spouse has, moreover, right of succession unless there are children.

In the case of cohabitation, there is no right to deferred community, such as exists in marriage. This is the upshot of a Supreme Court decision of 1975 in the case of *Holsbeck v Estate of Odenljung.*[98] A woman had lived with a man for ten years preceding his death. During the last few years he had been ill and she had taken care of him in their common home. After his death she claimed payment for her work from his estate (the issue of unjust enrichment was not raised). The Supreme Court rejected her claim. It conceded that as a general rule payment was due when a person had performed work on behalf of another, even in the absence of any contract to that effect. But it said that there were some exceptions to the rule, as, for example, where a child helped his legal parents at home or where friends helped one another on occasions where need arose. The court held that work performed by a woman for a man with whom she had been living in circumstances resembling marriage should be regarded as another exception to the general rule. It reasoned that, just as in marriage, the work should be considered as a part of their cohabitation. There is a remarkably similar decision in British Columbia, where a female cohabitant, who had helped her partner's advancement only to be abandoned when she became incapacitated, failed in her claim to be recompensed. The court considered that work of a kind spouses commonly perform did not carry a right to payment.[99]

Cohabiting partners are not under any legal obligation to pay maintenance for each other's subsistence either during the cohabitation or after. The fact that a couple is living together as a single economic unit is, however, taken account of in fiscal policies and social security arrangements. The reason for this is to ensure that married couples and those who cohabit should be treated equally. This does not in fact happen, since the tests for equal treatment insist on the satisfaction of such prerequisites as the birth of a child, cohabitation in circumstances resembling marriage, 'lasting cohabitation' and the existence of a common household. The tests are variable. No such limiting tests apply to married couples.

In private law also the fact that an unmarried couple maintain a common household is recognised. Legislation in 1978 repealed a provision in the Marriage Code which provided that the right of a divorced spouse to alimony should cease on remarriage. Now any award of alimony can be reviewed in the light of 'altered circumstances'.[100] One of the reasons for this amendment was a concern for marriage as an institution (the former rule was thought to encourage cohabitation rather than remarriage). The Parents and Children Code of 1978 also recognises financial obligations in a non-marital union. A parent liable to pay maintenance is entitled to reserve to himself a sum necessary for his own living expenses, and, if there are 'special reasons', for a spouse with whom he is living. 'Spouse' includes 'another person with whom the party liable to pay maintenance is cohabiting permanently, if they have a child together'. The sort of 'special reasons' envisaged are the inability of the 'spouse' to seek gainful employment and hence to provide for herself in some way. It may also be added that the Parents and Children Code of 1978 imposes a liability on a cohabitant to pay maintenance to the child of the partner, but only where the partners also have a child of their own together. The rationale for this is that all children in the new family unit should have a claim to the same economic standard whether they are children of both or only one of the parties. In this way Swedish law has extended the concept of step-parenthood beyond its usually accepted meaning. Although, therefore, there is no private law duty of maintenance between cohabiting couples in Swedish law, that legal system has made a number of accommodations both in its public and private law to the fact of cohabitation and its consequences for the parties and their children.

Economic dependence of a cohabitant is also taken cognisance of in Swedish pension law. An Act dating from 1962 states 'an unmarried or divorced woman or widow who was living permanently with an unmarried or divorced man or widower at the time of his death, and who has been married to him or had children by him, shall be put on equal footing with a widow for purposes of entitlement to widow's pension'.[101] This rule only applies to the basic pension. As Agell notes, the system is 'not applied very consistently'.[102] For example, under occupational injuries insurance schemes a female survivor may be entitled to a special 'widow's' pension not only if she has had a child by the deceased but also if she has otherwise 'lived together with [him] for a considerable period under circumstances resembling marriage'.[103] What 'resembles' marriage is left to a tribunal to decide: we are not aware of any case law settling the meaning of this expression, though it does not take much ingenuity to guess the factors that might be considered.

Swedish tax law also takes account of cohabitation. The Swedish tax system aggregates the income of spouses, unless they request separate assessment (which they have been able to do since 1965). As Sweden operates a progressive tax, it was financially advantageous to cohabit or, if married, to divorce and continue to live together. Sweden partially plugged this gap in the law in 1960 by providing that the rules applicable to a married taxpayer should be applied also to those who live together without being married 'if they have been married previously or if they have had children together'. Cohabitants without children were still more favourably treated than those with. The mischief the law was designed (if badly) to remove disappeared with separate assessment in 1965, but the provision about cohabitation remains in the statute book. The result is that every year each Swedish taxpayer is required to state in his tax return whether or not he is living with someone to whom he was previously married or with someone who has borne him a child.[104]

Swedish courts have extended legislation designed to protect creditors to deal with the cohabitation situation as well. For example, the Execution Act reverses the normal burden of proof and requires that the wife has the burden of proving that property in the spouses' common home belongs to her and, therefore, cannot be seized by a creditor of the husband. If she cannot produce such evidence, the property is presumed to belong to the husband and can be distrained upon by the creditor. Two cases in 1979 applied this rule by analogy to cohabitants. In one the parties had lived together for fourteen years, though there were no children. In the other there were children and the cohabitation had persisted for some years.[105] Similarly, under the Bankruptcy Act, there are provisions for the avoidance of transactions carried out to the disadvantage of creditors. The Act distinguishes transactions involving someone with whom the creditor is 'closely connected' from others (the time period is longer).[106] 'Closely connected' has been interpreted to include a person with whom the debtor cohabits under circumstances resembling marriage. This is not strictly an example of equating the two, because other relationships of close connections – for example, foster parent and child – are similarly regarded.

Swedish law does not contain rules to govern children born of unmarried but cohabiting parents. The rules on children born to unmarried mothers are therefore applicable. These differ very little from the rules concerning children of married parents. Swedish law dispensed with the terms 'legitimate' and 'illegitimate' in 1917, and 'child born in wedlock' and 'child born out of wedlock' in 1976, because such expressions 'might express a lingering moral evaluation to the disadvantage of children born to unmarried mothers'.[107] Despite this, differences do remain. First, there is a presumption that where a child is born to a married woman, her husband is the father of the child. The paternity of a child of an unmarried woman, on the other hand, must be established either through acknowledgement by the father or a court judgment. Child welfare committees have a duty to ensure that paternity is established for all children: if an unmarried mother cohabits with the father, the investigation may be simplified, though the same rules apply as where an unmarried mother is not living with a man. It may be noted that in Norway, where the attitude towards illegitimacy is similarly liberal, a committee in 1977 recommended the abolition of the legal presumption of the paternity of the husband where a child has been born in marriage. The paternity for all children would thus need to be established. The proposal was heavily criticised and is not followed in recent Norwegian legislation.[108]

The second difference relates to custody. If a child is born to married parents, both have custody and guardianship of the child. However, if the mother is not married to the father, she alone has legal custody, whether or not she is living with the father. Only upon marriage will the father acquire custody. A third difference is that the child of an unmarried mother takes the mother's surname, whereas a child of married parents is given his father's surname. An unmarried mother may, however, notify the civil registry that the child is to be given the father's name. This happens commonly but mainly where the mother and father are cohabiting.[109]

This discussion of Swedish law shows that it, like the neutrality principle it is said to embody, is full of contradictions and inconsistency. Take, for example, the way in which the economic community which exists in a stable cohabitation is recognised, even though the parties have no mutual legal obligations. Look at the way the recognition of cohabitation is limited by considerations of children or the need for the cohabitation to resemble marriage, whatever that might mean. The Swedish approach is to attribute legal consequences to cohabitation so as to eliminate discrimination against unmarried cohabitation. But, as Agell noted, it is not a clear-cut policy. It exists 'where there is a felt need for practical solutions'[110] and it does not aim at giving cohabitants full equality with married couples. Marriage still occupies in the minds of the Swedish legislators a central position, though it clearly no longer does so in the minds of a large number of the people of Sweden. There are three legal categories of cohabitation in Sweden today: there is marriage; there is unmarried cohabitation where there are children; and there is unmarried cohabitation without children. Nevertheless, in more and more cases the tendency is to equate cohabitation with marriage. Agell sees this leading to the encouragement of cohabitation, with the concomitant decline in the number of those marrying. This assumption seems to us questionable. Very few people, it is thought, consciously choose not to marry and to cohabit instead, after weighing up the social and legal benefits of the two statuses as well as their burdens and obligations.

At present the future of Swedish law remains uncertain and in flux. In the light of this it is of some significance that recent reports in both Denmark and Norway[111] have avoided an endorsement of the Swedish neutrality principle. The majority of the Norwegian committees did not express a particular ideological evaluation. A minority, however, repudiated the Swedish neutrality principle. The report generally favours a cautious and piecemeal approach to the phenomenon of cohabitation, with legislation limited to matters upon which it is thought there is a particular need for new rules. The Danish committee has taken a stance very similar to that of the Norwegian one. However, it does also stress the importance of giving marriage priority and of avoiding the construction by legislation of 'a marriage of second class'. A number of the proposals in both reports, if implemented, would bring their respective legal systems close in spirit to the Swedish.

Latin and South American approaches

In Latin and South America there have always been high rates of illegitimacy.[112] Stable non-marital unions have been common. Legal responses in the different states, sometimes within the same country, have not, however, been uniform.

At one end of the spectrum stands Brazil. Its 1969 Constitution proclaims that the family is constituted by matrimony and that only such families will be protected by public authority.[113] Though the Civil Code does not directly regulate cohabitation, it shows in some of its provisions hostility towards it.[114] Brazil did not provide for divorce until 1977.[115] Because of the absence of divorce and social changes generally, both legislature and courts have had to develop techniques to deal with cohabitation. Thus, there is special legislation in Brazil on road accidents and industrial injuries which provides that a female cohabitant (as in France the tendency is to use the word 'concubine') who is economically dependent on her partner should have the same rights as those enjoyed by other persons who are economically dependent.[116] Brazilian courts, rather like the French, have been prepared to find a partnership in fact between cohabitants so as to enable one to share in property accumulated by common effort. But Brazilian jurisprudence makes it clear that common effort is required: proof of the existence of cohabitation without more is insufficient.[117] Brazilian courts, on the other hand, are reluctant to enforce financial obligations between former cohabitants even where there is an agreement by one to support the other.[118] Clearly though, as Villela notes, Brazilian case law has come a long way from the position taken in the Constitution and Civil Code.

Mexico[119] has thirty-two Civil Codes. Generalisation about them is facilitated because the Code of the Federal District is the prevailing model. Neither the original Code of 1870 nor its successor of 1884 contain any reference to cohabitation, despite the fact that it constituted then as now a major social problem in Mexico. In Mexican legal literature, however, cohabitation (it tends to be called 'concubinage') is considered a factual relationship to which certain legal consequences are attributed when it is stable and prolonged. Sánchez-Cordero states that 'the cohabitation of man and woman – if both are single – is a lawful relation productive of legal effects'.[120] He lists a number of characteristic elements which correspond broadly to basic conditions of marriage. 'In sum', he states, 'the model of concubinage is derived from the marriage model'.[121] There is even a law in one Mexican state (Tamaulipas) which equates marriage to cohabitation, article 70 of the Civil Code stating, 'for all legal purposes, matrimony will be considered the continuous union, cohabitation and sexual relations of a single man with a single woman', provided they have no blood or affinity ties, have reached the minimum age for marriage etc. The Code provides facilities for registering such a relationship. The parallel of Bolivia and Guatemala was invoked by the legislator but, rather nearer home, the Scottish system of 'marriage by habit and repute'[122] is close in spirit to the Code in Tamaulipas.

Mexican Civil Codes provide considerable economic protection to female cohabitants. A testator must leave his cohabitant an allowance if he has lived with her as her husband during the five years immediately preceding his death, provided they remained unmarried during the cohabitation and she is unable to work and lacks insufficient means. This right subsists as long as she does not marry and 'behaves properly'.[123] However, if the testator lived with several women, none of them has the right to an allowance. A female cohabitant may also inherit on the intestacy of her partner.[124] Mexican social welfare law also allows benefits, in the absence of a widow, to accrue to persons who partially or totally depended on the deceased worker, and this may include a 'concubine' with whom the worker shared a common life. A further example is the Social Security Law, which, in the absence of a wife, entitles a cohabitant to a survivor's pension if she lived with the deceased for the five years preceding his death and both remained unmarried during the cohabitation.

Mexican law is firmly on the road to giving cohabitation virtually the same legal effects as marriage. A recent bill drafted by the 25th Legislative Congress of the Mexican Union provided for a family when founded as a relationship of cohabitation to have legal effects where the relationship implies complete community of life. According to Sánchez-Cordero, 'the partners in concubinage were charged with the responsibility of contributing to the maintenance of the family on a fifty–fifty basis, it being understood that care of the home be considered economically productive work and therefore the contribution of whomever performs it'.[125] The Bill apparently has no possibility of being enacted, but shows the trend in Mexican thinking clearly.

Other Latin and South American countries barely distinguish marriage and cohabitation. Article 131 of the Bolivian Constitution, for example, recognises as marriage 'any union in concubinage' with only two years of life in common, verified by proof or by the birth of a child, provided the parties had legal capacity to marry. Guatemala recognises the legal union in fact of a man and a woman, with a capacity to marry and for the purpose of living together, to beget, feed and educate their children and help each other, kept in public manner and consecutive for over three years, provided that they had made a home together and conducted themselves as a legal union.[126] In Cuba also non-marital unions are recognised. Article 43 of the Cuban Constitution requires the courts to determine when, for reasons of equity, a union between persons with capacity to marry who have not formally done so shall, by reason of its stability, be equated with civil matrimony. Cuban law does not deal with the economic consequences of cohabitation, but Venezuela's Code of 1942 does. This creates a presumption of community of property in all cases of cohabitation where the woman demonstrates that she has lived permanently in such a state and has contributed by her labour to the acquisition of or increase in her cohabitant's assets. The Brazilian solution, as already indicated, is not dissimilar.

The countries considered here by no means have uniform solutions. Yet all of them, and this includes Brazil, are pushing in the same direction. Brazil has not got as far and may not do so. The direction, however, is plain. The legal systems confronted by widespread cohabitation (invariably called concubinage) have responded by giving it as many legal effects as possible: sometimes, even calling it marriage. In some of the systems (Bolivia, Guatemala, Cuba) there is little or no distinction between a formal marriage and a long-standing cohabitation. The motive, where one can be detected and where it goes beyond expediency, seems to be the protection of the female cohabitant. Much of the legislation is, as might be expected in these countries, overtly sexist. It is essentially pragmatic. There is little or no detectable theory.

The Yugoslav response

Responses to cohabitation in the different republics and provinces of Yugoslavia have been by no means uniform. The number of cohabiting couples is not insignificant. But, according to Mladenovic, though legislators have anticipated the 'revolutionary' changes taking place in family formation and structure, they have 'not been able fully to grasp the essence of these changes, i.e. that marriage is inevitably moving away from the "oppressed, compulsive form of formal marriage" towards the "free, humane, informal relationship in cohabitation without formal marriage" that is threatening to eliminate the institution of marriage'.[127] This statement is interesting, since it fuses socialist ideology and typical bourgeois scaremongering to be found in Western legal literature.

Before the Second World War a negative attitude was taken to cohabitation. This is thought to have reflected the influence of the different ecclesiastical authorities of the various religious groups in Yugoslavia. There were no legal provisions on the subject in 1945. The Federal Constitution of 1946 guarantees to protect the family. It does not indicate which families are entitled to protection but is thought to cover the family outside marriage as well as the traditional family.[128] The Federal Basic Law on Marriage in 1946, however, granted parties to non-marital unions no rights whatsoever. The reasoning was that, since almost all persons were able to marry, it was unnecessary to protect non-marital unions. But, since there were even then a large number of cohabitants, the courts were forced to protect the exploitation of what were called 'unmarried "wives" '.[129] A Directive of the Federal Supreme Court in 1954 declared that relations in a non-marital union were not equal to those of marriage; there were no support obligations, though if support had been given, a refund could not be requested. There were, furthermore, no inheritance rights; if, however, the Directive continued, one of the unmarried partners had worked or run the household for the other, he or she had the right to claim an amount equivalent to his or her contribution to the other.[130] This Directive did not bind lower courts but had the force of a persuasive precedent and influenced other courts in their decision-making. Consequently, Šarčević notes, 'the directive . . . was accepted in judicial practice, and in this manner cohabitation without formal marriage was granted a certain amount of protection without direct legal regulation'.[131] In time this practice broadened. For example, a cohabitant was recognised as a member of the family and in certain cases granted the right to tenancy of the common home after the death of the tenant partner.

Constitutional amendments in 1971 and 1974 have transferred jurisdiction over marriage and the family to the individual republics and provinces. The responses of the different republics and provinces have varied. Slovenia has actually equalised the legal status of unmarried couples who have been cohabiting for a long period of time with that of married couples, provided a marriage in the actual circumstances would be valid.[132] Other republics and provinces have not granted non-marital unions equality with marriage, though certain rights have been accorded cohabitants. For example, in Croatia legislation from 1978 provides for mutual support obligations and other property rights and obligations for cohabitation. An unmarried person may receive support from his partner after the end of their common life if he has no means of supporting himself and is incapable of working or is unemployed.[133] Property acquired by unmarried partners becomes their joint property and is to be distributed as a married couple's property would.[134] The law of Bosnia and Herzegovina is very similar.[135] In Kosovo rights depend on the relationship having existed for several years and being 'similar to marriage'.[136] In Serbia there are mutual support obligations where there are children or the relationship is of long-lasting character. Serbian law also regulates agreements between cohabitants. The courts will not enforce the contract if the claimant was 'rude or behaved unbecomingly in the non-marital union, if he deserted his partner maliciously or without justified reason or if his claim would incur obvious injustice to the other unmarried partner'.[137] This is a remarkable proviso to find in a world, Yugoslavia included, where the matrimonial offence is taboo. The Serbian provision apart, all the remaining Yugoslav legislation requires a cohabiting couple to have lived together for a long time or a specified period before rights and obligations arise. Marriage and cohabitation are, accordingly, not treated equally, even in Slovenia where equality is the expressed goal, because there is no requirement for a marital union to have lasted for a long time in order to be subject to legal effect.

Yugoslav legal commentators share a number of the concerns of jurists of other countries. Šarčević is concerned that 'legal protection' should be extended to all families whether they are based on marriage or not.[138] At the same time he quotes with approval a comment of Stevanov[139] to the effect that cohabitation without formal marriage might lose some of its freedom and consequently the essence of its advantages over marriage if it were completely equalised with marriage. It is significant that this tension between protection and autonomy is to be found in such a different cultural setting from ours.[140]

A concluding comment

This survey has highlighted a number of points. Despite the increase in cohabitation outside marriage, marriage still occupies a central position in all the societies surveyed in this chapter. The main social and legal developments have emerged as in this country, where *Diwell v Farnes*[141] was still the leading case in 1972, during the last decade. It is noticeable how codified systems, the norm outside the common law world, tend not to provide in their codes for the problems created by non-marital unions. Many codes, we have seen, ignore cohabitation as a phenomenon altogether. Others either expressly or by implication are critical of it. As in the common law world, there are gaps in the legislation, and judges worldwide, it seems, have had their minds exercised by problems such as what to do with property acquired by common effort but placed in one partner's hands and whether to impose any mutual obligation of support on cohabiting partners. Like divorce a quarter of a century ago, attitudes to cohabitation are in a state of flux. Little stigma attaches now to divorce: ten years ago in Europe (perhaps not in some of the Latin American countries discussed) cohabitation was frowned upon at least in middle-class society. It occupied some kind of twilight zone, a *demi-monde.* There have been adjustments in social attitudes since then. There may still, however, be a feeling prevalent in society that, while stigma should not attach to living together outside marriage, those who cohabit, who choose not to marry, should not take the 'benefits' of marriage. If, in other words, there is resistance to treating cohabitation like marriage (and there are movements in this direction in all the countries discussed), it comes in the main not from those who want to preserve freedom for those who do not wish to marry, but from those who want to preserve a special status for marriage, and who do not think that the advantages, as they see them, of marriage should be given away to those not prepared to pay the price.

A dominant theme, as we might expect, has been the determination to protect the weaker, the more economically dependent of the partners. This in most cases is the female partner or former partner. Most of the legislation and case law is general and therefore gender-neutral, though some is explicitly sexist. Most of the countries surveyed believe in the equality of the sexes, especially Sweden and Yugoslavia: all are beginning at the very least to pay lip-service to the ideal. But hardly anywhere, not even in Sweden or in 'socialist' countries, have women been placed in a true position of equality. It is from this absence of equality that the need to protect springs. There is also, rightly, a desire to protect children born of non-marital unions. This extends beyond the children of cohabitations. A number of the countries in our survey – New Zealand, Sweden, to a lesser extent France – have dispensed with the legitimacy–illegitimacy distinction. More important is the necessity to ensure that children, all children but especially those who might be more vulnerable, are provided for. This is one of the underlying reasons why both legislatures and courts have been more ready to accord recognition to cohabitants who have children.

None of the countries under consideration imposes legal effects on all sexual relationships. Most, for example, insist that the relationship be heterosexual. This may be the next barrier to fall. Some American case law already suggests a trend towards the recognition of homosexual relationships as well.[142] As yet, of course, they cannot marry[143] and so can only cohabit. All the systems surveyed try to avoid giving legal effects to partners in transitory sexual relationships. This is one of the reasons why we have seen that legislation often distinguishes between 'lasting' cohabiting relationships and others. Some legislation actually prescribes a minimum period of cohabitation. Some go further to insist that a cohabitation should 'resemble' marriage, whatever this may mean. It is common for legislation only to accord recognition to relationships where the parties could have married each other. An under-age relationship or one not permitted by rules of consanguinity and affinity thus does not produce the effects that one not so tainted might. In the same way it is implicitly recognised (and expressed in some Yugoslav and Latin American legislation) that the relationship must be 'monogamous': if you can only have one wife, you are not entitled to a plurality of non-marital partners.

Once a state has decided that it will accord recognition to certain relationships outside marriage, and once it has decided which of those relationships is meritorious, a number of decisions still have to be taken. This suggests a conscious process, a deliberate policy. In fact in many systems, not just the uncodified ones, these decisions have been left to the judges to determine in a pragmatic way as problems have arisen. Judges have then often reasoned by analogy, sometimes looking at marriage, particularly matrimonial property systems, sometimes at partnership law. Doctrines of unjust enrichment have also been invoked. Where deliberate policies have been pursued, in Sweden, in South Australia, in Slovenia, in parts of Latin and South America, a decision still has to be taken whether those cohabiting are to be given full equality or whether legislation is to be extended to them as thought necessary, and hence in a piecemeal fashion. More thought has been given to this question in Sweden than elsewhere. But, as indicated earlier, Sweden's famous 'neutrality principle' is not without its difficulties or its ambivalences. Does it mean giving individuals the liberty to choose what norms are to govern their relationship, putting the emphasis, in other words, on a cohabitation contract? Or does it mean that the state should apply the same rules to those who cohabit as it does to those who marry? Sweden, it appears, does not apply a consistent line of thought, preferring, as it does, the first interpretation in marriage law, the second in social welfare and fiscal legislation. Contract poses problems, for situations are not foreseen and new circumstances occur. Hence systems which put the onus on cohabiting partners to agree upon their mutual rights and obligations often find it necessary to inject elements of equity when something goes wrong.

But, if we do not discover a consistent policy even in a country like Sweden where serious thought has been given to the phenomenon of cohabitation, it is hardly surprising to find that in countries where the approach is piecemeal and the responses pragmatic no real understanding of the issues emerges. The general trend is towards the recognition of more and more effects of cohabitation: most of the countries in our survey recognise cohabitation for tax, pensions and social welfare purposes, even if they do not do so fully. An increasing number grant succession and inheritance rights. Some construct quasi-matrimonial regimes to deal with commonly used property. Some are trying to construct obligations of support. The movement, in other words, is towards treating cohabitation like marriage. Only in Sweden are there occasional glimpses of a reverse policy: treating marriage like cohabitation. If this comparative survey has taught us anything, it is that we are not groping in the dark alone; that even in Sweden, where experts have given sustained and serious attention to the theory, no long-lasting and satisfactory answer has been formulated. One of the goals of comparative law is to open our eyes and minds to different approaches. What our exercise demonstrates is that the value of this hinges on the other systems having something to offer. We can learn from their errors; we can avoid some of their difficulties; but, outside Sweden, and probably not there either, for, as indicated, confusion reigns there too, we will not find a coherent policy. Everywhere, it appears, the law has been unable to come to grips with cohabitation.

It is easy to blame legislatures and judges, but their hesitancies, inconsistencies and doubts reflect those of the societies of which they are parts. Is this an area of life where law-makers should lead or follow? What evidence[144] we have suggests that in 'expressive'[145] areas of life, areas rooted in emotion, tradition, custom and religion, attempts to use legislation to forge public opinion are seldom successful. But public opinion is changing, in part a response to the campaigns of women's movements. It cannot, therefore, be long before serious attention is given to a reconsideration of the issues and reformulation of the laws considered in this chapter. It is important, as we have stressed throughout, for a consistent policy to be pursued.

Notes

1 See, generally, H.C. Gutteridge, *Comparative Law*, Cambridge U.P., 1946.

2 A. Agell, 'The Swedish Legislation on Marriage and Cohabitation: A Journey without a Destination', *Amer. J. of Comparative Law*, 29 (1981) p. 285.

3 The most thorough examination of this is K. Llewellyn, *The Common Law Tradition*, Little Brown, 1960.

4 410 U.S. 113 (1973).

5 See *post*, p. 171.

6 [1972], 2 All E.R. 38.

7 [1975], 3 All E.R. 768.

8 83 D.L.R. 3d 289, 303 (1978).

9 *Idem*, see also *Pettkus v Becker*, 117 D.L.R. (3d) 257 (1981).

10 *Ogilvie v Ryan* [1976], 2 N.S.W. L.R. 504; *Nemeth v Nemeth* (1977), 17 A.L.R. 500. See also R. Bailey, 'Legal Recognition of De Facto Relationships', *Aust. L.J.*, 52 (1978), p.174.

11 *Fraser v Gough* [1975], 1 N.Z. L.R. 138.

12 For example, Bagnall J, in *Cowcher v Cowcher* [1972], 1 All E.R. 943.

13 [1977] 2 N.S.W. L.R. 685, 694.

14 'De Facto Relationship and the Imputed Trust', *Sydney L. Rev.*, 8 (1979) pp. 571, 576.

15 See *Tanner v Tanner* [1975], 3 All E.R. 776.

16 The theories underlying unjust enrichment are examined by D. Friedmann, 'Restitution of Benefits', *Columbia L.R.*, 80 (1980), p. 504.

17 *Op. cit.*, note 8, p. 303. See also *Pettkus v Becker, op. cit.*, note 9, p. 260.

18 *Tyranski v Piggins*, 205 N.W. 2d 595 (1973); *Levar v Elkins*, 604 P. 2d 602 (1980); *Keene v Keene*, 371 P. 2d 329 (1962); *Beal v Beal* 577 P. 2d 507 (1978) and, of course, *Marvin v Marvin*. A useful account of the cases (*pre-Marvin*) is C. Bruch, 'Property Rights of De Facto Spouses including Thoughts on the Value of Homemakers' Services', *Fam. L.Q.*, 10 (1976), p. 101. The tort case is isolated. It is *Wilke v Oldenburg*, 6 Fam. L. Rep. (BNA) 2086 (1979).

19 557 P. 2d 106 (1976).

20 *Post*, p. 194 *et seq.*

21 238 S.E. 2d 81, 82 (1977).

22 'Marriage and the State: the Withering Away of Marriage', 62 *Virginia L. Rev.*, 62 (1976) p. 663.

23 A point also made by C. Bruch, 'Nonmarital Cohabitation in Common Law Countries', *Amer. J. of Comparative Law*, 29 (1981) pp. 217, 224, quoting judicial testimony to a California Senate Committee inquiring into *Marvin*.

24 *Wirth v Wirth*, 366 N.Y.S. 2d 308 (1971).

25 429 N.Y.S. 2d 592 (1980).

26 S.11.

27 Now Maintenance Act 1967 s. 16.

28 Law Reform Commission of Tasmania, *Report on Obligations Arising From De Facto Relationships*, 1976. There are accounts of it in E. Evatt *et al.*, 'The Legal and Social Aspects of Cohabitation', and F. Bates, 'The Changing Nature of Marriage', in J. Eekelaar and S. Katz (eds), *Marriage and Cohabitation in Contemporary Societies*, Butterworths, 1980, pp. 398 and 104 respectively.

29 S.52. On which see J. O'Hoski, 'The Legal Recognition of Domestic Contracts', in Eekelaar and Katz (eds), *op. cit.*, note 28, at p. 228.

30 S.52.
31 S.64(b).
32 Ss.13 and 14.
33 *Re Feehan and Attwells Sr.* (1979), 24 O.R. (2d) 248.
34 *Donheim v Irwin* (1979) 6 R.F.L. (2d) 242.
35 Family Law Reform Act 1978 ss.15(a), 19(4)(a) and (c) and 52.
36 S.1.
37 See Vaver, 'The Legal Effects of De Facto Relationships', 2 *N.Z. Recent Law* (n.s.), (1976) p. 161.
38 See, *e.g. Re Edilson* (1976) 2 N.Z. Recent Law (n.s.), 11 and *Re Sanderson* (1975) 1 N.Z. Recent Law (n.s.), 51.
39 See New Zealand Matrimonial Property Bill, 1975.
40 See R. Keeton, *Venturing To Do Justice,* Harvard U.P., 1969; L. Jaffe, *English and American Judges as Lawmakers,* Oxford U.P., 1969.
41 Proposals referred to by Bruch, *op. cit.,* note 23, p. 226, and D. Foster and H. Freed, '*Marvin v Marvin* – New Wine in Old Bottles', *Fam. L. Rep.,* 5 (1979), pp. 4001, 4009.
42 See *Fam. L. Rep.,* 5 (1979), (BNA) p. 2624.
43 N.H. Rev. Stat. Ann. S457: 39 (1968).
44 On which see P. Bromley, *Family Law* (6th ed.), Butterworths, 1981, pp. 28–30.
45 Ch. 3 of *State, Law and Family,* North Holland Publishing Co., Amsterdam, 1977, p. 78.
46 A good introduction to these is vol. 4 of *International Encyclopedia of Comparative Law* (chapter 4, *Interspousal Relations* by M. Rheinstein and M. Glendon), Mohr, Tubingen, 1980. See also *op. cit.,* note 45, ch. 4.
47 Rodière in '*Le ménage de fait*', *Travaux de l'Association Capitant,* tome XI, Dalloz éd., Paris (1960), p. 60.
48 Glendon's expression: *op. cit.,* note 45, p. 85.
49 There was no divorce in France between 1816 and 1884.
50 '*L'avenèment du concubinat*', *Dalloz* (Recueil Hebdomadaire de Jurisprudence), 45 (1932).
51 '*Le Probleme de l'Union libre*', *idem,* 49 (1935).
52 *Op. cit.,* note 45, p. 85.
53 'Mariage et Concubinage en Droit Francais Contemporain', *Archives de Philosphie du Droit,* vol. 20 (1975), p. 17, at p. 25.
54 Code Civil, art. 1402, para. 1.
55 *Idem,* art.270.
56 *Idem,* arts. 271, 272.
57 *Idem,* art. 266.
58 H. Mazeaud and L. Mazeaud, *Leçons de Droit Civil,* I 3 (1972), p. 852.
59 Code Civil, art. 281.
60 Cass. civ. 12 Nov 1959, Dalloz, 1960, p. 447.
61 *Per* Malaurie, *op. cit.,* note 53, p. 27.
62 *Idem,* p. 26.
63 See R. Nerson, '*Les Couples non-mariés en France*', in J. Eekelaar and S. Katz (eds), *op. cit.,* note 28, pp. 198, 205.
64 The expression belongs to D. Huet-Weiller, '*L'Union libre*', *Amer. J. of Comparative Law,* 29 (1981), pp. 247, 259.
65 *Op. cit.,* note 45, p. 86.
66 A subsidiary action (see Huet-Weiller, *op. cit.,* note 64, pp. 260–1).
67 See J. Carbonnier, 2 *Droit Civil* 192–3 (1972); Huet-Weiller, *op. cit.,* note 64, pp. 262–3.
68 See, e.g., Huet-Weiller, *op. cit.,* note 64, p. 263.
69 See Cass. civ. 6 Oct 1959, Dalloz 1959, Dalloz 1960, 515 (note by Malaurie).
70 Trib. Paris, 13 Nov 1959, Dalloz 1960, 360.
71 Using the concept of *un ménage apparent.*
72 A point stressed by Malaurie, *op. cit.,* note 53, p. 29.
73 See Nerson *op. cit.,* note 63, p. 206.
74 *Idem.*
75 *Op. cit.,* note 45, p. 87.
76 Cass. crim., 20 Apr 1972, Juris-Classeur Périodique 1972 II 17278, note by Vidal. See also Huet-Weiller, *op. cit.,* note 64, p. 265.

77 Trib. Paris 24 Nov 1972, Recueil Dalloz Sirey 1973, Jur. 414, note Groslière.
78 'Le Coeur de la Cour de Cassation', Recueil Dalloz Sirey 1975, Chr. 41.
79 'De l'union libre au mariage à travers L'art 301, Dalloz 75 Chr. 123 (1975).
80 *Op. cit.,* note 53, p. 27.
81 *Op. cit.,* note 64, p. 249.
82 Ministerial response, 11 February 1980, quoted *idem,* p. 250.
83 *Op. cit.,* note 45, p. 91.
84 In *Carmen,* Act 1.
85 These statistics are official Swedish statistics and are quoted by Agell, *op. cit.,* note 2, pp. 287–91.
86 See, generally, J. Trost, *Unmarried Cohabitation,* International Library, Vasteras, 1979. See also J. Trost, 'Dissolution of Marriage and Cohabitation in Sweden', *Journal of Divorce,* vol. 2 (1979), p. 415.
87 According to research quoted by Agell, *op. cit.,* note 2, p. 289.
88 'Recent Changes in Swedish Family Law: Experiment Repeated', *Amer. J. of Comparative Law,* 23 (1975) p. 34. The same theme is presented in J. Sundberg's earlier article, 'Marriage or No Marriage', *I.C.L.Q.,* 20 (1971), p. 223.
89 On which see R. Schlesinger, *The Family in the U.S.S.R.,* R.K.P. 1949, pp. 33, 154.
90 In much the same way as the English presumption in favour of marriage (see, e.g., *Re Taplin* [1937], 3 All E.R. 105) and system of common law marriage tend to do.
91 Extracts are to be found in both Sundberg articles (note 88) and in Agell, *op. cit.,* note 2.
92 *Op. cit.,* note 2, p. 292.
93 *Idem,* p. 293.
94 *Idem.*
95 This may seem radical but the same result was achieved in English cases such as *Eves* and *Tanner* (notes 7 and 15); and in the context of marriage in cases like *Martin v Martin* [1978], Fam. 12; *Bassett v Bassett* [1975], 1 All E.R. 513; and *Browne v Pritchard* [1975], 3 All E.R. 721.
96 *Op. cit.,* note 2, p. 294. We must add 'in Sweden'.
97 As to which, see *op. cit.,* note 46, p. 100. A Family Law Commission Report (1981) has proposed modifications.
98 (1975) N.J.A. 298 (referred to by A. Agell, 'International Society of Family Law', *Newsletter* (1977), p. 82.) Changes have recently been recommended. See *op. cit.,* note 97.
99 *Holli v Kost* [1972], 7 R.C.L. 77.
100 As it may be in England. See Matrimonial Causes Act 1973, s.31. The Swedish provision is in the Marriage Code ch. 11, § 15.
101 S.8:2 (in Sundberg's translation *Am. J. of Comp. L.,* 23, pp. 34, 38).
102 *Op. cit.,* note 2, p. 297.
103 Occupational Injuries Insurance Act 1976, ch. 5, §6.
104 See Sundberg, *op. cit.,* note 88, at p. 39.
105 N.J.A. I 1979, p. 302 (I and II) (see A. Agell, *op. cit.,* note 2, pp. 299–300).
106 Bankruptcy Act (1921) §29a (from 1975).
107 *Per* A. Agell, *op. cit.,* note 2, p. 300.
108 As to which, see P. Lødrup, in Eekelaar and Katz (eds), *op. cit.,* note 28, p. 413.
109 These differences demonstrate that Sundberg is going too far when he asserts (*Am. J. of Comp. Law,* 23, pp. 34, 36) that 'the legal relationship between the parents does not affect the relationship between the parents and their children'.
110 *Op. cit.,* note 2, p. 306.
111 Agell dismisses these, *op. cit.,* note 2, pp. 315–14. Earlier Danish developments are discussed by I. Pedersen, 'Danish Law relating to Non-Marital Relationships', *I.C.L.Q.,* 28 (1979) p. 117.
112 See W. Goode, *World Revolution and Family Patterns,* Free Press, 1963.
113 Art. 175.
114 See J. Villela in Eekelaar and Katz (eds), *op. cit.,* note 28, p. 172.
115 By a ninth amendment to the Constitution.
116 Law no. 2681 of 1912 and 7036 of 1944.
117 *Op. cit.,* note 114, pp. 173–4.
118 As in the famous *Ira de Fürstemberg v 'Baby' Pignatari* case (see *op. cit.,* note 114, pp. 175–6).

119 See A. Sánchez-Cordero, 'Cohabitation Without Marriage in Mexico', in *Amer. J. of Comparative Law,* 19 (1981), p. 279.
120 *Idem,* p. 280.
121 *Idem.*
122 As to which, see Scottish Home and Health Department, *The Marriage Law of Scotland,* Cmnd. 4011 (1969), HMSO, ch. 9.
123 *Per* Sánchez-Cordero, *op. cit.,* note 119, p. 283.
124 Civil Code Art. 1636.
125 *Op. cit.,* note 119, p. 284.
126 Art. 1 of Statute of November 1947. Provision is also made for Indians where relationships celebrated in accordance with their customs are deemed to be unions in fact, entitled to rights established by the law even though they have not lasted three years. They must, however, be registered.
127 *Basics of the Sociology of the Family,* 1979, p. 188, quoted by Šarčević, *Amer. J. of Comparative Law,* 29 (1981), pp. 315, 317.
128 Art. 190 I.
129 A point made by Stevanov, 'The Non-Marital Union' (1978), quoted by Šarčević, *op. cit.,* note 127, p. 319.
130 No Su 42/54, quoted *idem.*
131 *Idem,* p. 320, quoting Stevanov.
132 Art. 12 of Slovenian Law on Marital and Other Family Relations of 1976.
133 Arts. 254–8.
134 Art. 293.
135 Effective 1 January 1980 (Art. 14).
136 Art. 46 of Law of Marriage of 1974.
137 Dating from 1980. See Art. 16 for the general provision: also Arts. 293–6, 338–9.
138 *Op. cit.,* note 127, p. 338.
139 From *op. cit.,* note 129, p. 92.
140 For the experience of another 'socialist' country (Hungary), see M. Soltesz, 'Les Questions Juridiques des Rapports Existant Entre Les Personnes Cohabitant Sans Mariage en Hongrie', in Eekelaar and Katz (eds), *op. cit.,* note 28, p. 179. Marriage occupies a central position in Hungarian law but cohabitants get some protection in social security, pension and housing law. The 1977 Civil Code extends community of property notions to cohabitants whose common life is ruptured.
141 [1959], 2 All E.R. 379.
142 See, for example, *Weeks v Gray* 256 S.E. 2d 901 (1979) (Georgia) and *Bramlett v Selman* 597 S.W. 2d 80 (1980) (Arkansas).
143 As to which, see E. Veitch, 'The Essence of Marriage – A Comment on the Homosexual Challenge', *Anglo-American Law Review,* 5 (1976), p. 41.
144 See Y. Dror, 'Law and Social Change', *Tulane Law Review,* 33 (1959), p. 749.
145 See G. Massell 'Law as an Instrument of Revolutionary Change in a Traditional Milieu', *Law and Society Review,* 2 (1968), p. 179.

6 Justifications for Equivalent Treatment

There is no lack in English[1] or American[2] case law of concern for the plight of cohabitants who come before the courts, or of the view that they should be treated in more or less the same way as married couples.[3] Some judges are, however, more confident of their ability to judge prevailing social mores and accordingly to decide cases in favour of cohabitants[4] than others, who prefer to seek support for their approach from legislation.[5] The problem with deriving assistance from the few legislative provisions which embody the equivalence principle is that it presumes that these measures are the result of a clearly argued and properly formulated policy towards cohabitation. This is simply not the case. Sweden is the exception in this area rather than the rule, though even there there is some confusion as to precisely what the neutrality principle entails.[6] The statutory provisions and the case law enforcing equivalent treatment, discussed in the previous two chapters, reveal a variety of reasons behind the adoption of the equivalence approach in the countries surveyed. No one reason, however, has emerged as being sufficiently compelling to structure a general policy around it, although the fulfilment of family functions has been a very common basis for attracting equivalent treatment. The laudable aim of eliminating inequalities between legitimate and illegitimate children has also fostered the trend to equivalent treatment, but thorough consideration has yet to be given to the consequences for family life, marriage and the law generally if proposals to abolish the status of illegitimacy are to be pursued to their logical conclusion. An additional factor encouraging moves towards the equivalence approach has been the desire of the courts and the legislatures to protect the economically and physically weaker family partner, usually the woman, from what is seen as male exploitation or abuse. Just how misguided the extension of equivalent treatment could be for cohabiting women can be seen from the quality of 'protection' presently enjoyed by married women who have subsequently divorced and are forced to rely on inadequate maintenance awards, supplemented by state assistance to support themselves and their children.[7] Yet, as we have seen, moves have been made in many countries to throw this mantle of protection around the cohabiting weaker sex, and few questions have been raised as to why this sort of protection should be extended, and even fewer explanations given, where it has already been done. The fault, though, does not only lie with Governments in having failed to formulate a coherent policy based on cogently argued reasons, but also with the elected representatives of the people and the media in failing to challenge the bases upon which such legislative provisions are drafted or judicial decisions made. The question remains to be answered: why should cohabiting couples be treated in the same way as married couples?

The justifications advanced in England

Very few of the legislative provisions embodying the equivalence principle have been adequately debated in England before they have reached the statute book, and therefore discussion of policy considerations has been rare. Thus, for example, little or no debate occurred in Parliament on the cohabitation rule before it was embodied in one of the most important statutes of the day, the Ministry of Social Security Act 1966.[8] It would seem that the then Government would not in any event have expected any debate,[9] for the rule was apparently taken so much for granted that it had not been included in the National Assistance Act 1948, and was only specifically embodied in the 1966 Act because that statute had increased the emphasis on a clear basis of entitlement for all claimants. Before its inclusion in this statute, the rule had been administered on a discretionary basis by the National Assistance Board, and was also applied under the National Insurance and Industrial Injuries schemes and under the War Widows' Pension scheme. Not only the Government but Parliament also in 1966 took it so much for granted that it was not debated on the floor of either House or in Committee, and it is clear[10] that successive governments have been surprised by subsequent controversy surrounding the existence and administration of the rule. So the approach which favoured treating a man and a woman who were cohabiting as man and wife, regardless of their wishes, had a relatively smooth passage into a major piece of legislation, destined to affect the lives of millions. The phrase 'cohabiting as man and wife' was subsequently changed to 'living together as husband and wife',[11] but it was still to gain increasing currency in statutory provisions and to attract comparatively little debate in Parliament. In public law statutes the principle of equivalent treatment was used again and again, chiefly to the benefit of the state's coffers and to the burden of the individual concerned, as was the case with virtually all the social security legislation. Occasionally the principle could work to the advantage of cohabitants, as under section 1 of the Family Income Supplement Act 1970, the Housing Finance Act 1972,[12] the Child Benefit Act 1975,[13] the Housing (Homeless Persons) Act 1977[14] and the Housing Act 1980.[15]

Since there is such a dearth of debate on many of the public law provisions and therefore a lack of Government response justifying the adoption of the equivalence principle, it is necessary to look to other sources to find policy justifications. Although there was no debate in Parliament on the cohabitation rule at the time of its introduction, it has since provoked considerable criticism from many quarters[16] and, as a result, has been debated in the House of Commons.[17] This in turn has prompted two reports commissioned by Governments[18] on the rule, and in another, which discussed the rule in relation to one-parent families,[19] attempts have at least been made to justify this prime example of equivalent treatment. The arguments used to support the equivalence approach are all essentially financial and therefore punitive. The first argument is based on the premise that an unmarried couple should not be placed in a more favourable position than the married couple, by allowing a cohabiting woman to claim benefit in her own right where a married woman cannot so claim. While acknowledging the trend towards equality, and the movement away from dependence on men by women, the Supplementary Benefits Commission states that it would be far too costly to allow all women to claim benefit in their own right regardless of the income of the man with whom they were living.[20] Accordingly, it concludes that 'so long as a married couple are treated as an economic unit for the purpose of supplementary benefit . . . it will be necessary to decide whether other couples, not married to each other, should be treated in the same way'.[21] As for the argument that a cohabiting woman does not have the same rights to enforce maintenance as a wife does, the Commission states that this is largely irrelevant, since most men do support the women with whom they are living.[22] The suggestion that the Commission should look more closely at actual financial arrangements than at anything else provoked the expected response that this would be unrealistic, as attempts would be made to conceal the real position in an effort to maximise entitlement to benefit.[23] The Commission's two reports are clearly very much in sympathy with the conclusion of the Finer Committee that the one overwhelming argument in favour of the cohabitation rule is that 'it cannot be right to treat unmarried women who have the support of a partner both as if they had no such support and better than if they were married'.[24]

Despite the fact that most of the legislative provisions embodying the equivalence approach have uniformly adopted the phrase 'living together as husband and wife' as the qualifying description for the imposition of burdens and occasionally benefits, two statutory provisions of recent times have used the phrase 'reputed husband or wife'[25] or reputed spouse.[26] Again, when such a term has been used by the draftsman, little question has been made as to its inclusion and use, although if such usage is queried, it is not unknown for a Government spokesman to declare that the concept is well-known in English law.[27] This could come as a considerable shock to all English lawyers. Since it is nowhere actually defined within English law, the concept of the 'reputed spouse' may yet give rise to difficulty, but it does imply, perhaps even more than the phrase 'living together as husband and wife', a complete assimilation of the position of the 'de facto' and 'de jure' spouse.

The principle of equivalent treatment through the application of the cohabitation rule has therefore gained some currency in legislative provisions in England. It remains to be seen what justifications are advanced for extending this approach, not only by means of legislation but also by judicial decision-making.

(i) *The fulfilment of family functions*

The principal justification for granting equivalent rights to, and enforcing equivalent responsibilities on, cohabitants, is that they fulfil exactly the same family functions as do married couples. Many cohabitants are concerned with the rearing of children, the building of a home, and the giving of emotional and financial support within a family setting, all of which are considered by the state to be important factors contributing to the ordered running of society. For this reason, many of the legislative provisions granting financial benefits for families with children extend equally to the unmarried as well as the married unit. In addition, judicial awareness of the changes which have occurred in family life-styles has been evident in several cases, and the courts bear a large part of the responsibility for the considerable extension of the principle of equivalent treatment for unmarried couples on the basis of their fulfilment of family functions. Whereas the courts would once have viewed only the 'legitimate' family as capable of performing such functions, they now acknowledge that cohabiting couples may perform a similar role.

The most forthright example of such acknowledgement is probably the judgment of James LJ in *Dyson Holdings v Fox* in 1975. In the course of reviewing earlier authorities, his lordship stated that

> in 1949 the popular meaning of family did not include the male consort of a female tenant whose relationship had all the incidents of a marriage short of the birth of a child and all the outward appearances of marriage. Between 1950 and 1975 there have been many changes in the law effected by statutes and the decisions of the courts. Many changes have their foundation in the changed needs and views of society. Such changes have occurred in the field of family law and equitable interests in property. The popular meaning given to the word family is not fixed once and for all time. I have no doubt that with the passage of years it has changed. The cases reveal that it is not restricted to blood relationships and those created by the marriage ceremony. It can include de facto as well as de jure relationships.

He then concluded that in 1975 the popular meaning of 'family' would include in that case the deceased tenant's cohabitant. He continued: 'this is not to say that every mistress should be so regarded. Relationships of a casual or intermittent character and those bearing indications of impermanence would not come within the popular concept of a family unit'.[28]

This caveat was to be seized upon three years later in *Helby v Rafferty*,[29] where the lack of the 'normal' incidents of marriage such as children, joint bank accounts and the use of the same surname, coupled with the 'short' (five year) duration of the relationship, all prevented the couple being described as a 'family'. By 1980 such factors were no longer so crucial, and Stephenson LJ in *Watson v Lucas* declared that 'the ordinary man often has or at any rate knows a man who has one family by his wife and another by his mistress'.[30] He said that the relevant question to be asked was would the ordinary man consider an association which has every outward appearance of marriage except the false pretence of being married as not constituting a family. He went on to say that 'the time has gone by when the courts can hold such a union not to be "familial" simply because the parties to it do not pretend to be married in due form of law'. He concluded that he had no wish to differ from an experienced county judge on the meaning and application of what ought to be plain English words *'but we are bound to move with the times'.*[31]

Thus, cohabitants may be granted rights equivalent to those of married couples if their relationship can be characterised as 'familial'. What are the factors which have been crucial in influencing the legislature's and the courts' determination as to whether cohabitants have established this familial nexus? Three criteria have been considered important: the presence of children, the length of the relationship, and finally the behaviour of the parties.

(a) The presence of children. The Family Income Supplement Act 1970, as amended,[32] provides by s.1 that for the purposes of qualifying for this benefit a family can consist of an unmarried couple and the child or children whose requirements are provided for, in whole or in part, by that member of the couple who is engaged in remunerative full-time work. The legislature has therefore defined a family as including cohabitants, provided there is at least one child living with the parties, and this in 1970, some five years before James LJ's interpretation of the meaning of the word 'family'. Entitlement to the supplement is dependent on the presence of a child, 'though it does not have to be a child of both parties'. The same is true of the conditions for the receipt of child benefit,[33] which is also paid without discrimination as to the legal status of the family. According to the guidelines laid down in the Supplementary Benefits *Handbook,*[34] the presence of children is one of the criteria which is indicative of whether a couple can be treated as living together as husband and wife. The *Handbook* states that 'when a couple are caring for a child or children of their union there is a strong presumption that they are living together as husband and wife'. The presence of children is only one item influencing the officer's decision, though it is interesting to note that this strong presumption only operates where they are caring for children of the union. If the couple is designated as 'living together as husband and wife', they will of course receive increases in respect of any of their dependent children, and such increases also are not restricted to children of the union.

The importance of such legislative provisions is that, while the judiciary has felt reluctant to act as lone arbiters of social change, they have on several occasions[35] quoted these statutes as proof of the legislature's desire that 'family' status should not be withheld from unmarried couples performing family functions. Although the judiciary at first resisted extending rights to unmarried couples, it was the judges in *Gammans v Ekins*[36] who, in a sense, opened up a loophole (namely the presence of children) through which 'illegitimate' families could slip to press home their claims to family membership in subsequent cases brought under the Rent Acts.[37] It then became only a matter of time before success in claiming to be a member of a cohabitant's family did not have to depend on the presence of a child or, as the court in *Hawes v Evenden* put it, 'the natural consequences of marriage'. Stephenson LJ in *Watson v Lucas* did, however, draw support for his decision that the survivor of a couple whose relationship had borne none of the usual incidents of marriage could be a member of the deceased partner's family from the thought that considerations for the reduction of illicit unions and the support of marriage were now deemed by Parliament to be irrelevant. He noted that Parliament had recognised the importance of this in several statutes, most directly in its concept of a family in the context of the Family Income Supplement Act 1970. In fact, it is most unlikely that Parliament had intended that any such inference should be drawn from its attempt to recognise the fulfilment of family functions by unmarried couples.

The presence of children is also now becoming a crucial factor in attracting quasi-matrimonial relief on the breakdown of a cohabiting relationship. In an attempt to provide for the children, the courts have not only favoured a type of maintenance support for the mothers[38] but are also determining property disputes by reference to the children's interests.[39] The inevitable result is that the procedures used to resolve such problems are becoming indistinguishable from those used in divorce cases. Early developments in awarding maintenance support to women were spearheaded by the judiciary,[40] yet in extending the principle the courts are now able to derive support from recent legislative measures.[41]

Initially, financial provision on breakdown was achieved by covert, and somewhat devious, means. In *Eves v Eves,* for example, the Court of Appeal held that since Janet Eves had done a lot of work on the house, she was entitled by way of constructive trust to 'such a share as was fair in view of all that she had done and was doing for him and the children'.[42] The constructive trust has been used to good effect in a number of cases concerning cohabitants in both England[43] and in Commonwealth countries[44] and it was of valuable assistance in Janet Eves's case. Lord Denning MR added here that he hoped that the interest he had awarded her 'would be regarded by her as more in the nature of a provision for the children than for her'.[45] Two days later, in *Tanner v Tanner,* Lord Denning MR was to uncover the existence of a new legal duty of provision for the cohabitant who looks after the children born of the cohabitation. The last part of the judgment[46] in the case illustrates the true basis upon which his Lordship assessed the compensation for the loss of her contractual licence at a figure as high as £2,000. In computing the compensation Lord Denning MR made it clear that in his view such a sum was by way of provision for the children and the person who cared for them. Again in *K v J.M.P. Ltd*[47] the court found a means of granting some provision for the mother of children born of a cohabiting relationship by increasing the amount of the children's damages to take account of the cessation of the father's payments to meet the mother's expenses when she accompanied the children on holiday. Similarly in *Haroutunian v Jennings,*[47a] a case under the old affiliation law, the court in awarding financial provision for the children indirectly provided some support for the mother, who was looking after them. In 1978, in pursuance of a policy clearly aimed at eliminating differences between legitimate and illegitimate children, the Domestic Proceedings and Magistrates' Courts Act amended the affiliation laws.[48] The new provision (see s.50(2)) allows the court to consider such factors as the mother's income, resources and earning capacity, and also her financial needs, obligations and responsibilities in determining the amount of an affiliation order. Just how widely such provisions will be interpreted by magistrates remains to be seen, but one Court of Appeal judge has seen the amendment as extending the principle of maintenance to mothers.[49] It would therefore seem possible that all mothers, regardless of status, may qualify for some sort of maintenance award. In debates on this measure[50] concern for the children was uppermost in everyone's mind; no one seemed to question the effect which such an extension might potentially have on the position of marriage within English society.

The presence of children has also been important in encouraging the courts to interfere with the exercise of property rights between cohabitants on the breakdown of their relationship. It seems that cohabitants will be given greater rights the closer they approximate to a legitimate family. The Court of Appeal's decision in *Chandler v Kerley* did recognise obligations arising from cohabitation, even if only of a temporary, general support nature in the form of housing. The extent of the licence given was partly dictated by the presence of children, although they only qualified for limited consideration, since they were not offspring of the relationship. As Lord Scarman said, 'it would be wrong to infer that the plaintiff was assuming the burden of housing another man's wife and children indefinitely, and long after his relationship with them has ended'.[51] In *Re Evers's Trust* and *Dennis v McDonald* the cohabiting couples were treated, insofar as the courts were able, in exactly the same way as married couples. The justifications advanced by the court in each case for equivalent treatment rested on the presence of children of the relationship. Ormrod LJ in *Re Evers's Trust* recognised that problems over the property of unmarried couples would increasingly come before the courts and that the case before him was novel. The frequency of cohabiting arrangements was characterised by him as 'a social development of considerable importance with which courts are now likely to have to deal from time to time'.[52] After reviewing decisions concerned with orders under s.30 of the Law of Property Act 1925 on the breakdown of marriages, Ormrod LJ considered whether the same approach should be taken in applications by cohabitants, and concluded without hesitation that it should. He said:

> This approach to the exercise of the discretion given by s.30 has considerable advantages in these family cases. It enables the

court to deal with substance, that is reality rather than form; it brings the exercise of its discretion under this section so far as is possible into line with the exercise of discretion given by s.24 Matrimonial Causes Act 1973; and it goes some way to eliminating differences between legitimate and illegitimate children in accordance with present legislative policy.[53]

At no stage was Ormrod LJ worried as to the effects of his decision on the institution of marriage, his concern was quite simply with 'the family', regardless of status. Similar considerations for the children, and the provision of a family, have influenced the decision of Purchas J in *Dennis v McDonald.* The presence of children can therefore be of great importance in attracting resolution of the unmarried couple's problems along the lines similar to those adopted in relation to the married couple.

(b) Duration of the relationship. The duration of the couple's relationship has also been an important factor in determining whether cohabitants should be accorded rights similar to those possessed by married couples, although the legislature has tended to accept much shorter periods of cohabitation as the basis for equivalent treatment than have the courts. Thus the Supplementary Benefit Act 1976, the Consumer Credit Act 1974, the Housing (Homeless Persons) Act 1977 and the Pneumoconiosis Act 1979, require no specific qualifying cohabitation period, and where they exist, other sources of guidance have to be consulted. Specific guidance in respect of the Supplementary Benefit legislation is provided in the *Handbook,*[54] which also applies to the Family Income Supplement scheme. Under the heading 'Stability' the handbook states that

> living together as husband and wife clearly implies more than an occasional or very brief association. When a couple first live together it may be clear from the start that the relationship is similar to that of husband and wife e.g. the woman has taken the man's name and has borne his child but in cases where the nature of the relationship is less clear the woman may continue to receive benefit for a short time in order to avoid discouraging the formation of a stable relationship.

The state is clearly anxious that the woman should form such a relationship, but its duration is not crucial and behaviour seems to be more important. The Domestic Violence and Matrimonial Proceedings Act 1976 lays down no qualifying period and, indeed, some have thought this omission unwise; the Inheritance (Provision for Family and Dependants) Act 1975 concentrates much more on the financial relationship between the parties. The Consumer Credit Act 1974 and the Pneumoconiosis Act 1979 are also silent on the length of time required to be spent living together in order to qualify as 'reputed spouses'. The Housing Act 1980, in providing that partners living together as husband and wife can qualify as family members, does require that the surviving cohabitant should have resided with the deceased tenant throughout the period of twelve months ending with the tenant's death.[55]

In contrast, the courts have in the past required much longer periods of cohabitation before according cohabitants without children rights roughly equivalent to those possessed by married couples. A few decisions which span a generation are illustrative of the gradual change in the courts' attitude. In *Gammans v Ekins* Asquith LJ described the parties to a relationship which had endured for some twelve years thus: 'to say of two people masquerading as these two were as husband and wife, that they are members of the same family seems to be an abuse of the English language'.[56] By 1975 the Court of Appeal had recognised that the degree of permanence in the relationship could make a difference, and in *Dyson Holdings v Fox* found that a cohabitant of some forty years' standing could be considered as a member of the deceased partner's family. The couple's 'unmarriage-like behaviour' and the fact that their relationship had only lasted some five years led the Court of Appeal in *Helby v Rafferty* to conclude that the quality of permanence was lacking, and Mr Rafferty could not qualify as a member of Miss Taylor's family. In *Watson v Lucas* the court was to hold that despite the absence of any pretence to marriage the ordinary man looking at the couple would have characterised them as a family, especially since their relationship had endured for nineteen years.

(c) Behaviour of the parties. Helby v Rafferty and *Watson v Lucas* also have important implications in relation to another factor upon which the English courts rely in justifying equivalent treatment for cohabitants, namely the manner in which the parties to the cohabitation behave. The behaviour to which the courts will have regard is of two types: first, and more importantly, the 'marriage-like behaviour' of the parties;[57] and secondly, whether the parties have expressed any intentions as to marriage during the course of the relationship.[58]

(i) *'Marriage-like behaviour'.* Again, in this area, the courts' requirements relating to the relevant factor have until recently been much more stringent than any laid down in legislation. Most of the statutes require neither a specific period of cohabitation nor behaviour of a particular nature during that cohabitation. The Supplementary Benefits *Handbook* and a certain number of cases in the social security field do, however, contain some guidance as to the behavioural characteristics which will influence the authorities in determining whether claimants are living together as husband and wife. The four remaining official criteria in the *Handbook*[59] all relate to the parties' behaviour. The cohabitants must actually be living together in the same house, there must be a degree of financial support or sharing of household expenses, and they should normally be having a sexual relationship, though the *Handbook* states that 'its absence does not necessarily prove that the couple are not living as husband and wife nor does its presence prove that they are'. Finally, the *Handbook* states that 'whether the couple have represented themselves to other people as husband and wife is relevant. But many couples living together do not wish to pretend that they are actually married. The fact that they retain their identity publicly as unmarried people does not mean that they cannot be regarded as living together as husband and wife'. It would seem that the authorities are determined to save public money whatever the effect on the institution of marriage.

Cases clarifying the terms of the cohabitation rule and its application are occasionally brought before the National Insurance Commissioners, since the rule also affects entitlement to widows' and other benefits. These too have concentrated on behavioural aspects. In a very early decision in 1950[60] the National Insurance Commissioner ruled that a man and a woman are cohabiting 'if he and she are carrying on a common home in the manner in which husbands and wives do'.[61] He went on to say that, 'in determining this question it is their general relationship which has to be looked at. Neither their habits with relation to sexual intercourse, nor the manner in which the common household fund from which they are maintained is spent or provided is conclusive'.[62] In a more recent case[63] a Commissioner stated: 'it is generally accepted that the question of whether a woman is cohabiting with a man as his wife within the meaning of the statutes, requires an examination of three main matters:

(1) their relationship in relation to sex,
(2) their relationship in relation to money, and
(3) their general relationship.

Although all three are as a rule relevant no single one of them is necessarily conclusive'. The Child Poverty Action Group study[64] of fifty cases of couples treated by the DHSS as living together as husband and wife found that only five women so regarded themselves, and that one other was treated as such by outsiders. In only four cases was there a pooling or sharing of resources, but there was direct or indirect evidence of sexual relations in more than thirty-two cases, and it seemed that it was this aspect of behaviour which, despite the Commission's frequent assurances to the contrary, most influences the Department in its determination. It is an indication of the perhaps unconscious devaluing of marriage that Government departments should treat couples as if they are living together as husband and wife merely because they are having a sexual relationship. The professed reason may be to save money and to ensure that unmarried women are not more favourably treated than married women, but the effect is to undermine, not to enhance, the position of marriage. If the true basis of the rule is really to save money, then, as Lister says,[65] the crucial question in deciding whether cohabitation exists should be that of financial arrangements.

The courts in fact have frequently looked to the financial arrangements existing between the parties as an instance of behaviour indicative of a marriage-like relationship. In *Crisp v Mullings* Russell LJ set considerable store by the 'man-and-wife' discussions the parties had in relation to their financial arrangements, whereas in *Helby v Rafferty* the fact that the parties kept separate bank accounts, though they shared expenses, was a factor deemed relevant by the court in denying Mr Rafferty the status of 'family member'. While sharing expenses has been considered a relevant factor, the courts have not been totally consistent in determining the weight to be attached to it, particularly in cases on the Inheritance (Provision for Family and Dependants) Act 1975. Thus, in *Re Beaumont*[66] the court found that the couple's very businesslike arrangement militated against any finding that the surviving man could in any sense be a dependant of the deceased woman. Reeve J in *HA v HG and D*[67] in early 1980 followed a similar line of reasoning, but in *Jelley v Iliffe,*[68] later in 1980, the Court of Appeal said that the court should take 'a broad commonsense view of the relationship between the parties and had to strike a balance between the benefits received by the applicant from the deceased against those provided by the applicant to the deceased'. Since the court went on to disapprove of Megarry V–C's approach in *Re Beaumont,* it is probable that *Jelley v Iliffe* is now the correct line.

Like the Supplementary Benefits Commission, the courts have looked at the issue of whether the parties attempt to present themselves to others as being married. Back in 1953, in *Hawes v Evenden,* the fact that the woman had not taken the man's name did not seem to enter into the court's consideration as to whether or not a family relationship existed. There were children of the union and that was sufficient. The case of *Helby v Rafferty,* on the other hand, indicated that the retention of separate surnames combined with no effort to pass themselves off as married substantially diminished the male claimant's case. The majority decision in *Watson v Lucas* indicates that now the retention of separate names and the absence of any pretence to marriage will not necessarily be fatal. The test henceforth is whether the ordinary man would, looking at all the circumstances – the parties' general behaviour, and the stability of the relationship – characterise that relationship as 'familial'.[69] If he can so characterise it, the parties can be treated in exactly the same way as a married couple.

Other cases illustrate the courts' predilection towards what could be described as the traditional pattern of marital behaviour. Thus, where the parties have clearly adhered to the stereotype marital roles within a relationship enduring over a considerable period of time, they have more easily attracted the courts' sympathy. In *Kokosinski v Kokosinski,* for example, Wood J held that he was able to take the wife's conduct during the twenty-five-year pre-marital cohabitation period into account when assessing financial provision because it had been so admirably 'wife-like'. 'This wife,' he said, 'has given the best years of her life to this husband. She has been faithful, loving and hardworking. She has helped him to build what is in every sense a family business. She has managed his home and been a mother to and helped him to bring up a son . . . '.[70] By way of contrast a period of six years' 'on-off' cohabitation was discounted by Balcombe J in *H v H*[71] partly because the parties had no children and had separated on various occasions, but also because they had considered themselves free to take another partner in the intervals between periods of cohabitation. Similarly, in *Hodges v Hodges,*[72] where the man had made it plain that he viewed the relationship as one of convenience and the woman merely as a mistress in the old sense of the term, the court refused to listen to the woman's assertion that she was anything more.

Doing *more* than a normal spouse does may also assist in engaging the courts' sympathy with the difficulties arising on the breakdown of cohabitation. The behaviour of Janet Eves[73] in wielding a hammer and clearing rubble and rubbish, and that of Miss Cooke[74] in doing work that most women do not contemplate (using a sledge hammer, working a cement mixer and filling up a wheelbarrow!) undoubtedly had a considerable effect on the judges' hearing of their cases. Both were 'rewarded' by being dealt with on equitable principles, which in *Cooke v Head* were described as 'equally applicable in the case of a husband and wife who have built a home together'.[75] This decision flew in the face of the declaration some thirteen years earlier by the Court of Appeal in *Diwell v Farnes*[76] that property disputes between unmarried cohabitants could not be resolved in the same way as those of spouses. It remains the case, however, that female cohabitants may have to work much harder in the house, and do jobs which are traditionally thought the preserve of males, before they can establish an interest in real property.

Perhaps the strangest case of all concerning the conduct of cohabitants is that of *Adeoso v Adeoso,*[77] where the couple's relationship had reached such a low ebb that they slept in separate rooms and communicated only by notes. In deciding whether to grant an application for an injunction under the Domestic Violence and Matrimonial Proceedings Act 1976, the Court of Appeal had, of course, to decide whether the parties were living with each other in the same household as if they were husband and wife.[78] The court stated that 'on an objective view the parties were living together in the flat as if they were husband and wife, *their relationship being comparable to a marriage in the last stages of breakdown*'.[79] Where the court is prepared to make such a comparison in order to justify relief, cohabitation can have very little further to go along the road of assimilation with marriage. English law now has not only the concept of 'living together as husband and wife' but also of 'living apart as husband and wife'!

(ii) *Expressions of future intentions to marry.* On occasion the courts have been persuaded that the expression by the parties of their future intentions to marry could be a sufficient justification for treating former cohabitants as if they had actually married. This may, of course, be of particular importance in societies like England, where most cohabitation currently seems to be a trial marriage experience.[80] Cretney[81] has urged that, where appropriate, more imaginative use could be made of s.2(2) of the Law Reform (Miscellaneous Provisions) Act 1970, to come to the aid of cohabitants who had, at some stage, professed intentions to marry. Doubts remain, however, about its real utility.[82] Effectively, s.2 provides that where an agreement to marry has been terminated, the property provisions which govern husband and wife apply to any property the couple acquired or worked on during the currency of the agreement. Cretney expresses surprise that no reliance has been placed on this provision in any reported case, and asks, 'surely in many cases it must at least be arguable, that the parties had agreed to marry'.[83] This certainly may be arguable, but it is likely that there would be considerable difficulties of proof in establishing such an agreement. Parliament, after all, does seem to have envisaged some sort of formal arrangement in the use of the word 'termination', and the section titles talk about 'engaged couples'.[84] Such a provision would therefore seem to be of limited application in the cohabitation context, since in none of the reported cases has there been anything approaching what the ordinary man or woman would describe as a formal engagement. If the courts have experienced difficulty in finding express or implied agreements as to the sharing of property interests where there has clearly been a joint effort, they might have even greater difficulty in discovering or constructing a formal agreement to marry where there is a complete lack of evidence of a joint agreement. By all means allow cohabitants access to the courts, but they should not be allowed to dress up in borrowed clothes, for in deliberately choosing to cohabit they have indicated either that they do not wish to marry at all, or at the very least that they do not wish to be treated like a married couple for some time yet.

Caution should be exercised by the courts, which have thus far been influenced to some extent by evidence of an intention to marry. Too much weight should not be attached to one party's view, where expectation of subsequent marriage may simply have been an unfounded hope and not the commonly expressed intention of both parties. Evidence of such joint intention was established in *Cooke v Head,* where Lord Denning MR said that the couple had bought the land and worked on it, 'in the hope that Mr Head's wife would divorce him and they would be able to marry'.[85] In *Eves v Eves* the court found as a matter of fact that the parties originally intended to marry when they were free to do so, and the court also took such intention into account in *Lawrence v McFarlane.*[86] Although evidence of the express rejection of marriage has in the past resulted in harsher treatment for surviving or deserted claimants, as illustrated by cases such as *Richards v Dove,*[87] *Helby v Rafferty* and *Hodges v Hodges,* it was by no means fatal in cases such as *Pascoe v Turner.*[88] Further, Stephenson LJ made it quite clear in *Watson v Lucas* that, although Mr Lucas had taken no steps to obtain a divorce from his wife, despite a separation of some twenty years, and could thus be said to have deliberately ruled out the possibility of marriage, this could nevertheless be discounted in view of other factors in the case. The expression of a future intention to marry can therefore be seen as of assistance in claiming equivalent treatment, but its absence will not necessarily be a hindrance.

(iii) *The elimination of inequalities between legitimate and illegitimate children.* Ormrod LJ in *Re Evers's Trust* adopted the same approach to the case, in which there was an application for the sale of the family home of an unmarried couple, as he would have done if the couple had been married. The reason for this quite simply was that there were children, and he argued that if he exercised the court's discretion in refusing a sale, then 'such exercise would go some way to eliminating differences between legitimate and illegitimate children in accordance with present legislative policy'.[89] The Law Commission has quite recently made further proposals which purport to abolish the status of illegitimacy altogether.[90] Such a move would inevitably have an effect on cases of cohabitants with children, since there would then be even stronger reasons for not discriminating between married and unmarried couples with children. While it is no doubt right that it is the parents' relationship which should be characterised as legitimate or not, rather than the offspring, the inevitable result of such a policy must be to undermine marriage as the lawful basis for family life. Hand in hand with a policy that aims to eradicate the differences between the children must go a policy that treats parents equally, whatever the status of their relationship, at least insofar as that relationship can in any way impinge upon the lives of the children. It must further be made clear precisely what this would entail, for the Law Commission does not seem to have considered the ramifications of its proposal. Present restrictive social security provisions which deny surviving partners of a deceased cohabitant benefits like widow's allowance, industrial injuries death benefit, child's special allowance, and other legislative provisions such as the Fatal Accidents Act or the Inheritance (Provision for Family and Dependants) Act 1975, would all have to be amended so that whenever children were born of a cohabiting relationship, they would not be adversely affected by discriminatory provisions operating against their parents. Such amendments would be in accordance with the Commission's stated desire to remove 'all statutory provisions whose consequences are adverse to the child',[91] and therefore married and unmarried parents would have to be treated equally.

It is thus clear that there cannot be a partial abolition of the status of illegitimacy, which is, in effect, what the Law Commission has so far proposed, and if a complete abolition is proposed, this must affect the position of marriage. The Law Commission does, it is true, purport to consider the effect its proposals would have on marriage, but its views seem curiously vague and ill-argued. Acknowledging the importance of stable family backgrounds in children's lives, it nevertheless argues that, since so many marriages today are unstable, to preserve the status of illegitmacy may simply 'encourage young couples to enter precipitately into marriages which may have little chance of success'.[92] Abolishing illegitimacy, however, is unlikely to improve the chances of stability in children's lives and may do much to diminish it, but this argument also lends little support to the institution of marriage, of which the Commission expresses its wholehearted approval. The Commission next discusses the argument that the legal relationship between the child's parents should be relevant in determining the child's legal status.[93] This proposition is rejected by the Commission, which declares: 'it is after all the child's status and the nature of the relationship between his parents need not and should not affect this'.[94] The point surely is, as can be seen from statutory provisions and from the cases, that the way the law views the parents' relationship must affect the way in which the child is treated. In almost all cases in which children are concerned there can never be true equality between the child born to a married couple and one born to an unmarried couple unless there is equality of treatment between the parents.

In recognition of this problem Meteyard,[95] in a recent article arguing against continued support of the institution of marriage, proposes the status of parenthood in its place. This, she argues, would achieve the elimination of all differences between children but assure the assignation of support, rights and duties. Oliver[96] would probably also favour such a move. She advocates[97] the extension of quasi-matrimonial rights, duties and obligations where an association has reduced one party, usually the woman, to a dependent position, normally because of the children. Clayton[98] too seems to support the idea of equating wives and female cohabitants who have dependent children, and argues that it is the fact of parenthood which must establish the right to equivalent treatment. The problem with such a proposal is that it only goes so far, and little consideration has been given to the issue of what should be done with all those couples, married or unmarried, who have no children. Is the rest of family law to be radically reformed to deal with their problems, or perhaps scrapped altogether? Is parenthood to become a privileged status in the same way as marriage was once, or is it to be merely different? Before we rush in to establish a new status, we should look more closely at what it would entail, particularly in relation to the position of women. In considering changes we should be careful not to throw the baby out with the bath water.

If complete abolition of the status of illegitimacy, with all that this must entail, is really what the Law Commission desires, then it must say so. But if the special status of marriage is to disappear, it should not be done under the guise of abolishing the status of illegitimacy. The reasons for, and the terms of, its elimination should be made clear.

(iv) *Protection of the weaker family partner.* Another justification advanced for according cohabitants equal treatment with married couples has been the desire of the courts[99] and to some extent of the legislature[100] to protect the economically and physically weaker family partner, i.e. the woman. This response has also received a measure of support from writers, including Oliver,[101] Pearl[102] and Clayton.[103] Where the woman has been forced into an economically dependent role by virtue of being a child's caretaker, the courts have attempted to provide some sort of compensation. This was evident in cases like *Eves v Eves, Tanner v Tanner, K v J.M.P. Ltd.* and more recently in *Re Evers's Trust.* In the absence of children the courts have not been slow in coming to the aid of the older weaker woman who has been scurrilously treated by a partner or his dependants. Thus, in *Pascoe v Turner,* Cumming Bruce LJ declared that 'the court must grant a remedy effective to protect her against future manifestations of his ruthlessness'.[104] The facts of *Greasley v Cook*[105] aroused to an even greater degree the protective instincts of the court. It was decided that the beneficiaries under the estate could not be allowed to go back on promises made to the woman, although she had not, in acting upon them, actually expended any money or positively acted to her own detriment. She had merely remained, in reliance upon the promises, and the court decided that she could stay. It is difficult to see how these last two cases can be reconciled with the principle that equity will not assist a volunteer. In fact, they are clear examples of the court being influenced by protective and paternalistic motives.

Less sympathy for the economically independent woman can be detected in various decisions of the courts, and there is even less for the position of men. Walton J, in *Richards v Dove,* was unimpressed by the woman's claim to any interest in the property, chiefly because, although she had paid some household expenses, she did not use her salary to contribute to the purchase of the house. On the basis therefore of her wages at the time of the case, the judge thought that any award would have been inappropriate. Similarly in *H.A. v H.G. and D*[163] Reeve J thought it relevant that both parties had been working. Simply pooling their resources while they shared a house together could not, be intimated, establish any sort of dependence by the woman. The position of the male cohabitant coming before the courts has until recently evoked very little sympathy. This was apparent from cases such as *Helby v Rafferty* and *Re Beaumont,* although attempts to be less obviously discriminatory have emerged from decisions such as *Watson v Lucas* and *Jelley v Iliffe.*

Parliament has also played its part in promoting the protection of the weaker family partner. In the course of the second reading of the Inheritance (Provision for Family and Dependants) Act 1975, the Solicitor-General, Peter Archer, answering inevitable criticisms that the Act would reward immorality, said, 'many of us who have practised in this area have come across tragic cases of a common law wife who has devoted years to the deceased and perhaps helped him to build up a business and who then finds that she is deprived of any benefit or redress because she cannot produce a marriage certificate'.[106] Such women are now protected by the provisions of this Act.[107]

A further statutory provision of a protective nature, which recognises the fact that cohabitants equally with spouses need physical protection from their violent partners, is the Domestic Violence and Matrimonial Proceedings Act 1976. In justifying s.1(2) of the Act, which extends certain rights to cohabitants, the Bill's sponsor, Miss Jo Richardson,[108] said that:

> in many cases it would be impossible for the woman to leave her home and to escape from violence. This is particularly so where children of the association are involved, though in some cases, even where there are no children, the association may have grown up over a period and there may be nowhere for the spouse who is assaulted or molested to go. Therefore she deserves protection . . . The President of the Family Division stated in his evidence to the Select Committee[109] that there was a need for women in such

relationships to be protected, and he suggested that, if the law relating to injunctions were to be amended, it should be extended to cover these cases.

The courts and lawyers, however, were plainly worried by this extension and sought in cases such as *B v B*[110] to characterise s.1(2) as being procedural only. The disputes between differently constituted courts eventually led to the convening of a five-member Court of Appeal in *Davis v Johnson*[111] to consider the scope of the provision. Lord Denning MR thought the Act perfectly clear, and specifically designed to protect cohabiting women in Miss Davis's position. Sir George Baker, the President of the Family Division, sitting in the Court of Appeal, rebuffed any suggestion that the 'provision was only a tiny miserable mouse incapable of even a nibble at the evil of domestic hooliganism'.[112] The majority found that the Act did apply to cohabitants in Miss Davis's position and overruled the earlier decisions. The House of Lords confirmed the Court of Appeal's ruling.[113] Viscount Dilhorne insisted that the provision was not concerned with property rights: 'It was not intended to provide a means for the enforcement of property rights but to give protection from domestic violence and from eviction'.[114] Lord Salmon saw the whole purpose of the Act as being to afford 'some protection to "unmarried battered wives" in particular'.[115] That cohabitants are entitled to receive the protection of the 1976 Act is now beyond dispute.

Cohabitation – a mirror institution?

It seems, therefore, that in an ever increasing number of situations the legal position of cohabitants in England is being assimilated to that of married couples, though that position has not yet achieved the status of a mirror institution. Several commentators who do favour the many recent moves towards equivalent treatment are nonetheless concerned by the contradictions currently to be found in the law. Oliver, for example, comments that, 'there is one trend to reduce the special status of marriage by measures such as those which treat married and unmarried couples alike', and 'the opposite trend to increasing the special status of marriage by measures such as those allowing capital transfers between spouses to go untaxed'.[116] 'If,' she asks, 'we have been unable to decide which way the law should develop in relation to marriage, can we decide coherently what legal policy should be toward unmarried relationships?'[117] Like Clayton,[118] we would point to yet another conflicting trend in current legislative thinking, which must inevitably contribute to even greater confusion as to the legal treatment of cohabitation.

As indicated in Chapter 2, many women have now thrown off the mantle of domesticity and are active participants in the labour market. In recognition of this fact, legislation concerned with sex discrimination and equal pay, and the establishment of the Equal Opportunities Commission, both encourage equality and economic independence for women.[119] But, at the same time, England has legislation, such as the Matrimonial Causes Act 1973 and the Inheritance (Provision for Family and Dependants) Act 1975, which encourages women to become what Germaine Greer once referred to as 'professional parasites'.[120] As Clayton says,[121] 'if the objective of these various legislative endeavours was to do with justice and equality between sexes then in the general dithering between being paternalistic and progressive the target has been missed'. By 1982 it should be possible to determine the role of women in society and thus to reach a rational conclusion as to how they should be treated within the context of cohabitation. To suggest, as do Meteyard,[122] Oliver[123] and Clayton[124] that a new status, that of 'parenthood', could provide a solution to the present difficulties is to be wilfully blind to what has happened in the past. If such a status were introduced it could create more problems than it might solve. In addition, the areas of child maintenance and custody are much less difficult in any event than those relating to property matters between partners. Such a status would therefore have no effect at all on the problems encountered by the vast majority of cohabiting couples who do not have children.

The many judicial decisions and the various Parliamentary debates concerned with the issue of equivalent treatment reveal the problems of attempting to resolve several conflicting values in the absence of any authoritative guidance. If equivalent treatment across the board is not to emerge by default, or as a result of muddled thinking, or by the enactment of incrementalist measures to meet particular problems, then those responsible for determining legislative policy must, before it is too late, sit down and formulate a coherent strategy. Cohabitation is becoming an increasingly popular life-style in England, and the decision must be made as to whether it should be accorded a status equivalent to marriage and the parties treated according to conventional principles of family law. If so, the motives and policy considerations behind such a decision must be clearly stated.

The trend towards cohabitation is not, as we have seen, limited to England. Examination of the justifications advanced in other jurisdictions for treating cohabitants in the same or an equivalent way as married couples, and the solutions which have been adopted, may accordingly prove helpful.

Justifications advanced in other jurisdictions

Few states have embodied the principle of equivalent treatment in statutory form to quite the same extent as England. The chief reason for this is that most of the English statutes which embody the principle are concerned with public law income provision, and whenever possible the state has sought to reduce its expenditure and to shift support obligations to some other source. With the exception of Sweden, none of the other countries discussed here has quite the same highly developed and wide-ranging scheme of social security provision and there has been less need to be quite so systematic in enacting 'cohabitation rules'. In some jurisdictions, therefore (the United States is an example), there has been little or no legislation dealing with the problems caused by cohabitation. In the case of the United States, Bruch indicates,[125] this results in part from the preference of legislatures to let the judiciary be the arbiters of social change. Any public censure which might then arise from the extension of cohabitants' rights falls upon the judiciary and not the elected representatives. It is, according to Bruch, 'pragmatism, combined with a genuine conviction that the common law rather than the legislature is the best testing ground for societal change' that has forestalled efforts in California to redefine the California Supreme Court's holding in the *Marvin* case.[126] Legislative hearings have apparently twice concluded that only time and judicial experience will provide social insights into the need for legislative intervention. Commonwealth countries such as Australia, New Zealand and Canada have enacted some provisions[127] to deal with the problems caused by cohabitation, chiefly in the less controversial areas, such as provision on death. More contentious issues like *inter vivos* support and property division have been left to be resolved by the judiciary. Sweden is alone in having attempted to formulate a legislative policy which aims at real equality,[128] but it falls down at those points where that policy conflicts with other stated policy goals, such as full economic independence for all adults[129] and the central position of marriage within society.[130] Whatever means have been used to resolve cohabitants' legal problems, whether these have been legislative or judicial, the influential factors in engaging assistance have been similar to those identified in England.

(i) The fulfilment of family functions

Those factors which encourage the application of the principle of equivalent treatment on the basis that the couple are fulfilling family functions include the presence of children, the length of the relationship, and the behaviour of the parties.

(a) Presence of children. The presence of children as a factor to which the courts have referred in concluding that a couple has been behaving like a family, and should be treated accordingly, has been of less importance in the United States than it has in England. The American courts seem to have preferred to look at the totality of the relationship, and the presence of children has rather been one of a list of factors which have encouraged the courts to treat cohabitants as if they had been married. Thus, in *Re Cary,*[131] the California Supreme Court considered the fact that the Carys had had four children as one of the indicia of a family relationship sufficient to bring them within the adjustive jurisdiction of that state's family law. Similarly, in *Estate of Thornton,*[132] the court set store by the fact that the female claimant had borne and raised four children with the deceased in what was therefore classified as a family relationship. The Oregon Court of Appeals also stated in the course of its judgment in *Rissberger v Gorton*[133] that the conception and birth of the child were persuasive evidence of an intent to share equally in household items, but not in the event persuasive enough.

The Commonwealth jurisdictions, on the other hand, seem to place considerably more emphasis on the presence of children, and several legislatures have enacted statutes granting more generous provisions for cohabitants with children. Thus, discrimination between childless cohabiting couples and those with children, the latter more obviously conforming to the 'family type', emerges in both Ontario's Family Law Reform Act 1978[134] and South Australia's Inheritance Family Provision Act 1972.[135] Under both provisions, partners to a relationship which has resulted in the birth of a child qualify automatically as persons entitled to make a claim against a deceased partner's estate. Ontario's law does include a further requirement that the relationship should possess some permanence, whereas South Australia's statute envisages claims by reference to cohabitation and the birth of a child.[136] The position in New Zealand is much more restrictive, and looks only to the existence of a child in allowing indirect provision for a surviving female cohabitant. New Zealand's Family Protection Act provides that a mother's needs can be taken into account only where the illegitimate child makes a claim on the father's estate.[137] In some states rights to *inter vivos* support from the other partner have been made easier where the claimant, usually a woman, can show that a child was born of the union and she is now looking after the child. A parent automatically qualifies as a 'putative spouse' under South Australia's Family Relationships Act 1975. In Canada a parent living in a relationship of some permanence can claim support under the Ontario Family Law Reform Act, while in Newfoundland[138] and Manitoba[139] parenthood must be accompanied by one year's cohabitation before a claim for support can be made.

In Sweden, home of the neutrality principle, it would appear that the presence of children can assist in ensuring that cohabitants are treated in the same way as married persons. A widow's pension, for example, is only available to a female cohabitant where she and the male partner had a child together,[140] and the presence of a child is probably sufficient to endow a relationship with marriage-like qualities so as to entitle a cohabiting couple to the housing allowance.[141] The cohabitant's right to property, principally the home, is dealt with by the new reformed law, which provides that on the dissolution of a marriage-like cohabitation the rental or tenant owner's right to the parties' jointly occupied residence can be transferred to the other party, who may have greater need. Such need is usually that one partner has been given custody of the children, and if there are no children, a transfer can occur 'if very special reasons so indicate'.[142] The position of cohabitants with children on the breakdown of their relationship is thus subject to provisions almost identical to those applied to married couples. This is, no doubt, a direct result of the attempt to pursue the neutrality principle, at least in relation to cohabiting couples with children.[143] In the circumstances it is not surprising that the Swedish legislators have used a limited approach and enacted laws where there was greatest need and a consensus about appropriate solutions.[144] From the current state of Swedish law it would appear that the consensus has focused on the presence of children as the basis for equivalent treatment.

(b) The duration of the relationship. The duration of the cohabiting relationship has been deemed to be a very relevant factor by both legislatures and courts in determining the application of equivalent treatment, though there is considerable discrepancy over the length of the qualifying period.[145] In many of the countries, as well, the judiciary seem to require much longer periods of cohabitation before they will treat a couple as if they had been married.

In the United States, New Hampshire, one of the very few states with a legislative provision dealing with cohabitants, has opened up the full range of public law survivorship claims to one 'who has cohabited with another for at least 3 years immediately preceding the partner's death in a relationship in which they held themselves out to be husband and wife'.[146] The judiciary, on the other hand, has been more impressed with relationships which have endured for somewhat longer than three years. The courts were more disposed to be sympathetic in *Keene v Keene,*[147] where the relationship had lasted eighteen years; *Estate of Atherley,*[148] where it had lasted for twenty-two years; and *Estate of Thornton,*[149] where it had endured for sixteen years; than they were in *Marvin v Marvin,*[150] where Michelle and Lee had lived together for only six years.

As is the case in England, several states are less concerned with the duration of a relationship in the case of public law income provision. Canada, Australia[151] and New Zealand[152] have rules which operate to effect the withdrawal of certain welfare and social security benefits from a woman who is living with a man as his wife. The assumption that male cohabitants will conform to a husband-like role and support their female partners is a convenient one to adopt, yet none of these countries grant the woman, who, without any option, is characterised as economically dependent, any right of support during the relationship. Limited provision is nevertheless made to grant support rights enforceable on breakdown or death,[153] although in such cases the duration of the relationship may suddenly become relevant. Australian law provides that if a cohabiting relationship has endured for three years the woman may thereafter qualify for certain old age pension and widow's benefits, as long as she can also prove total or substantial dependence upon the partner.[154] The time factor in indicating the marriage-like stability of the relationship also appears to be important in other areas: for example, under the Workmen's Compensation legislation in British Columbia,[155] Australian Capital Territory, Northern Territory and South Australia,[156] claims can be made by de facto spouses, provided the relationship has lasted for seven years in British Columbia and for three years in the other jurisdictions. Family provision on death of the partner where there are no children depends in both South Australia[157] and Ontario[158] on the relationship having endured for five years, and in the latter state the five years must be those immediately preceding death. In the areas of rights to *inter vivos* maintenance support, Ontario[159] recognises a right to bring an action where the relationship was childless but had lasted five years, whereas British Columbia recognises only two years' cohabitation,[160] and Tasmania twelve months',[161] provided certain other conditions are satisfied. The duration of the relationship has also impressed the Commonwealth courts when they have been called upon to make decisions as to property rights, more especially when such decisions have been based on the principles of constructive trust doctrine.[162] The court in *Becker v Pettkus* was helped to reach its decision by the fact that the woman had lived and worked with the respondent for more than twenty years. Similarly, the courts were influenced by the marriage-like stability of the relationship in *Ogilvie v Ryan,*[163] where it had lasted twenty years; in *Olsen v Olsen,*[164] where, in the court's words, they had lived together for 'many years'; and in *Horton v Public Trustee,*[165] where the relationship had endured some twenty-four years up to the partner's death.

There seems, therefore, to be little consensus either between state legislatures of the same country, or between courts and legislatures, as to the duration of the relationship required to establish a right to equivalent treatment. This lack of agreement, and the fact that both statutes and case law look also to other factors, would tend to indicate that the time factor alone is regarded as an inadequate basis for attracting the principle of equivalent treatment.

(c) Behaviour of the parties. Although many of the statutory provisions of the Commonwealth and Scandinavia talk about the parties 'living together as husband and wife'[166] or living in a 'marriage-like relationship',[167] few expand on precisely what is meant by such phrases, presumably because they are thought to be self-explanatory. The courts, on the other hand, have looked much more closely at whether the parties are behaving in the same way as married couples before they have extended equal rights to cohabitants.

The New Hampshire statute,[168] which provides certain rights of survivorship, insists that the partners to the relationship should have held themselves out to be husband and wife. The effect of such a requirement may well be fatal, for, as Bruch says,[169] such a condition is of decreasing utility in an era in which representations of marital status by cohabitants are increasingly rare. Elsewhere in the United States courts have been prepared to recognise implied support agreements in circumstances where the female partner has performed wife-like services.[170] Many women have sought to allege that the provision of such services was in return for some sort of continuing lifelong financial support. The decisions in *Marvin v Marvin, Kozlowski v Kozlowski,* and *Levar v Elkins*[171] have recognised such support agreement as enforceable between cohabitants. In *Marvin v Marvin* it was eventually decided that no such agreement existed, but a sum was awarded by way of rehabilitative damages.[172] The women in *Kozlowski v Kozlowski* and *Levar v Elkins* were able to establish implied agreements, their consideration for these being their performance of wife-like services. These services had to be the basis for awards, since they had made no other contribution to the building of family assets. The problem with recognition of such services by courts is that it may encourage the professional parasitism of women. Judicial intervention in the United States has, however, proceeded predominantly on the basis of fair treatment in the case (*Levar v Elkins* is a good example). The court's conception of what is fair may have been strongly influenced by protective instincts towards those women who have been fulfilling a wife-like role within cohabitation.

The American courts are prepared to invoke all sorts of remedies[173] where the relationship displays marriage-like qualities. In *Re Marriage of Cary,*[174] for example, the court was bombarded with evidence to this effect, including Janet's use of Paul's surname, their use of joint credit cards and filing of joint income tax returns, and the parties' fulfilment of traditional family roles, with husband as breadwinner, wife as homemaker. Similarly, in *Re Estate of Atherley* it was stressed that the parties had conducted their relationship as 'man and wife'. The decision of the Michigan Court of Appeal in *Tyranski v Piggins*[175] turned chiefly on the finding that the plaintiff's wifely services rendered to her deceased cohabitant, including cooking meals, laundering clothes and caring for him when sick, constituted good consideration for a promise of lifelong support. In allowing the female cohabitant an equal share in the assets accumulated during a nineteen-year relationship, the Oregon Supreme Court in *Latham v Latham*[176] stressed that the parties' agreement had 'contemplated all the burdens and amenities of married life'.

Similar considerations have influenced the courts in Commonwealth jurisdictions, though the basis upon which they have justified relief have not been so wide. Thus, in *Ogilvie v Ryan* the New South Wales Supreme Court was clearly impressed not only by the woman's performing all the normal wifely duties, but also by the way in which she cared for and looked after Ogilvie 'as well as any devoted wife might have done'.[177] Occasionally, the expression of future intentions to marry has also been considered relevant, as in *Horton v Public Trustee,*[178] where the parties originally began building up a home together on the basis that they would marry when the woman was free to do so, but in fact, though she later obtained a divorce, they never did.

Under Swedish law the home can only be transferred on the breakdown of a childless cohabiting relationship from the tenant or owning partner to the other partner if 'very special reasons so indicate'.[179] The judiciary is left with the task of interpreting the circumstances giving rise to 'very special reasons'. The purport of certain statements by the Swedish Minister of Justice was that these 'reasons' should be restrictively interpreted,[180] so as to cover only those situations where the evidence suggested that the relationship was sufficiently marriage-like. As Sage comments, 'determining whether a relationship is marriage-like would seem to open enormous possibilities for the courts to investigate the personal circumstances of the parties, an approach the reform had systematically sought to avoid'.[181] Such an approach is scarcely neutral to this different form of living together. Rather, it endorses a certain moral view. It entails treating everyone as though they *should* have married.

(ii) The elimination of inequalities between legitimate and illegitimate children

The desire on the part of the legislatures and courts worldwide[182] to improve the position of the illegitimate child has inevitably further encouraged moves towards equivalent treatment for those cohabiting couples who have children. In some countries this has perhaps been more evident than in others, but it is also true to say that such moves have not been without considerable opposition.

The housing position in Sweden ensures that, where there are children, cohabiting couples will be treated in the same way as married couples, but the parents' status will still affect the legal rights which they have over the child. Thus, the child's surname and guardianship are in the control of the mother where the child is illegitimate,[183] and in both parents' control where the child is legitimate. As far as rights over children are concerned, the balance is still tipped in favour of married couples, at least in respect of fathers' rights. The law in Norway is similar, although recent proposals for reform[184] have emphasised that all children should be treated equally, and a children's code in draft form has been based on such a philosophy. As Lødrup points out, special provisions for children born out of wedlock have been included only where it seemed indispensable, notably 'concerning the establishment of paternity where this has not been recognised'.

The position of the child of cohabiting parents is not quite so favourable in the United States of America. Several decisions[185] of the Supreme Court have attempted to effect equivalent treatment in the face of state legislation seeking to uphold discriminatory provisions. The basis for the Court's decisions is, as several commentators[186] have indicated, rather unclear. The Court has even, probably with some justification, been accused of suffering from judicial schizophrenia. In some of its decisions[187] the Supreme Court has indicated that it realises that the result of applying the equal protection clause to illegitimate children will do much to destroy the preferential status of marriage in the law. It has also stressed the state's interests in fostering marriage and legitimate family life and even recognised these interests as compelling.[188] Yet the Court has struck down various statutes discriminating against illegitimate children, either because the challenged statute has not sufficiently promoted these interests, as for example in *Weber v Aetna Casualty & Surety Co.*, or because the statute has exceeded the limits necessary to serve them, as in *Levy v Louisiana.*

Further confusion in the Supreme Court's approach is demonstrated in the consideration accorded to administrative convenience in cases such as *Matthews v Lucas,*[189] *Trimble v Gordon*[190] and *Lalli v Lalli.*[191] The Court was concerned in each case to emphasise that the state's interests served by the restrictive statutory provisions affecting illegitimate children were those of establishing a method of disposing of property,[192] the avoidance of spurious claims to estates,[193] the earlier termination of probate[194] and the protection of the reputations of alleged fathers.[195] More recent decisions of the Supreme Court indicate a continuing failure to resolve the various competing interests of the state and the individual. *Califano v Boles,*[196] in denying mothers' insurance benefits to mothers of illegitimate children, lies uneasily in the same bed as *New Jersey Welfare Rights Organization v Cahill.*[197] Similarly, *Parham v Hughes,*[198] in denying a father the right to sue for his child's wrongful death, goes against the earlier decision of the Court in *Glona v American Guarantee and Liability Ins. Co.*[199] In *Caban v Mohammed,*[200] on the other hand, the Court openly rejected the stance it had previously taken towards unmarried fathers in *Orsini v Blasi,*[201] and declared that an illegitimate child could not be adopted without the father's consent where he had participated in the rearing of the child. While this decision is of considerable importance to cohabiting fathers and their children, and is to be welcomed, the other recent decisions referred to indicate a reverse trend against illegitimate families. The result is now utter confusion as to the legal position of the illegitimate child and his parents. The situation in the United States is a good indication of the virtual impossibility of recognising a right to equal treatment and reconciling it with the preferential status of marriage and the compelling state interests in fostering legitimate family life.

The law in Australia also falls short of the generally accepted goal of equality of treatment of children irrespective of their parents' status. There is a lack of uniformity in the approach to illegitimate children, with New South Wales, Victoria, South Australia and Tasmania having abolished the status of illegitimacy, while it is retained in varying degrees in the other states. The Report of the Australian Royal Commission on Human Relationships surveyed the differing levels of recognition accorded to the rights of illegitimate children within the country and concluded that 'uniformity was desirable in regard to the status and rights of all Australian children'.[202] A necessary corollary of such uniformity is the recognition of equality between the parents of such children. Although in provisions such as s.11(1) of South Australia's Family Relationships Act the position of cohabiting mothers has been equated with that of married mothers, there still remain many areas of inequality which will affect the children as much as their parents. As was the case with England, the possible ramifications of this desired uniformity, especially the effects on marriage and legitimate family life, escaped the detailed consideration of the Royal Commission's Report.

A possible interim solution to the legal problem of children born of cohabiting relationships could be a contract governing such matters as child maintenance and support. Such contracts are certainly allowed under the laws of Ontario[203] and Prince Edward Island.[204] While such a contract might ensure equality as between the children of parents who do contract, especially in Ontario, where the arrangements can be varied to accord with what is in the best interests of the child, the position of children whose parents do not contract would remain unaffected. The additional problem with attempting to use private contracts as a means to achieve equality of treatment is that such contracts cannot affect rights to state benefits. Until, therefore, the state resolves the many conflicting interests which beset it wherever it confronts the issue of equality of treatment for children, little progress in achieving real equality will be realised.

(iii) Protection of the weaker family partner

The desire to protect the family partner, usually the woman, who is said to be in a weaker economic bargaining position as a result of cohabiting, emerges from various legislative provisions which grant rights to *inter vivos* maintenance support. Thus, the 1978 Acts in Ontario and Prince Edward Island allow agreements for *inter vivos* support to be set aside on the grounds that they are unconscionable, and Tasmanian law[205] allows a woman to recover support from the man with whom she has cohabited for at least twelve months if he has wrongfully abandoned her or committed other specified acts of misconduct. These laws and proposals to extend them are based largely on the premise that the female cohabitant performs the role of a traditional wife in the home: the reasoning being that she becomes economically dependent on the man, and suffers hardship should the relationship break up.

In Sweden, on the other hand, there is no legislation granting a right to support for persons who cohabit, although the Committee charged with the reform of Family Law did discuss the desirability of instituting support provisions for the economically weaker party in a marriage-like cohabitation.[206] They concluded against such provision, however, since one of the reform's objectives was to achieve a society where every adult individual could take responsibility for himself without being economically dependent on relatives, and where equality between men and women would be a reality.[207] A proposal for maintenance provision for the weaker cohabitant seemed in any event somewhat absurd, when a major part of the discussion in Committee was concentrated on suggestions that alimony be abolished. A further inhibiting factor was, as Sage comments,[208] 'that the complexities in legislating for unmarried persons would seem to be particularly acute in the area of economic relations'.

Despite the fact that the California State Court was unable to find an implied agreement that Lee Marvin should share all the assets accumulated during his relationship with Michelle, or that he would continue to support her after the breakdown of the relationship, the Los Angeles County Court[209] subsequently awarded her a sum of $104,000 by way of rehabilitative maintenance. Such an award was clearly based on the recognition by the court that she, by virtue of her performance of all the wifely duties within the relationship, had achieved a wife-like dependence upon him. She was therefore deemed to be in need of some protective financial provision before she could be thrown back into the harsh reality of earning a living for herself in the outside world. Similar, though perhaps stronger, arguments influenced the courts' findings as to the existence of implied agreements in *Kozlowski v Kozlowski* and in *Levar v Elkins.* The rather disturbing feature of these cases, which encourage claims by female cohabitants based on wife-like dependence on the male, is that the courts nowhere consider the woman's exercise of her free choice to enter the relationship, nor the value of the man's economic support of the woman during the relationship. Surely these ought also to feature in the balance?

Although the provisions for *inter vivos* support have been somewhat restricted, the degree of provision for a cohabitant on the death of a partner is, as we have seen, noticeably more widespread and generous. One explanation for this, often reflected in the qualifying criteria for the award of support, is concern that the economically dependent partner, normally the woman who has borne children of the relationship, should not be left destitute on the death of her partner. Concern for the public purse plays a part in this, for, where the man's estate is sufficient to bear the burden of support, the less likely it is that the woman with children will have to fall back on state benefits. Public opinion is also more likely to acknowledge the justice and the morality of this situation than it is to allow the necessity for alimony rights arising from cohabitation. Recognition of the morality of allowing claims to be made in these circumstances is specifically provided for in Western Australia's Inheritance (Family and Dependants Provision) Act 1972.[210] Thus, the Act requires de facto *widows* not only to prove economic dependence, and membership of the same household as the deceased, but also that the deceased 'had in the opinion of the Court some special moral responsibility to make provision'. The statute, by confining its attention to widows, is clearly discriminatory, though the basis of the provisions – protection of the economically dependent weaker woman – is thereby made obvious. Under the provisions of South Australia's Family Provision Act 1972,[211] and Ontario's Family Reform Act,[212] claims for provision on death are based on establishing economic dependence. Thus, under the former, the court can only entertain claims where the applicant 'has not been adequately provided for', and under the latter the court is only authorised to make 'such provision as it considers adequate for the proper support of the claimant'. There have been proposals to extend succession rights to cohabitants in Tasmania,[213] New South Wales,[214] and Quebec,[215] chiefly based on the argument that women in these relationships become as dependent on the men as the wives are upon husbands, though these suggestions have not yet been put into legislative form. Economic dependence is also the qualifying condition for applying for maintenance provision out of the deceased cohabitant's estate in Sweden.[216]

In the area of the division of property upon the breakdown of the relationship, legislatures have been more reluctant to provide cohabitants with specific rights. Legislation in Ontario and Prince Edward Island, however, to which reference has been made,[217] allows cohabitants to enter into contracts governing property rights during and on breakdown of the relationship, subject to the same conditions as those applied to parties entering ante-nuptial and marriage agreements, and the conditions relating to unconscionable terms are equally applicable. The intention is to ensure the protection of the weaker bargaining partner. The United States has no legislative provisions dealing directly with the property rights of cohabitants, which have been left to judicial innovation. The judiciary, though, as indicated in the last chapter,[218] has not been slow in devising remedies to solve the novel problems arising from cohabitation, based on well-established principles of law not normally applied in the area of domestic relationships. The courts, however, have gone beyond ordinary legal principles and have justified decisions by reference to other factors, particularly the need to protect the female partner who has been behaving like a wife. Implied partnership theory, for example, merely required evidence in *Re Thornton*[219] of a couple sharing in the running of a ranch and in taking profits from it. Yet Justice Finely felt compelled to say that a surviving meretricious spouse should be entitled to a share in the couple's property through an implied partnership agreement by a showing of a relatively long-term stable relationship in which the partners hold themselves out as husband and wife. Significantly, the court also went on to hold that this relationship created in the survivor 'a right similar to that of a legal wife in the community property of the spousal unit'.[220] Similarly, in *Latham v Latham,* the Oregon Supreme Court found that an express agreement between cohabitants to share equally all property accumulated during a nineteen-year relationship did exist, and that they could enforce it because it contemplated 'all the burdens and amenities of married life'[221] and so differed from agreements where the primary consideration was sexual intercourse. Refusal to enforce agreements such as this, the Court said, 'often resulted in the male keeping the assets accumulated in the relationship and the female being deprived of what she jointly accumulated'. If the woman has contributed jointly or there is in existence an express agreement, there is no need to talk in terms of marital behaviour and protection of women. She should be able to sue in just the same way as anyone else for what is rightfully hers.

The characterisation of the cohabiting woman as a sort of 'second class wife' is found also in academic writing in the United States, For example, Folberg and Buren's proposals[222] on domestic partnership as a 'no-fault remedy for cohabitants' on breakdown start promisingly enough. They reject the idea of fault playing a relevant part in determining cohabitants' rights when it has ceased to be relevant in relation to married couples' rights and accordingly propose that 'partnership property be disposed of in proportion to the parties' economic contributions'.[223] This makes good sense, but the woman's contributions are to include, we are told, 'the provision of domestic services whilst the other party goes out to work'. On the other hand, Folberg and Buren seem reluctant to give any credit to the male for the provision of economic support, and in this they appear to agree with the American courts.

Elsewhere there has been little legislative support for the idea of granting cohabitants property rights. A proposal to extend property-sharing principles in New Zealand to cohabitants whose relationship had endured for two years was rejected,[224] while South Australia's Family Relationship Act 1975 only as yet provides a basis upon which extensions of property rights to putative spouses could be made at some time in the future. Such relief is likely to be granted on the grounds of economic dependence arising from the relationship, and possibly also the need to provide a home for any children of the cohabiting couple. As Bailey comments,[225] recognition of the effect of de facto relationships on property rights has been left to the courts. It is clear from many of the decisions that the courts have been influenced by a desire to protect the woman, who by virtue of the relationship has been reduced to a much weaker bargaining position. In part, of course, this emerges from the very use of the constructive trust, more especially since Commonwealth judges have been concerned to emphasise the precise legal basis of constructive trusts. But, if this is the basis of relief, why did the Australian courts in particular feel the need to refer to marriage-like qualities such as the stability of the relationship, as they did in *Ogilvie v Ryan, Olsen v Olsen* and *Horton v Public Trustee;* the marriage-like behaviour in *Ogilvie v Ryan;* and the presence of children in *Valent v Salomon*?[226]

The courts in characterising the relationship as marriage-like imply that the partners have quasi-marital rights and expectations and that it would therefore be going against the demands of justice or good conscience to deny relief to cohabitants, usually women, simply because they were not married. In reality, however, in all the cases quoted the marriage-like relationship could have been ignored and exactly the same result achieved. There is really no need to characterise cohabitation as some sort of quasi-marriage in order to achieve justice between the parties upon the breakdown of their relationship.

Conclusion

Economic considerations have undoubtedly played a large part in influencing the legislatures and the courts of the United States, Scandinavia, the Commonwealth and England in according cohabitants rights and duties equivalent to those possessed by spouses. A concern to lighten state liability and to ease bureaucratic administration has meant that it has been more convenient for the state to categorise cohabitants, usually women, as dependent de facto spouses, and therefore as creatures needing support from the ex-partner or his estate. Such a process is rendered easier by evidence of marriage-like behaviour, more especially the birth of a child. Moreover, the desire to achieve equality between children regardless of their status has encouraged moves which tend to eliminate many of the differences between mothers. Thus, whether they desire it or not, cohabiting women and men are being forced into the limited, sexist-based model of traditional marriage, with all the attendant dangers of such a process. The judiciary too has helped to foster this quasi-marital model for relief. The attractive prospect of escaping from the stereotypical roles and incidents of marriage to cohabitation is becoming progressively more difficult to achieve. The outlook for cohabiting men looks very bleak – no escape – simply the same situation with the same incidents but a different name, and for cohabiting women the position is scarcely better. Such women may well wish to escape the fate of being professional parasites but various jurisdictions seem concerned to encourage them to adopt such a role. The cry of 'back to the kitchen, we have protected you' could thus be applied to all cohabiting women, regardless of their desire to remain independent and at considerable cost to the recent reforms effected for married women.

The risks of extending equivalent treatment to cohabitants are sizeable, and the effects of such extensions as yet ill-considered. It is therefore worthwhile examining the arguments which have been advanced for treating the married and the unmarried couple differently.

Notes

1 See, generally, judgments of Cumming-Bruce LJ in *Pascoe v Turner* [1979], 2 All E.R. 945, 951; Ormrod LJ in *Re Evers's Trust* [1980], 3 All E.R. 399, 400.

2 E.g., in *Kozlowski v Kozlowski* 403A. 2d 902; *Re Estate of Thornton* 541 P. 2d 1243; in *Re Marriage of Cary* 34 Cal. App. 3d 345.

3 E.g., in *Watson v Lucas* 1980, 3 All E.R. 647, 653; in *Re Marriage of Cary, op. cit.,* note 2, at p. 349.

4 E.g., in England Ormrod LJ in *Re Evers's Trust, op. cit.,* note 1, at p. 401; and in USA Tobriner J in *Marvin v Marvin,* 557 P. 2d 106.

5 E.g., Wood J in *Kokosinski v Kokosinski* [1980], 1 All E.R. 1106 at 1119–20; and

Underwood J in *Hewitt v Hewitt* 394 NE 2d 1204, (1979).

6 See *post,* and also in Z. Sage, 'Dissolution of the Family under Swedish Law', *Fam. L.Q.*, 10 (1975), p. 398.

7 See *ante,* ch. 4, pp. 74–75.

8 Ministry of Social Security Act 1966, Schedule 2, para. 3(1).

9 *Living Together as Husband and Wife,* pp. 2–3 Supplementary Benefits Administration Papers No. 5, HMSO, 1976.

10 *Idem,* pp. 5–7.

11 See Supplementary Benefits Act 1976, Schedule 2, para. 3(1). The change was proposed in *op. cit.*, note 9, paras. 48–52.

12 See Schedule 3, para. 2.

13 See s.3(1).

14 See s.1(1)(a).

15 See s.50(3).

16 See, e.g., Ruth Lister, *As Man and Wife – A Study of the Cohabitation Rule,* Child Poverty Action Group, 1973; and also *The Times* (9, 10, 11 May and 9 June 1972); *The Guardian* (6 and 9 May 1972); *Daily Mail* (9 May and 9 June 1972).

17 H.C. Deb. vol. 813, 9 May 1972; vol. 837, 26 May 1972; vol. 840, 11 July 1972.

18 *Cohabitation – the administration of the relevant provisions of the Ministry of Social Security Act 1966,* HMSO, 1971, was the first, and *Living Together as Husband and Wife, op. cit.*, note 9, the second.

19 *Report of the Committee on One-Parent Families* (the Finer Report), Cmnd. 3629, HMSO, 1974. See also the Fisher Report, *Abuse of Social Security Benefits,* Cmnd. 5228, 1973.

20 *Op. cit.*, note 9, paras. 15 and 16.

21 *Idem,* para.19.

22 *Idem,* para.22.

23 *Idem,* para.55(3).

24 *Op. cit.*, note 19, at para. 5. 269.

25 Consumer Credit Act 1974 s.184(5).

26 Pneumoconiosis, etc. (Workers' Compensation) Act 1979, s.3(1)(c).

27 An example is Harold Walker in Committee stage of the Pneumoconiosis Bill (H.C. Deb. vol. 965, col. 1126).

28 [1975], 3 All E.R. 1030, 1035.

29 [1978], 3 All E.R. 1016.

30 [1980], 3 All E.R. 647, 651.

31 *Idem,* p. 653 (the emphasis is ours).

32 By s.7 of the Social Security Act (no.1) 1980.

33 Child Benefit Act 1975, s.3(1).

34 Para. 2.12(e) published by HMSO, for the DHSS (1980).

35 See, for example, Wood J in *Kokosinski v Kokosinski, op. cit.*, note 5, and Stephenson LJ in *Watson v Lucas, op. cit.*, note 3.

36 [1950], 2 K.B. 328.

37 E.g., *Hawes v Evenden* [1953], 2 All E.R. 737.

38 E.g., *Haroutunian v Jennings* (1980), 1 *F.L.R.* 62, and *Tanner v Tanner* [1975], 3 All E.R. 776 at 779.

39 E.g., *Re Evers's Trust* [1980], 3 All E.R. 399, and *Dennis v McDonald* [1981], 2 All E.R. 632.

40 See *Haroutunian v Jennings; Eves v Eves* [1975], 3 All E.R. 768; *Tanner v Tanner.*

41 An example is in the judgment of Ormrod LJ in *Re Evers's Trust, op. cit.*, note 39, at p. 400.

42 *Op. cit.*, note 40, at p. 772.

43 E.g., *Eves v Eves; Cooke v Head* [1972], 2 All E.R. 38.

44 E.g., *Becker v Pettkus* (1978) 87 D.L.R. (3d) 101; *Ogilvie v Ryan* [1976] 2 N.S.W. L.R. 504.

45 *Op. cit.*, note 40, at p. 772.

46 [1975], 3 All E.R. 776, 780.

47 [1975], 1 All E.R. 1130.

47a [1980] 1 F.L.R. 62.

48 See s.50, amending s.4(2) of the Affiliation Proceedings Act 1957.

49 See the judgment of Ormrod LJ in *Re Evers's Trust, op. cit.,* note 39, at p. 404.
50 E.g., see H.C. Deb. vol. 950, cols. 1043–7.
51 [1978], 2 All E.R. 942, 947.
52 *Op. cit.,* note 39, p. 401.
53 *Idem,* at p. 403.
54 *Op. cit.,* note 34, at p. 28.
55 See s.30(2)(b).
56 *Op. cit.,* note 36, p. 331.
57 E.g., as in *Kokosinski v Kokosinski, op. cit.,* note 5, and *Crisp v Mullings, The Times* (4 July 1975).
58 E.g., as in *Cooke v Head, op. cit.,* note 43.
59 *Op. cit.,* note 34, p. 28, para. 2.12(a), (c), (d) and (f).
60 G214/50 K.L. Digest of Commissioner's Decisions, HMSO.
61 *Idem.*
62 *Idem.*
63 R(G) 3/71.
64 *Op. cit.,* note 16.
65 *Idem,* at p. 41.
66 [1980] Ch. 444.
67 [1980], 10 Fam. Law 98.
68 [1981], 2 All E.R. 29.
69 *Op. cit.,* note 3, at p. 653.
70 *Op. cit.,* note 5, at p. 1117.
71 *The Times* (16 May 1981).
72 [1980], 10 C.L.3.
73 *Op. cit.,* note 40, at p. 770.
74 *Op. cit.,* note 43, at p. 40.
75 *Idem,* at p. 43.
76 [1959], 1 W.L.R. 624.
77 [1981], 1 All E.R. 107.
78 S.1(2) of the Act requires this to be proved before relief can be given.
79 *Op. cit.,* note 77 at p. 109 (emphasis ours). See further J.T. Younger, 'Marital Regimes' Cornell L.R., 67 (1981), p. 45, 94–102.
80 See *ante,* p. 55.
81 In 'The Law Relating to Unmarried partners from the Perspective of a Law Reform Agency', in J. Eekelaar and S. Katz (eds), *Marriage and Cohabitation in Contemporary Societies,* Butterworths, 1980, p. 357 at p. 362.
82 See e.g. A. Zuckerman, 'Formality and the Family – Reform and the Status Quo', *L.Q.R.* 96 (1980), p. 255.
83 *Op. cit.,* note 81, at p. 362.
84 See ss.1–3 of the Law Reform (Miscellaneous Provisions) Act 1970.
85 *Op. cit.,* note 43, at p. 40.
86 *The Times* (19 May 1976).
87 [1974], 1 All E.R. 888.
88 [1979], 2 All E.R. 945.
89 *Op. cit.,* note 1, at p. 403.
90 See generally the Law Commission Working Paper no. 74, *Illegitimacy,* HMSO, 1979, especially pp. 27–32.
91 This aim is included even in the Commission's proposal for partial abolition: see *op. cit.,* note 9 at para. 3.8.
92 *Idem,* at para. 3.4.
93 *Idem,* at para. 3.5.
94 *Idem.*
95 B. Meteyard, 'Parenthood and Marriage', *Family Law,* 10 (1980), p. 206.
96 D. Oliver, 'The Mistress in Law', *Current Legal Problems,* 31 (1978), p. 81.
97 *Idem,* at p. 103; see also D. Oliver, 'Why do people live together?', *J.S.W.L.* (1982), 209–222.
98 P. Clayton, *The Cohabitation Guide,* Wildwood House, pp. 152–4.
99 E.g., in *Pascoe v Turner, op. cit.,* note 1; *Greasley v Cooke* [1980], 3 All E.R. 710; *Davis v Johnson* [1978], 2 W.L.R. 553; *Spindlow v Spindlow* [1979], 1 All E.R. 169.

100 E.g., Inheritance (Provision for Family and Dependants) Act 1975 and Domestic Violence and Matrimonial Proceedings Act 1976.
101 *Op. cit.*, note 96.
102 D. Pearl, 'The Legal Implications of a Relationship Outside Marriage', *C.L.J.* (1978), pp. 252–69.
103 *Op. cit.*, note 98.
104 *Op. cit.*, note 1, p. 951.
105 [1980], 3 All E.R. 710.
106 H.C. Deb. vol. 895, col. 1686.
107 By s.1(1)(e).
108 Standing Committee, col. 9.
109 On *Violence in Marriage:* see *Minutes*, paras 1804–1806, H.C. 553 (1975).
110 [1978], 1 All E.R. 821. See also *Cantliff v Jenkins* [1978], 1 All E.R. 836.
111 [1978], 1 All E.R. 841.
112 *Idem*, p. 860.
113 [1978], 1 All E.R. 1132.
114 *Idem*, p. 1145.
115 *Idem*, p. 1150. For further discussion of the violence issue see M.D.A. Freeman, *Violence in the Home – A Socio-Legal Study*, Gower Press, 1979, ch. 8.
116 *Op. cit.*, note 96, p.102.
117 *Idem.*
118 *Op. cit.*, note 98, pp. 153–4.
119 But for an indication as to how the laws work in practice, see J. Gregory, 'The Great Conciliation Fraud', *New Statesman* 3 July 1981, pp. 6–7.
120 *The Female Eunuch*, MacGibbon and Kee, 1971.
121 *Op. cit.*, note 98, p. 153.
122 *Op. cit.*, note 95.
123 *Op. cit.*, note 97.
124 *Op. cit.*, note 98.
125 'Nonmarital Cohabitation in the Common Law Countries', *American Journal of Comparative Law*, 29 (1981), p. 217.
126 *Idem*, p. 226.
127 See *ante*, ch. 5.
128 See *ante*, ch. 5 and also Z. Sage *op. cit.*, note 6, p. 393.
129 *Idem*, p. 388 and pp. 400–2.
130 *Idem*, p. 400.
131 *Op. cit.*, note 2, p. 252, 255.
132 *Op. cit.*, note 2.
133 497 P. 2d 366 at p. 366 and p. 370.
134 S.14.
135 S.3 – as amended by s.11(1) of the Family Relationships Act 1975.
136 Family Relationships Act 1975 s.11(1)(b).
137 Under s.9 of the Family Protection Act 1975. See also *ante*, p. 122.
138 See s.10A of the Maintenance Act, R.S.N. 1970 added by s.5 the Maintenance (Amendment) Act 1973.
139 See s.11(1) of the Family Maintenance Act, S.M. 1978.
140 See s.2 of the Act on National Insurance 1962, as amended. On Sweden, see *ante*, p. 130–1.
141 See s.18 of the Ordinance on State Housing Allowances to Families with Children 1976.
142 See *ante*, p. 130.
143 See the discussion of the Minister of Justice's Protocol, *ante*, p. 128.
144 *Per* Z. Sage, *op. cit.*, note 6, p. 377. See, further, A. Agell, 'Cohabitation Without Marriage in Swedish Law' in J. Eekelaar and S. Katz, *op. cit.*, note 81, p. 245.
145 Thus one year is sufficient in Manitoba, Newfoundland and Tasmania under legislative provisions, whereas the courts are more impressed by much longer periods. See *Becker v Pettkus* (twenty years) and *Ogilvie v Ryan* (twenty-four years).
146 N.H. Rev. Stat. Ann 457:39 (1968). See also *ante*, p. 123.
147 47 Cal 2d 657 (1962).
148 44 Cal App 3d 758 (1975).
149 541 P 2d 1243 (1975).

150 *Op. cit.,* note 4.

151 See examples quoted in R. Sackville, 'Social Security and Family Law in Australia', *I.C.L.Q.,* 27, p. 127 at pp. 156–9.

152 See provision discussed in Hughes, 'Domestic Purposes Benefit: Lessons from the Furmage Case', *N.Z. L.J.,* (1979), p. 32 at p. 39.

153 See *ante,* p. 121 and p. 172.

154 S.3(c) and (d) although also note (f) Superannuation Act 1976.

155 S.17(2)(h) Workmens' Compensation Act 1968.

156 These are cited in E. Evatt, R. Watson and D. McKenzie, 'The Legal and Social Aspects of Cohabitation and the Reconstituted Family as a Social Problem', in J. Eekelaar and S. Katz, *op. cit.,* note 81, p. 398 at p. 404.

157 S.11(1) of the Family Relationships Act 1975 (SA).

158 S.64 of the Succession Law Reform Act 1977.

159 S.14(b)(i) of the Family Law Reform Act 1978.

160 S.15 (e)(iii) of the Family Relations Act 1972.

161 See *ante,* p. 121.

162 The Commonwealth courts pride themselves on a strict application of these principles. See, e.g. Wilson J in *Becker v Pettkus,* 87, *D.L.R.,* p. 101 at pp. 105–9.

163 [1976], 2 N.S.W. L.R. 504.

164 [1977], 1 N.S.W. L.R. 189.

165 [1977], 1 N.S.W. L.R. 182.

166 E.g., Commonwealth Superannuation Act 1976 (Cth); Family Relationships Act 1975 (SA).

167 E.g., Swedish Ordinance on State Housing Allowances to Families with Children 1976. See *ante,* p. 129.

168 *Op. cit.,* note 146.

169 *Op. cit.,* note 125.

170 See e.g., *Kozlowski v Kozlowski, op. cit.,* note 2.

171 604 P 2d 602 (Alaska).

172 B.N.A., *Family Law Reporter,* 5, pp. 3077, 1085.

173 See *ante,* p. 119–120.

174 *Op. cit.,* note 3.

175 44 Mich. App. 570.

176 547 P. 2d 144.

177 (1976) 2 N.S.W. L.R. 504, 508. See also the New Zealand case of *Fraser v Gough,* 1 *N.Z. L.R.* (1975), p. 138.

178 *Op. cit.,* note 165 at p. 184.

179 *Op. cit.,* note 144.

180 Government Bill 1973: 72 at 169.

181 *Op. cit.,* note 6, p. 399.

182 See, e.g., the Council of Europe, *Convention on the Legal Status of Children Born out of Wedlock,* 1975, and *post,* pp. 171–173.

183 Parents Code 6:12 (1974), See, Further, *ante,* p. 132.

184 See P. Lødrop, 'The Position of Children of Unmarried but Cohabiting Parents', in J. Eekelaar and S. Katz, *op. cit.,* note 81, pp. 413–19, at p. 414.

185 E.g., *Levy v Louisiana* 391 US 68 (1968) and *Weber v Aetna Casualty and Surety Co.* 406 US 164 (1972), *Gomez v Perez* 409 US 535 (1973).

186 E.g., Riga, 'The Supreme Court's View of Marriage and the Family: Tradition or Transition?', *JFL,* 18 (1979), p. 301; J. Noonan, 'The Family and the Supreme Court', *Catholic Univ. Law Rev.,* 23 (1973), p. 255.

187 For example, in *Weber v Aetna Casualty and Surety Co.*

188 *Labine v Vincent,* 401 US 532 (1971).

189 427 US 495 (1976). *Cf Jiminez v Weinberger,* 417 US 628 (1974).

190 430 US 762 (1977).

191 99 S.Ct. 518 (1978).

192 *Op. cit.,* note 190 at pp. 770–1.

193 *Idem.* (See also *Lalli v Lalli, op. cit.,* note 191, at p. 526.)

194 *Idem.*

195 *Idem.*

196 99 S. Ct. 2767 (1979).

197 349 F. Supp. 491.
198 99 S. Ct. 1742 (1979).
199 391 US 73 (1968).
200 441 US 380 (1979).
201 423 US 1042 (1977).
202 *Final Report,* vol. 4, pp. 68–9.
203 See s.53 of the Family Law Reform Act 1978 (Ont.).
204 See s.52 of the Family Law Reform Act 1978 (P.E.I.).
205 Maintenance Act 1967 s.16.
206 Swedish Government, *Official Reports,* 1972: 41, 93.
207 *Abstract* of Protocol on Justice Department Matters, 1968, pp. 3, 10–11.
208 *Op. cit.,* note 6, at p. 400.
209 *Op. cit.,* note 172.
210 S.7(1)(f).
211 Ss.4, 7(1).
212 S.64(b).
213 Proposal made in 1976 to extend the provisions of Tasmania's Family Maintenance Act 1912 to surviving de facto spouses as well as legal spouses. See Evatt, Watson and McKenzie, *op. cit.,* note 156, at p. 403.
214 New South Wales Law Reform Commission proposed in 1977 that the court should be authorised to make an award to any person who was at any time a member of the deceased's household or partially or wholly dependent upon the decedent, if the court concludes that the survivor is a 'person whom the deceased person ought not to have left without provision for his proper maintenance, education or advancement in life'. See Evatt *et al, op. cit.,* note 156, at p. 403–4.
215 Quebec Civil Code Revision Office, *Report on the Quebec Civil Code* vol. 1 (Draft Civil Code) s.42.
216 See, e.g., Tort Liability Act 1972, s.2; Occupational Injuries Insurance Act 1976, s.6.
217 *Ante,* p. 121.
218 *Ante,* p. 119–120.
219 541 P. 2d, p.1243.
220 *Idem,* p. 1250.
221 *Op. cit.,* note 176, p. 366.
222 'Domestic Partnership: A Proposal For Dividing The Property of Unmarried Families', *Willamette LJ.,* 12 (1976), p. 453.
223 *Idem,* p. 458.
224 Referred to by H. Finlay, 'The Battered Mistress and the Violent Paramour', *Aust. L.J.,* 54 (1978), pp. 613, 614.
225 'Legal Recognition of De Facto Relationships', *Aust. L.J.,* 52 (1976), p. 174.
226 Unreported decision of N.S.W. Supreme Court (8 December 1976).

7 Justifications for Differential Treatment

That cohabitation should be treated differently from marriage is the argument both of those who seek to uphold marriage on public policy[1] grounds and of those who wish to support the private autonomy of cohabiting couples.[2] Both arguments are used by legislatures and courts of many countries, and each has attracted a degree of academic support. The goal of differential treatment entails much of which lawyers approve.[3] It also appears to accord more with the supposed[4] intention of parties who have adopted an informal life-style. Such an approach does not mean that cohabitants are unable to resort to the law when difficulties arise, for the judiciary, when freed from the straitjacket of quasi-marital relief, has adopted some remarkably innovative legal solutions[5] to the problems of the unmarried couple. A note of caution should, however, be sounded in respect of this approach also: thus the law should not seek to impose rights and duties where such were never the expressed, implied or reasonable expectations of both the parties. Human relationships, despite comparisons with contract and business partnerships, cannot be reduced to the level of the market place. To use language reminiscent of the Wolfenden report, there is an area of human relationships which is quite simply 'not the law's business'.[6]

Justifications advanced in England

(i) *Public policy and public morality*

Expression of the sentiment that marriage still occupies a central position in English society can be found in both statutory[7] and case law.[8] Most of the differences between marriage and cohabitation analysed in Chapter 4 stem from a deliberate policy to foster marriage as the legitimate basis for family life. Lenore Weitzman believes that legal regulation of marriage is thought to serve four state interests: 'promoting public morality, ensuring family stability, assuring support obligations and assigning responsibility for the care of children'.[9]

All of these are legitimate public policy considerations, and all contribute to the good order of society, which is a primary aim of the government of any state. Nowhere in recent years have these differing considerations been so clearly articulated as in the debates in both Houses of Parliament on the Inheritance (Provision for Family and Dependants) Act 1975. In calling for the exclusion of clause 1(1)(e) of the bill (discussed at p. 80) Mr Ivor Stanbrook described the clause as 'a blow to family life and to the institution of marriage', and called for the Archbishop of Canterbury to consider it in the context of his 'recent appeal for the restoration of fundamental standards in the community including family life'.[10] Mr Ivan Lawrence declared that 'those who believe that the family is a vital and fundamental unit in our free society must be greatly uneasy that this bill will extend the benefits of the family system to a unit outside the family'. He continued: 'in a sense the sanctity of the family is undermined when the good things of family life are readily available without the constraints of that unit. Marriage creates obligations as well as rights and, if the rights are easily obtained outside marriage and without the obligations, how long will it be before no one wants the obligations and the family concept collapses?'[11] Lord Simon of Glaisdale in the House of Lords defended the anti-avoidance provisions contained in clause 10 of the same bill on the basis that 'there will be unreasonable testators, anxious to cast aside moral obligations to a family in favour of other obligations, however worthy, which society feels ought to rank behind the obligations to a family'.[12] It emerged from the debates that speakers were seriously worried about the effects which the bill could have in undermining family life in England. In consequence, both the Solicitor General[13] and the Lord Chancellor[14] were moved to point out that the courts were unlikely to award the whole estate to an undeserving 'mistress' at the expense of a blameless wife. The Act's provisions do, in any event, differentiate between legitimate spouses and cohabitants, no doubt on grounds of public policy. Spouses are entitled to provision both of a capital and maintenance nature, regardless of dependence. Cohabitants, on the other hand, are only entitled to reasonable provision by way of maintenance, having regard to the degree of support afforded by the deceased immediately before death. To a large extent, therefore, the Act ensures that 'the good things of family life' are still not quite so accessible to unmarried couples.

Similar considerations of promoting public morality and social stability have also played a part in influencing the state's denial of social security survivors' benefits to unmarried couples,[15] and its unsympathetic response to any proposals for the extension of support rights in the private law field.[16] We have seen on many occasions how administratively convenient it is for marriage to be the criterion by reference to which support obligations are assigned,[17] but there is also a strong feeling that those who assume the burdens of marriage should reap its benefits.[18] There is considerable reluctance to extend such benefits to cohabitants who, by choosing such an open-ended and potentially unstable life-style, are deemed to be rejecting the long-term benefits and burdens offered by what is still intended to be a lifelong institution.

Marriage is protected by a special law complex because it does promote the ends of social stability. It not only provides the means for assuring support obligations, which is an important state concern, but also, and equally importantly, it is thought that marriage is more likely to provide the background in which stable family relationships will develop.[19] The marriage partnership is thus characterised as promoting a depth of relationship by virtue of its lifelong commitment which cohabitation cannot provide. This, in part, explains why married partners can claim damages for loss of consortium whereas cohabitants cannot, though it does not explain why such relief was reserved for men.[20] Similarly, in relation to children, the level of support for the institution of marriage has been justified by the English Law Commission on the basis that a married relationship between parents should be more stable than an unmarried one. Thus, the English law of adoption prevents a cohabiting couple as a couple from adopting children.[21] It is the theory of marriage that it expresses lifelong commitment. The legitimate family also serves as the more desirable model for socialising children into acceptable standards of behaviour. not the least because it emphasises the monogamous nature of marriage, this too connects the considerations of public morality and social stability, the achievement of the latter generally flowing from success in upholding the former.

Legal monogamous marriage, emphasising as it does sexual fidelity within the relationship, operates as a force for the social regulation of sexuality.[22] Without monogamy some, for example Devlin, have argued that there would be utter anarchy in the field of human relationships and those state interests identified previously would be difficult if not impossible of realisation.[23] The criteria for the assigning of support and custody rights in relation to children could become very complicated, which in turn could severely threaten the established social order. Although the penalties for breaching the accepted norm of marital fidelity are not as severe as they once were,[24] adultery, or even lesser forms of sexual misconduct, still constitute grounds for, or facts on which, to base divorce in most jurisdictions. In consequence, the blameworthy spouse risks losing spouse, children, property, income and friends. J.M. McMurtry, in his critique of monogamy, comments that in this way possibly the most compelling natural force towards expanded intimate relations with others is strictly confined within the narrowest possible circle for the whole of adult life (barring delinquency). The sheer weight and totality of this restriction is surely one of the great wonders in the history of institutional control.[25] Far from wondering at it, Lord Devlin sees the institutional marriage as most necessary to promote the stability of society.[26] Without its supposed shared morality, of which such marriage is a part, English society would come perilously close to disintegration. This is why, he argues, marriage is accorded a specially protected position within English law.[27]

Such concern for English public morality has also influenced the support for differential treatment which can be found in several judicial decisions, including very recent ones.[28] Some of the judiciary, it must be said, seem scarcely to have advanced much from the attitude displayed by Bucknill LJ in *Upfill v Wright* in 1911. He stated that it had been put to him in argument 'that prostitution is one thing and living as one man's mistress is quite a different thing. In my opinion, however,' he said, 'they may differ in degree but they both stand on the same plane'.[29] Similarly, Asquith LJ in *Gammans v Ekins* in 1952 said 'if the relationship involves sexual relations it seems to me anomalous that a person can acquire a status of irremovability by living or having lived in sin, even if the liaison has not been a casual encounter but protracted in time and exclusive in character'.[30] Sir Raymond Evershed MR added: 'it may not be a bad thing that by this decision it is shown that, in the Christian society in which we live, one, at any rate, of the privileges which may be derived from marriage is not equally enjoyed by those who are living together as man and wife but who are not married'.[31]

Some of the judiciary, like the Government and members of the legislature, have also indicated their support for the special legal, moral and emotional commitment represented by entry into marriage, by refusing to award cohabitants rights equivalent to those possessed by married couples. Thus, Walton J in *Richards v Dove* in 1972 declared that 'it is impossible to leave out of the picture the fact that as husband and wife the husband has certain legal duties in relation to maintaining his wife, whereas between man and mistress the whole relationship is consensual, if you like contractual with no legal obligation superimposed'.[32] The opening sentences of Lawton LJ's judgment in *Colin Smith Music Ltd. v Ridge* express much the same sentiments. 'The starting point', he said, 'for deciding what is the right order in this case is to look at the status of the defendant when she and Mr Venn were cohabiting together. She was not his wife so she did not enjoy the special position recognised by the common law for wives; . . . he was under no legal obligation to support her.'[33] He continued: 'there is nothing in the authorities which justifies this court or any other courts adjudging that a mistress in her capacity as a lodger or indeed in any other capacity, is in any position analogous to that of the wife'. Cairns LJ, in the same case, stated that, 'counsel seeks to say that in these days possession by a mistress who has borne children to the protected tenant is analogous to possession by a wife but in my view this is not so'.[34]

As if acting out the prophecy of the Solicitor General,[35] the court in *Horrocks v Forray,*[36] in settling a claim under the Inheritance (Provision for Family and Dependants) Act 1975, decided that possession of a house occupied by a 'mistress' should be surrendered to enure to the benefit of the deceased's widow. Any other course would have resulted in the deceased's lawful spouse being left almost penniless as a result of his extravagance in setting up and supporting a 'mistress' in a home bought in his name. Megaw LJ made great play of the fact that the widow had had no idea of her husband's infidelity, and that it would add insult to injury if she were further to be left destitute as a result of his extravagant and immoral behaviour. A distinct odour of moralistic censure emerges from his judgment. Are we to conclude that when faced with a blameless widow, a 'mistress' and insufficient resources to provide for both, courts will ensure the widow comes off best? The 'other woman' in this case, though, could perhaps be seen as less 'deserving' than those other classes of 'worthy women' considered in debates on the Act.[37] In fact she tended to fit in more with the class of women of whose continued existence Lord Kilbrandon doubted in *Davis v Johnson,*[38] namely, 'a woman installed in a clandestine way by someone of substance, normally married for his intermittent sexual enjoyment'. The surviving female cohabitant in *H v H.D. and G,*[39] however, had lived with the deceased for a couple of years as though they were husband and wife, and they had pooled all their financial resources. In dismissing her claim for provision under the same Act, Reeve J expressed very clearly his preference for legitimate family life based on marriage. Looking at the circumstances of the case, he characterised the woman's application as 'impertinent'. In addition, he considered it 'important that the interests of legitimate family dependants should be protected'.

Claims that periods of cohabitation should rank equally with periods of marriage in computing financial provision on divorce, on the basis of the marriage-like qualities of the relationship, have also provoked sharp criticism from the judiciary. The justification for such criticism has been quite simply that these suggestions degrade marriage. A prime example of such criticism can be found in the judgment of Baker P in *Campbell v Campbell*[40] in 1976. He stated that

> there is an increasing tendency . . . to regard and indeed to speak of the celebration of marriage as 'the paper work'. The phrase used is we were living together but we never got around to the paper work. Well that is to my mind an entirely misconceived outlook. It is the ceremony of marriage and the sanctity of marriage which count; rights, duties and obligations begin on the marriage and not before. It is a complete cheapening of the marriage relationship which is essential to the well-being of our society to suggest that pre-marital periods, particularly in the circumstances of the case, should as it were by a doctrine of relation back of matrimony be taken as a part of marriage to count in favour of the wife, performing as it is put wifely duties before marriage.

Even in *Kokosinski v Kokosinski*[41] in 1980, where Wood J was prepared to take into account 20 years of pre-marital cohabitation, he was concerned to make it clear that his decision was confined to the facts of the case and to stress that it would 'do nothing to undermine the institution of marriage'. More recently in *H v H*,[42] in 1981, Balcombe J said that 'to consider a period of six years on-off cohabitation as equivalent to a true period of marriage would be cynical in the extreme'. Only a few days later, in *Foley v Foley*,[43] Eveleigh J said that 'ten years of cohabitation would not necessarily have the same effect as ten years of marriage. Public opinion still generally recognised a stronger claim founded upon years of marriage than one which was founded upon years of cohabitation'.

The writings of ideologues like Lord Devlin and Mia Kellmer-Pringle[44] apart, it is not easy to find in the writings of English legal academics any very strong *arguments* for the specially protected position of marriage under the law. There is, however, some *support* for its continued protection. Thus, Samuels,[45] while writing approvingly of the Law Commission's tentative proposal for the abolition of the status of illegitimacy, feels compelled to urge that 'marriage as an institution should certainly be strongly encouraged and supported in every possible way'. He neglects to say why. Blake,[46] discussing the greater recognition the law now accords cohabitants, states that 'if the declining popularity of marriage is due in part to the law of marriage rather than to an alteration in moral views then it may be that the law of marriage should be changed to stem that decline'. Blake's solution to the problem is not concerned with maintaining the differentials between marriage and cohabitation but rather in equalising them so as to stem the decline in marriage. Since such a move to equalisation entails the removal of so many provisions which favour marriage, it is difficult to see how it might stem the decline, but in any case Blake nowhere indicates *why* the decline should be stemmed. Pearl,[47] on the other hand, while not avowedly supporting the special position of marriage under the law, simply seems resigned to the fact that any real changes in English law relating to couples and their relationships 'will occur at a stage long in the future and for the present at least, the law must acknowledge that public policy supports the status of the marital tie'.[48]

(ii) The private autonomy approach

This approach postulates the view that those who cohabit have chosen not to marry and the law should therefore respect that choice, preserve their autonomy, and not attempt to treat them as if they were married. This justification for the differential treatment of cohabitants has attracted some support amongst academics,[49] and also has on occasion commended itself to the judiciary[50] and to members of Parliament.[51] It should, however, be admitted that its popular appeal to cohabitants, particularly women, might be described as suspect,[52] although this does not unduly worry us. After all, the law in England currently provides everyone, even women, with the choice of marriage or cohabitation. The freedom once offered by cohabitation is being severely circumscribed, and escaping from marriage by cohabiting is becoming increasingly difficult. In an age in which the State concerns itself in, and restricts, so many aspects of our existence, we should be cautious about giving it any greater control over our private lives.

Mr John Horam, in a House of Commons debate on the Housing Finance Bill expressed serious reservations as to the characterisation of a couple as 'living together as husband and wife' merely because they were living together under the same roof.[53] Although the provision meant that cohabitants and married couples would be treated equally, Mr Horam was disturbed by its implications and urged that 'cohabiting couples be given the choice to elect in writing whether they wished to be so treated.[54] He described the existing provision as a 'threat to the natural right of privacy' and went on to picture the sort of ridiculous investigations which might ensue if the cohabiting couple also happened to be on supplementary benefit. Thus, he said,

> not only is there one set of people investigating on behalf of the Supplementary Benefits Commission, there is now a man in a

mackintosh outside a council house front door deciding whether in fact the first man is right. This is the kind of French farce situation which will develop as a result of this further erosion of the personal privacy. I also think that it is indelicate.

He went on to say that he felt his amendment was a small price to pay 'for allowing people to decide what they reveal of the state of their relationships and not to have it decided for them by the council'.[55] In the event, however, his amendment was defeated.

While Parliament and various Government departments may, for all sorts of reasons, not be inclined to be influenced by such considerations of privacy and freedom of the individual, a few decisions of the courts indicate a willingness to adopt the private autonomy approach. For example, in *Helby v Rafferty,*[56] Stamp LJ took special note of the woman's attitude towards the cohabiting relationship. 'Miss Taylor', he said, 'had deliberately chosen to avoid any permanence in the relationship; she wanted freedom among other things to withdraw from the relationship with the minimum of fuss and without legal formalities.'[57] Similarly, in *Re Beaumont,*[58] Megarry VC commented that 'the whole picture presented by the plaintiff is one of two people each with their own earnings . . . who chose to pool such of their individual resources as were needed for them to be able to live with each other without either undertaking any responsibility for maintaining the other'. Similarly, in his dissenting judgment in *Watson v Lucas,*[59] Oliver LJ stressed the fact that the parties had deliberately chosen cohabitation (what he called 'concubinage') in preference to marriage. In trying to decide whether such a couple could be described as a family, he stated:

> if they themselves openly treated themselves as engaged only in concubinage which each was free to continue or not and from which each was free to withdraw at will and without obligation, then this does appear to me to be at least a factor to be taken into account in considering whether the relationship had a sufficient degree of apparent permanence . . . They did not seek to put themselves in a position in which they could commit themselves *de jure* to a permanent relationship involving mutual obligations although they knew that they could do so, and the judge inferred from this that they had elected to preserve their independence.

The obvious question arising from such a decision is whether the first instance judge was entitled to make such an inference. Are such inferences permissible where the facts indicate a conscious, freely entered into, non-marital union? We would tend to the view that they are, as would Deech,[60] Poulter[61] and Zuckerman[62] but Dawn Oliver[63] is dubious about the legitimacy of such an inference. We argued in an earlier article[64] that couples who live together should not be subject to legal regulation similar to that applicable to married couples. By their adoption of such a life-style one, if not, both cohabitants have indicated an unwillingness to assume marital status. While it is probably wrong to characterise such cohabiting couples in England as permanently rejecting marriage, since so many of them subsequently get married, the actual decision to marry indicates at that stage a readiness to make that degree of commitment to another person exemplified by marriage. During a period of cohabitation it is wrong to impose upon them the consequences of a commitment which they have not been prepared to make, and where such cohabitation fails, it is doubly wrong to impose upon them the penalties of a failed marriage, when, as Deech says, they were probably experimenting precisely in order to avoid that outcome.[65]

Oliver[66] has described our arguments and those of Ruth Deech as based on two untested assumptions: that unmarried couples reject the legal incidents of marriage; and, conversely, that couples who marry do so partly at least because they accept the legal obligations of marriage. She asserts that no empirical research supports these assumptions and then goes on to demonstrate from the results of a very small-scale survey,[67] conducted amongst seven cohabiting couples, that few of these couples knew the precise legal incidents of marriage, though most were aware that it created certain legal obligations of support; a few thought cohabitation had similar legal effects. This is to miss the point entirely. What we and Deech are saying is that marriage is a voluntary institution in which the parties express their willingness to commit themselves to each other for life. Whether they are completely cognisant of all the legal effects of such a commitment is immaterial; the commitment is made, nevertheless, and marital rights and obligations inevitably follow. Cohabiting couples do not make that same commitment, and rights and duties akin to marriage should not as a result follow. The danger with imposing the incidents of marriage on a cohabiting couple is that it constitutes a denial of a fundamental freedom. As Deech says,[68] 'we are not arguing for the superiority of marriage or even its centrality but rather for the preservation of the freedom to try alternative forms of relationship'. This point is also made by Poulter.[69] He argues that 'it would hardly seem desirable for the law to be so radically reformed as to equate cohabitation with marriage in every respect. Apart from anything else this would deprive people of the freedom of choice presently open to them'. Similarly, Zuckerman,[70] arguing against calls for a special legislative code for cohabitants, declares that such a code would be 'unjustifiable in an age of increasing diversity in personal relationships and family patterns and of respect for individual choice, to confine those who have avoided matrimony into almost equally inflexible institutional categories'.

Another important factor militating against the imposition of such quasi-matrimonial rights and obligations is that they are most strongly urged upon breakdown of the relationship. The courts thereby find themselves in the position of artifically constructing a marriage, only to dissolve it in order to mete out what one of the partners, usually the woman, deems to be her just reward in the light of her expectations, arising from what she, unilaterally by this stage, wishes to call a marriage-like relationship. Additional objections to this extension of traditional family law stem from the tendency of the law to characterise the female partner in marriage necessarily as economically dependent. To encourage cohabiting women to jump on to the bandwagon of economic dependence would be to turn the clock back for married women also. In any event, the argument that the cohabiting woman has performed 'wife-like duties', and is therefore deserving of 'wife-like' support on breakdown, leaves out of the calculation the fact that in return for such services she usually has received economic support during the relationship. The difference with marriage is that the contract contains an implied term for such support to continue for life, with the necessary corollary being lifelong commitment. Cohabitation has no such commitment, and thus no similar corollary.

While an extension of quasi-marital rights to cohabiting women may be attractive to the state for financial reasons, it must be deplored as representing a backward step in the moves for women's equality. Any such extension would also adversely affect the courts' attitudes generally to support rights arising from marriage. The goal of social and economic independence for women, and the recent and welcome use by the courts of the 'clean break' principle[71] and the concept of genuine rehabilitative maintenance,[72] should not be jeopardised by paternalistic attitudes towards female cohabitants. As Deech says,[73] 'maintenance and property awards to former cohabiting partners . . . would . . . reinforce the outmoded view, upheld by the law, of the man as the head of the household and the woman as being under an obligation to provide domestic services and child care, a view which is too unsatisfactory in its application to married persons to permit of its extension to the unmarried'. The view that women need to be protected and that the cohabiting woman should be protected by outmoded principles of traditional family law is untenable. The value of remunerative employment to an individual has been demonstrated in so many ways. Whenever possible women should be encouraged to take such work.[74] Where they are bringing up children or have had to make sacrifices, they should receive adequate compensation, not a meal ticket for life. Moves to encourage women into roles of economic dependence because of high levels of unemployment are cynical in the extreme, and must be resisted at all costs.

Another problem relating to simple economics also operates against the extension of quasi-matrimonial rights to cohabitants and in favour of differential treatment, and that is the difficulty caused by trying to reconcile the claims of a wife and a cohabitant against the same man or against his estate.[75] Where the male partner is alive, the prospect of his being able to support a former cohabitant and a present wife is as unlikely as most men's ability adequately to support a wife and former wife.[76] The situation currently with divorce awards for maintenance is that once a man remarries and assumes new responsibilities, this constitutes grounds for variation,[77] and his former wife may encounter financial difficulties. Such a problem would be compounded if former cohabitants also had to be supported. Any means used to reconcile such claims would provoke allegations of injustice from one of the parties. Nor do the ramifications of providing for such claims extend only to support rights. The consequences for property rights would also be considerable, both in terms of effect on third parties and in determining the merits of claims between a spouse and former cohabitant. Thus, Deech comments:[78] 'in a society where earnings and housing are generally designed for the support of one family at the most, a choice has ultimately to be made between the claims of cohabitants and those of wives. Both cannot be afforded any more than can polygamy'.

If the problems arising from reconciling competing claims by partners appear difficult, those which could arise from a concerted attempt to introduce equivalent treatment throughout the law would be insurmountable. The scale and reach of the reforms necessary to achieve such a goal would be enormous.[79] To extend to unmarried couples treatment under the law equivalent to that possessed by married couples would be to open the floodgates – all in order that cohabitants can be treated according to the same outmoded principles of family law as are married couples. The inadequacy of traditional family law in adjusting to changed economic and social conditions has been frequently documented in this book. Before such a corpus of law is extended to cohabitants, we should question whether this is what is needed. There have already been tenuous moves by the judiciary towards the idea of seeing marriage as a partnership of equals[80] and against the idea of lifelong dependence by wives on husbands.[81] Such trends should be encouraged, not deflected by attempts to force cohabitants into a model beginning to be deemed inappropriate even for married couples.

Justifications advanced in other jurisdictions

(i) *Public policy approach*

This approach attracts varying levels of support in the USA,[82] which is perhaps understandable, given the variegated nature of its constituent states and the complete lack of legal uniformity as between the different state jurisdictions. It is consequently impossible to define American public policy as such. Particular policy considerations attract greater institutional support in one state than they do in another, and because of the nature of political life in America, the elected representatives must also pay close regard to those aspects of policy which attract or rebuff popular support. It is for this reason that the state legislatures are reluctant to enact laws which would either positively discriminate in favour of or against cohabitants. It is also more expedient for them to allow the courts to test out reaction, and then, after considering public response to any particular decision, determine whether the law should be altered. Sometimes such decisions are only made at state Supreme Court level[83] and are a good indication of public policy in that state, whereas others, which raise constitutional issues, go on appeal to the Federal Supreme Court,[84] the decisions of which have on occasion been criticised as being in advance of what the public or the state desires.[85]

In *Rehak v Mathis* the Georgia Supreme Court denied relief to a woman who had made all the payments on a house for the first two years and one-half for the next sixteen years, arguing that: 'all property and monetary claims [were] based upon a meretricious relationship, which claims [were] not recoverable because [they are] contrary to public policy'.[86] The Court stated that it was 'well settled that neither a court of law nor a court of equity will lend its aid to either party to a contract founded upon an illegal or immoral consideration'. Since the parties had admitted to cohabitation in the pleadings, said the court, 'this would constitute immoral consideration', within the terms of the state's statutes. Similarly, in *Roach v Button*[87] the Tennessee Chancery Court stated starkly that public policy would bar recovery between cohabitants in that state, and in *New Jersey Welfare Rights Organization v Cahill*[88] the New Jersey district court judge put very clearly the policy considerations justifying the denial of welfare services to illegitimate children. He stated:

> marriage, by itself, is a permanent or at least semi-permanent institution. The state has reinforced it with a great deal of protection in its statutory and case laws. Its whole domestic relations

law is designed to protect marriage and the family . . . It all results from a recognition by the State of New Jersey and every other state in the United States that the family is the basic social unit, and provides much of the norms for a person's action in society . . . The State has determined that it only works to subsidize what it considers to be legitimate families, ones where the likelihood is greater for the instillment of proper social norms. It is certainly both a proper and compelling state interest to refuse to subsidize a living unit which may lead to a state of anomie and which violates its laws against fornication and adultery.[89]

The Illinois Supreme Court in 1979 discussed the issues raised by the cohabitants' claims for quasi-matrimonial relief in even greater detail. In *Hewitt v Hewitt*[90] Underwood J said:

the issue of unmarried cohabitants' mutual property rights . . . cannot appropriately be characterised solely in terms of contract law . . . There are major public policy questions involved in determining whether, under what circumstances and to what extent it is desirable to accord some type of legal status to claims arising from such relationships. Of substantially greater importance than the rights of the immediate parties is the impact of such recognition upon our society and the institution of marriage. Will the fact that legal rights closely resembling those arising from conventional marriages can be acquired by those who deliberately choose to enter into what have heretofore been commonly referred to as 'illicit' or meretricious relationships encourage formation of such relationships and weaken marriage as the foundation of our family based society?

Underwood J proceeded to ask the question:

if resolution of this issue rests ultimately on grounds of public policy by what body should that policy be determined? . . . The issue realistically is whether it is appropriate for this court to grant a legal status to a private arrangement substituting for the institution of marriage sanctioned by the state. The question whether change is needed in the law governing the rights of parties in this delicate area of marriage-like relationships involves evaluations of sociological data and alternatives we believe best suited to the superior investigative and fact-finding facilities of the legislative branch in the exercise of its traditional authority to declare public policy in the domestic relations field. That belief is reinforced by

> the fact that judicial recognition of mutual property rights between unmarried cohabitants would in our opinion clearly violate the policy of our recently enacted Illinois Marriage and Dissolution of Marriage Act.[91]

After reading the preamble of the Act, the aims of which included the strengthening and preserving of the integrity of marriage, Underwood J concluded that the plaintiff's claim in the particular case was unenforceable as being in contravention of public policy.

According to some commentators,[92] the United States Supreme Court has ignored considerations of public policy and concern for legitimate family life by some of its recent decisions in respect of illegitimate children. Certainly, in cases such as *Levy v Louisiana*[93] and *Weber v Aetna Casualty and Surety Co*,[94] the Supreme Court has substituted its own view of the legitimate limits of public policy for those of the states concerned, in order to enforce the principle of equal protection guaranteed by the Constitution. Riga,[95] in the course of criticising the Supreme Court's attitude in such cases, comments that the attempt to remove the stigmatisation of children born out of wedlock by an equal treatment of the married and the unmarried does false service to both. He queries whether the court's approach is at all justified. He says:

> It is not at all necessary to resolve the difficult problem of illegitimacy and its legal disentitlements by having recourse to the equal protection clause. This course lessens public esteem for the normative family by placing family life on the same plane as unions resulting in illegitimacy. No legal system can remain a healthy one by equating and treating equally the married and unmarried parent and spouse since marriage has always enjoyed a privileged status in our society. The state has a fundamental interest in encouraging these values as a form of self-protection and self-defence. To tamper with the value and the esteem with which it is held in our society is to tamper with its vitals, which no court should be allowed to do. The law accords legal benefits to the married and legal disabilities to the unmarried for its own moral health and ultimate survival not because of religious, social or economic preference. That is why the interest of the state in the stability and encouragement of the family must be seen as fundamental even in the face of illegitimacy.

Riga's views are supported by Noonan,[96] who declares that 'to say that Equal Protection requires the equal treatment of the married and unmarried in all respects is to deny the hierarchy of values in our society'. Clark[97] too, after discussing the illegitimacy decisions of the Supreme

Court and the moves in the Californian courts to equate marriage and cohabitation, remains doubtful of society's approval of current judicial trends. Thus, he states that

> although sexual freedom is a current shibboleth of great popularity, there do seem to be substantial segments of American society that do not favour it, and that stoutly proclaim the virtues of conventional marriage. For these segments of society, social practice ideally at least remains what it has been for many years. To make radical changes in the law of marriage on the ground that such changes will bring the law into closer conformity with prevailing behaviour would be considered by these segments of society to be wrong-headed and probably immoral.

Clark further doubts whether in any event the courts are the best arbiters of what prevailing social practice is within the community, a view clearly shared by the Illinois Supreme Court but not by the California Supreme Court. Thus, Judge Tobriner in *Marvin v Marvin*[98] stated that 'the mores of the society have indeed changed so radically in regard to cohabitation that we cannot impose a standard based on alleged moral considerations that have apparently been so widely abandoned by so many'. Interestingly, though, Tobriner J went on to say

> lest we be misunderstood however we take the occasion to point out that the structure of society itself largely depends upon the institution of marriage and nothing we have said in this opinion should be taken to derogate from that institution. The joining of the man and woman in marriage is at once the most socially productive and individually fulfilling relationship that one can enjoy in the course of a liftime.

In Australia public policy is embodied in statutory form in the Family Law Act of 1975. The court is directed in cases coming before it to have regard to: '(a) the need to preserve and protect the institution of marriage as the union of a man and woman to the exclusion of all others voluntarily entered into for life'.[99] The Australian federal legislature has accordingly provided that marriage should be protected and should occupy a special position, and many laws preserve the difference between married and unmarried couples.[100] Several states have enacted laws which give cohabitants rights upon breakdown of the relationship,[101] or upon death,[102] and have also equalised the position of children[103] of such relationships with legitimate children. In addition to these provisions, a change in judicial attitudes has meant that few references, if any, are made to considerations of public policy when granting relief to cohabitants or to the children of cohabiting relationships.[104]

Such changes, while appearing inconsistent with the requirement to protect the institution of marriage, do comply with the second principle to which the Family Law Act directs the court, which is: '(b) the need to give the widest possible protection and assistance to the family as the natural and fundamental group unit of society particularly while it is responsible for the care and education of dependent children'.[105] Aside from the provisions requiring protection for marriage in the federal Family Law Act, the only positive support for marriage on the grounds of public policy is to be found in arguments such as that of the Tasmanian Law Reform Commission. In 1977 the Commission, though recommending an extension to the rights of cohabitants, declined to recommend the creation of a new de facto status coextensive with or similar to marriage, basing their objections on considerations of public policy.[106]

(ii) Private autonomy approach

Respect for the individual's freedom of choice was one of the main factors influencing Justice Clark, who gave the only dissenting judgment in *Marvin v Marvin.*[107] Disturbed by the possible ramifications of the majority's decision (with which in substantial part he did not disagree), Justice Clark felt that the court should have stopped short of attempting 'to determine all anticipated rights, duties and remedies within every meretricious relationship particularly in vague terms'. He went on to query whether 'upon termination of the relationship it is equitable to impose the economic obligations of lawful spouses on meretricious parties when the latter may have rejected matrimony to avoid such obligations'. In concluding his judgment, he stated laconically: 'by judicial overreach the majority perform a *nunc pro tunc* marriage, dissolve it and distribute its property on terms never contemplated by the parties, case law or the legislature'.[108] Weitzman,[109] after discussing these cases which have extended the 'benefits' of marital status to cohabitants, comments that while such a move may provide critical rights to some unwed partners and illegitimate children, it may also impose unwanted regulation and burden on others. 'It may have unanticipated negative consequences for individuals who are trying to establish alternative personal and family life-styles. Individuals who want to live together without a permanent commitment, and those who want to establish an egalitarian relationship, may be thwarted by the state's imposition of its conception of marital rights and obligations.'[110]

Concern for the individual's freedom to choose cohabitation in preference to marriage has also been evident in decisions from the Canadian courts. The British Columbian Supreme Court in *Prokop v Kohut,*[111] in denying quasi-matrimonial relief to a surviving female cohabitant, made special reference to the fact that the deceased had not believed in marriage, being of Communist beliefs. In *Dwyer v Love*[112] Darby J, sitting in the Prince Edward Island Supreme Court, described a union as one where there were 'two individuals both wanting to live their own lives – wanting a relationship that could end at any time – no marriage – no ties, no problem to enter and none of divorce to end'. Similar considerations influenced the Australian Royal Commission on Human Relationships which reported in 1977. 'In our view', the report stated, 'the recognition of *de facto* relationships as conferring interests in property should be approached with caution. If parties refrain from marrying because they do not want to incur the legal and financial obligations of marriage then the law should be slow to impose those obligations on them.'[113]

Sweden, as we have seen, has attempted to eliminate the financial dependence fostered by traditional marriage by encouraging generally a move towards economic independence for all individuals. Where such independence has not been achieved, then, on breakdown of marriage, alimony can still be awarded. Despite the declaration of the principle of neutrality, the right to alimony remained the exclusive preserve of married partners, the first portion of the Family Law reform programme affecting only rights to residence.[114] The reasons for not extending alimony were: first, the desire to limit economic dependence between adults, and secondly, as Sage states,[115] it seemed philosophically consistent and reasonable to allow some leeway in the law for those who did not want to have their personal relationships regulated by the State.

Although Sweden has adopted the general principle of neutrality, while preserving a few differences, Denmark has not evolved any clear policy towards cohabitants. Pedersen[116] notes that 'there is no general rule concerning free unions in Danish statute law, and case law on cohabitation was rare until about five years ago (1974). There is no case in which it has been argued that such relationships violate public policy. On the other hand, the courts have been reluctant to use analogies with rules concerning married couples'.[117] In the course of examining the policy problems relating to the treatment of cohabitation under the law, she states that 'the disadvantages in trying to formulate a general legal definition include the fact that a legal status may sometimes be forced upon couples very much against their will without any benefit to the community or interested third parties . . .'.[118] Pedersen concludes her discussion of recent developments in Danish law relating to the illegitimate family and its rights by warning that 'in giving information or taking policy decisions in this complicated field there are two equally dangerous pitfalls. One is to think that non-marital relationships are a moral danger and ought to be suppressed. The other is to think that a progressive attitude towards family law must necessarily result in a desire for full equality between married and non-married couples'.[119]

Conclusion

Many countries appear to have an interest in maintaining the differentials between marriage and cohabitation. Whether this interest springs from a desire to promote traditional family life based on legal marriage, or from a respect for the individual's freedom of choice, is a matter for debate – and concern. It would seem at the moment that cohabitation has not been totally corrupted by marriage; nor has marriage by cohabitation. But what does the future hold for each?

Notes

1 See *post*, p. 184.

2 See *post*, p. 189.

3 This approach opens up the possibility of a variety of legal remedies, which a status-based approach does not.

4 Some commentators, e.g. D. Oliver, quarrel with the drawing of such an inference from the fact of cohabitation. See J.S.W.L. (1982), p. 209–222.

5 E.g., in England the development of the principle of constructive trusts, as in *Cooke v Head* [1972], 2 All E.R. 38, and *Eves v Eves* [1975], 3 All E.R. 768; or in the USA of partnership, as in *Re Estate of Thornton* 541 P. 2d 1243.

6 Cf. Wolfenden, *Report on Prostitution and Homosexuality*, Cmnd. 247 (1957).

7 E.g., in the more generous provision for spouses under the terms of the Inheritance (Provision for Family and Dependants) Act 1975; Rent Act 1977; and Housing Act 1980.

8 See e.g., Baker P in *Campbell v Campbell* [1977], 1 All E.R. 1; Eveleigh LJ in *Foley v Foley* [1981], 2 All E.R. 857; and Balcombe J in *H v H, The Times* (16 May 1981).

9 'Legal Regulation of Marriage: Tradition and Change', *Calif. Law Rev.*, 62, p. 1242.

10 H.C. Deb. vol. 898, col. 172 (20 Oct 1975).

11 *Idem*, cols. 186, 187. See also A. Samuels, 120 S.J. 123 (1976).

12 H.L. Deb. vol. 359, col. 1086 (Committee stage).

13 Peter Archer in debate on the 2nd Reading H.C. Deb. vol. 895, col. 1686.

14 Elwyn Jones in debate on the 2nd Reading H.L. Deb. vol. 358, col. 935.

15 See *ante* ch. 4, pp. 82–83.

16 See *ante* ch. 4 and 6.

17 See *ante* ch. 3 and 6.

18 E.g., in debates in House of Commons on the Inheritance (Provision for Family and Dependants) Act 1975; especially speech of Ivor Lawrence *op. cit.*, note 10, at cols 186–9.

19 See comments of the Law Commission in its Working Paper No. 74 on *Illegitimacy*, HMSO, 1979, paras 3–4.

20 The action does not extend to a wife: see *Best v Samuel Fox* [1952], 2 All E.R. 394.

21 S.11 of Children Act 1975.

22 See L. Weitzman, *op. cit.*, note 9; Lord Devlin, *The Enforcement of Morals*, Oxford U.P., 1965, at pp. 8–16; J. McMurtry, 'Monogamy: A Critique', *Monist*, 56 (1972), p. 587 at p. 589.

23 See Devlin, *op. cit.*, note 22.

24 There are places where adultery is a crime, including many states in the USA. But, outside Islamic countries, penal sanctions are rarely invoked.

25 *Op. cit.*, note 22, p. 591.

26 *Op. cit.*, note 22, at p. 592.

27 Even some of Devlin's critics (e.g., H.L.A. Hart, *Law, Liberty and Morality*, Stanford U.P., 1963) believe in the appropriateness of using the law to uphold a particular institution which is central to society's whole way of life. Hart gives the example of monogamy in our society. See, further, his article 'Social Solidarity and the Enforcement of Morality', *Univ. of Chicago L.R.*, 35 (1967), p. 1.

28 Evershed, MR, in *Gammans v Ekins* [1950], 2 K.B. 328, and Balcombe J in *H v H, The Times* (16 May 1981).

29 [1911], 1 K.B. 506.

30 [1950], 2 K.B. 328.

31 *Idem*, p. 334.

32 [1974], 1 All E.R. 888, 894.

33 [1975], 1 All E.R. 290, 293.

34 *Idem.*

35 *Op. cit.*, note 13.

36 [1976], 1 All E.R. 737.

37 See comments of Peter Archer, 2nd Reading H.C. Deb. vol. 895, vol. 1686, and in debate on 2nd Reading amendments H.C. Deb. vol. 898, col. 175.

38 [1978], 1 All E.R. 1132, 1148.

39 [1980], 10 Fam. Law 98.

40 [1977], 1 All E.R. 1,6.

41 [1980], 1 All E.R. 1106, 1119.

42 [1981], 2 All E.R. 857, 861.

43 [1981], 2 All E.R. 857.

44 E.g., *The Needs of Children*, Hutchinson (2nd ed.), 1980.

45 'Abolish Illegitimacy', *Fam. Law*, 9 (1979) pp. 131, 132.

46 'To Marry or not to Marry?', *Fam. Law*, 10 (1980), p. 29.

47 'The Legal Implications of a Relationship outside Marriage', *C.L.J.*, (1978), p. 252.

48 *Idem*, p. 269.

49 See, e.g., R. Deech, 'The Case against Legal Recognition of Cohabitation', in *Marriage and Cohabitation in Contemporary Societies*, J. Eekelaar and S. Katz (eds), Butterworths, 1980, p. 300; and see also our earlier article, Freeman and Lyon, 'Towards a Justification of the Rights of Cohabitees', *N.L.J.*, 130 (1980) p. 228.

50 See, e.g., the judgment of Stamp LJ in *Helby v Rafferty* [1978], 3 All E.R. 1016; and Oliver LJ in *Watson v Lucas* [1980], 3 All E.R. 647.

51 See, e.g., Mr John Horam *post*, p. 189–90.

52 See D. Oliver's comments in 'Why Do People live together?', *J.S.W.L.*, (1981), pp. 209–222.

53 In Standing Committee F, H.C. 1971–72, vol. VI, col. 755.

54 *Idem*, at col. 756.

55 *Idem.*

56 [1978], 3 All E.R. 1016.

57 *Idem*, p. 203, quoting with approval the judgment of the first instance judge.

58 [1980], 1 All E.R. 266, 276.

59 [1980], 3 All E.R. 647, 657.

60 *Op. cit.*, note 49.

61 'The Death of a Lover', *N.L.J.*, 126 (1976), p. 427.

62 In 'Formality and the Family – Reform and the Status Quo', *L.Q.R.*, 96 (1980), p. 248, at pp. 278–80.

63 See *op. cit.*, note 52.

64 In *op. cit.*, note 49.

65 *Op. cit.*, note 49 at p. 302.

66 *Op. cit.*, note 52.

67 Of seven couples known personally to Dawn Oliver.

68 *Op. cit.*, note 49 at p. 302.

69 *Op. cit.*, note 61 at p. 428.

70 *Op. cit.*, note 62 at p. 279.

71 E.g., *Minton v Minton* [1979], A.C. 593.

72 See, e.g., *Khan v Khan* [1980], 1 All E.R. 497.

73 *Op. cit.*, note 49, p. 304.

74 See comments of Baker P. in *Brady v Brady, The Times* (23 February 1973).

75 E.g., as in *Re C* (1979), 123 Sol. Jo. 35, and *Malone v Harrison* [1979], 1 W.L.R. 1353. See, further, M. Bryan, 'The Mistress and the Multiplier', *L.Q.R.*, 96 (1980), p. 165.

76 See *ante*, ch. 3 and also Mary Hayes, 'Supplementary Benefit and Financial Provision Orders', *J.S.W.L.*, (1979), p. 216.

77 Under s.31 of the M.C.A. 1973. Responsibilities towards a cohabitant can also be taken into consideration in determining financial provision under s.23 in accordance with the terms of s.25(1)(b) M.C.A. 1973.

78 *Op. cit.*, note 49, p. 306.

79 See *ante*, ch. 6 at pp. 159–161.

80 *Khan v Khan, op. cit.*, note 72.

81 See, e.g., *Mesher v Mesher and Hall* [1980], 1 All E.R. 126; *Minton v Minton* [1979], A.C. 593; *Dunford v Dunford* [1980], 1 All E.R. 122; and *Dipper v Dipper* [1980], 2 All E.R. 722.

82 Its keenest supporters among academic commentators are Riga, Noonan and Clark; see *post*, pp. 196–197.

83 E.g., as in *Rehak v Mathis* 238 S.E. 2d 81; and *Hewitt v Hewitt* 394 N.E. 2d 1204.

84 E.g., *New Jersey Welfare Rights Organization v Cahill* 349 F. Supp. 491.

85 See P. Riga, 'The Supreme Court's View of Marriage and the Family: Tradition or Transition', *Journal of Family Law*, 18 (1979), p. 301.

86 *Op. cit.*, note 83, at p. 82.

87 6 Fam. L. Rep. (B.N.A.) 2355, 2356.

88 *Op. cit.*, note 84, p. 497.

89 See also *Palo Alto Tenants Union v Morgan* 321 F. Supp. 908 for a decision of a Californian district court revealing a similar bias in favour of marriage and against alternative family forms.

90 394 N.E. 2d 1204, 1207 (1979).

91 *Idem*, at p. 1209.

92 See Riga, *op. cit.*, note 85; and H. Clark, 'The New Marriage', *Willamette LJ*, (1976), p. 441 at p. 449.

93 381 U.S. 68 (1968).

94 406 U.S. 164 (1972).

95 *Op. cit.*, note 85 at p. 309.

96 'The Family and the Supreme Court', *Cath. U.L. Rev.*, 23 (1973), p. 255.

97 *Op. cit.*, note 92, at p. 452.

98 134 Cal. Rptr. 815, 831.

99 S.43.

100 For example, even the most recent legislation on domestic violence only extends to protect married and not unmarried persons; see s.114 of Family Law Act 1975 and also the decision of Demack J. in *Fitzwilliam v Beckman* [1978], Qd. R. 398.

101 S.16 Maintenance Act (Tas) 1967–73.

102 E.g., s.7(1)(f) Inheritance (Family and Dependants) Provision Act 1972 (W.A.); and s.11(i) Family Relationships Act 1975 (S.A.).

103 E.g., Children (Equality of Status) Act 1976 (N.S.W.); Status of Children Act 1974 (Vic.); Status of Children Act 1974 (Tas).

104 E.g., *Valent v Salamon*, Supreme Court of New South Wales, 8 Dec. 1976 (unreported decision).

105 S.43(b).

106 Law Reform Commission of Tasmania Report on Obligations arising from *de facto* Relationships, 1976, at p. 8.

107 *Op. cit.*, note 98 at p. 832.

108 *Idem*, at p. 833.

109 'To Love, Honor and Obey? Traditional Legal Marriage and Alternative Family Forms', *Family Coordinator* (1975), p. 531.

110 *Idem*, at p. 546.

111 54 D.L.R. (2d) 717, 719.

112 67 D.L.R. (3d) 550, 552.
113 Royal Commission on Human Relationships – Final Report, Vol. 4 (1977), at p. 73.
114 See Z Sage, 'Dissolution of the Family under Swedish Law', *Fam. L.Q.*, 9 (1975), p. 375 at p. 401.
115 *Idem.*
116 I. Pedersen, 'Danish Law relating to Non-Marital Relationships', *I.C.L.Q.*, 28 (1979), p. 117.
117 *Idem,* at p. 118.
118 *Idem,* at pp. 119–20.
119 *Idem,* at p. 127.

8 Conclusion: Further Directions

A study of cohabitation has proved illuminating. It has revealed that in the course of a decade there has been a profound change in legal ideology.[1] From being regarded as little more than a species of prostitution. law reformers both in legislatures and courts have come to extend increasing recognition to family units based on cohabitation outside marriage.[2] To a greater or lesser extent in each of the countries studied cohabitation has come to be regarded as like marriage, and accordingly worthy of being treated in similar terms. How are we to understand these processes? What do they signify and portend?

There is, of course, an official answer to these questions. It may be sought in the reports of government commissions, in parliamentary debates and in the reasoning of judges in decided cases. This stresses that cohabiting couples have set up family-like establishments, that their behaviour is quasi-marital. It is hardly surprising, as a result, that cohabiting couples with children should have been given special consideration in many of the recent developments. All children need to be nurtured irrespective of whether their parents are married.

In all the legal systems studied there has been a shift in the direction of equalisation of marriage and cohabitation. This has gone further in some countries, notably Sweden,[3] than others. The trend is, however, common to all countries discussed in this book.

Conservative paternalism once saw the family based on marriage as the foundation of the social order. Looked at in this way every change was seen as a threat to social integrity.[4] Obstacles were always placed in the way of divorce reform. The importance of differentiating the status of children born outside marriage from those conceived in lawful wedlock was constantly stressed. Extra-marital sexual relations were penalised: sinful women could not expect maintenance or custody of their children.

As indicated in Chapter 2, women have always been defined in terms of the family. The position they have occupied and continue to occupy throws light on the structure and dynamics of society itself. The formal legal position of married women has improved in the course of the last century. They can now own property, make contracts; they are entitled to, and usually get, custody of children on divorce or separation. They may acquire a beneficial interest in the matrimonial home even where they are not waged and do not make a financial contribution, though engaging in 'men's work'[5] is more likely to establish such an interest than doing stereotypical female tasks. For all these changes the law continues to support a family structure in which a married woman's dependence is fundamental.[6]

Rights in the family may be seen as an alternative to greater public rights. Women are still expected to be dependent on men and to be controlled by them. We still operate within an economic system that stresses a 'family wage'.[7] Fiscal policies and social security arrangements reflect at every turn the economic dependence of women. The cult of domesticity is supported throughout by tax and social security systems. We have passed equal pay legislation and purported to create equal opportunities through a Sex Discrimination Act, but the success of both pieces of legislation is so dubious that to describe them as pacification measures or exercises in symbolic politics[8] would not be far from the mark.

Less, then, has changed than might superficially appear to be the case. Those groups like the Campaign for Justice in Divorce and Families Need Fathers, who believe current laws and policies favour women, ignore the structural dependence of women in marriage. We would like to see an end to maintenance of ex-wives but we appreciate that the duty to maintain is the result of economic realities. Until women have equality in the economy there may be no alternative to accepting that on break-up of a family unit the economic provider continues to provide.

Marriage has been described, with considerable justification, as 'repressive benevolence'.[9] Women, it is said, have been 'given' (the imagery is significant for gifts are a way of expressing power)[10] rights and protection. But how are these gifts to be seen? As E.P. Thompson has noted,[11] the dominated tend to see their grievances in terms of rights granted by law, and expect justice; the system, in this case the patriarchy, to preserve its legitimacy, has to appear to be just. Indeed, on occasion it may actually be so. But instances of real justice, such as the powers given women by recent legislation to exclude violent husbands and cohabitants, may be smokescreens which hide more pervasive injustices. The notion of protection is similarly problematic. It was a Victorian judge[12] who saw protection and submission as correlatives. Much law is passed, or so it is said, to protect the weak. Experience has shown that the effect of such legislation is often the control of those whom those who design the legislation purport to protect.

Why then have the consequences of cohabitation gradually been assimilated to those of marriage? One can see these developments in terms of rights for cohabitants and protection of the weaker partner. This is the way that most lawmakers and commentators perceive contemporary developments. But if marriage is repressive benevolence, what are we to say of cohabitation? Is there to be no escape from marriage? Are those who exercise their autonomy by opting out of marriage to have the legal consequences of matrimony thrust on them willy-nilly? Marriage remains popular and is unlikely to be eclipsed by trends towards cohabitation for a generation or more, at least, that is, in Britain. Cohabitation may only delay marriage. Why should couples who have decided not to marry not have their decisions respected? The case for what one author has called 'freedom of intimate association'[13] is, we believe, a strong one.

Current developments in relation to cohabitation thus show the way the state is interfering with family autonomy. Interference is tantamount to control. Legal developments must not be seen as disembodied or neutral. The law helps to constitute and define social order. It has done this down the centuries in relation to marriage. It is now purporting to do the same in cases where couples live together outside marriage but behave like married couples. Recent developments thus have a broader significance than may appear superficially. They are about the family on one level; on another they dictate the place women are to occupy in society. They may seem to be permissive but in reality they are an attack on cultural diversity. The bourgeois family ideal is being imposed on those who wish to experiment with alternative life-styles.[14]

Individualism is an overworked concept. To Steven Lukes[15] it embraces a number of 'unit-ideas': the dignity of man, autonomy, privacy, self-development, and what he calls a concept of the 'abstract individual'. ('The crucial point about this conception is that the relevant features of individuals determining the ends which social arrangements are held (actually or ideally) to fulfil, whether these features are called instincts, faculties, needs, desires, rights, etc., are assumed as given, independently of a social context').[16] We see the move towards cohabitation as an example of individualism in practice. We find the debates about the moral propriety of allowing cohabitation outside marriage to continue and, if so, under what control, mirror views within political and moral philosophy about individualism generally. Thus, to A.D. Lindsay one of the elements of modern individualism is 'a high valuation set on the voluntary association and the relation of contract'.[17] Autonomy, as Lukes indicated, is a central idea of individualism. According to David Riesman in *The Lonely Crowd,* the autonomous are those who are 'free to choose whether to conform or not' to the behavioural norms of their society and are 'capable of transcending their culture'. There were, he thought, pressures which drove people into anomie and produced a 'wan conformity' in others. But despite these pressures towards conformism and adjustment, 'people may, in what is left of their private lives, be nurturing newly critical and creative standards'.[18]

Autonomy and privacy are both intimately connected with liberty, as that concept is understood in Sir Isaiah Berlin's essay 'Two Concepts of Liberty'.[19] Autonomy is closely related to 'positive' freedom or liberty: 'the wish on the part of the individual to be his own master'.[20] Berlin expresses that individual's wish as follows:

> I wish my life and decisions to depend on myself, not on external forces of whatever kind. I wish to be the instrument of my own, not other men's, acts of will. I wish to be a subject, not an object . . . I wish to be somebody . . . ; a doer deciding, not being decided for, self-directed and not acted upon by external nature or by other men as if I were a thing, or an animal, or a slave incapable of playing a human role, that is, of conceiving goals and policies of my own and realising them.[21]

Privacy is linked to what Berlin calls 'negative liberty',[22] or 'the desire not to be impinged upon, to be left to oneself'.[23] It demands an 'area of personal relationships as something sacred in its own right'.[24] In John Stuart Mill's language, there is 'a sphere of action in which society, as distinguished from the individual, has, if any, only an indirect interest'.[25] Liberty includes 'liberty of tastes and pursuits; of framing the plan of our life to suit our own character . . .'[26] There is a view which holds, to quote Riesman again, that 'conformity with society is not only a necessity but also a duty'.[27] We repudiate such a view. As Riesman notes, this is to 'destroy that margin of freedom which gives life its savour and its endless possibility for advance'. We must, he continues, and this is the kernel of our argument too, 'give every encouragement to people to develop their private selves . . .'[28]

There are some who interpret recent developments in the law relating to cohabitation as affirmations of this individualism. Eekelaar and Katz, for example, suggest that 'the last decade has seen an ever increasing focus on the needs and desires of individuals in contrast to the traditional emphasis on family and other personal relationships'.[29] This may be an accurate assessment of some developments, for example, in laws of divorce stressing breakdown rather than fault,[30] but we do not see it as a correct appraisal of developments in the law relating to cohabitation. What emphasis is there on the desires of individuals if, having chosen not to marry, the consequences of marriage are thrust upon them anyway?

One hundred and twenty years ago Sir Henry Maine had seen 'the emergence of the self-determining separate individual' as an important constituent in the movement he identified from status to contract. 'The movement of progressive societies', he noted, 'has been uniform in one respect. Through all its course it has been distinguished by the gradual dissolution of family dependency and the growth of individual obligation in its place. The Individual', so he argued, 'is steadily substituted for the Family as the unit of which civil laws take account.'[31] Is cohabitation to become a status-producing relationship or are cohabitants to be left to their own resources? Would it be more appropriate to allow cohabitants to deal with their problems by contract than to assimilate their position to that of married couples?[32]

There have been a number of suggestions as to how best to deal with the problem. The firmest espousal of individualism is found in the writings of Ruth Deech. She has argued, and her premise should be noted:

> Assuming that women are not simply tossed around by events but are to some extent in control of their lives, any foreseeable injury resulting from cohabitation ought to be fairly attributable to the payer of compensation. This means dealing with the problems . . . by contract between the cohabitants and by the application of ordinary principles of law.[33]

The 'ordinary' legal principles, contract aside, that Deech believes should be applied to cohabitants are those of property, torts and trusts. But she is critical of the judgment of Tobriner J in *Marvin v Marvin,*[34] for he held that in absence of an express contract the court should enquire into the conduct of the parties to see if it demonstrated an implied contract, and that if there were no grounds for finding one, resort should be had to equitable principles such as *quantum meruit,* constructive or resulting trusts. Deech comments: 'this determination to apply what are in practice special family-based laws or to force on the couple a legal framework when they have expressly rejected one by cohabiting without a contract is regrettable'.[35] The problem with putting express contracts in the forefront is that few people contemplating a non-commercial relationship will think of expressing their rights and obligations in contractual form.[36] Weyrauch is surely right when he notes that contract is 'particularly useful for women from the middle classes and of high educational attainment who are self-assertive and competitive in their relations with men. It is less adequate for parties of the lower classes and those who, because of the continued differential treatment of the sexes, lack equal bargaining power'.[37] Autonomy presumes equality of bargaining power. It will be some time before women as a whole enjoy this.

Deech believes it to be anomalous that, as she puts it, 'at a time when most women are establishing social and economic independence, a few should try to capitalize on the myth of the weak woman'.[38] We too think this parasitism, where such it is, regrettable, and like Deech deplore the antics of the Michelle Marvins of this world. But the basic issue remains. Given the structure of today's society, the position of many women remains weak. The question is whether the breakthrough will come by ignoring inequality in power in marriage and other relationships or whether the change must be initiated in the public realms before the private. Women have been given increasingly formal equality but the structural inequalities remain. One cannot analyse the position of women at the level of individual members of the family. Deech does just this. The future may lie with express contracts; we would certainly encourage prospective cohabitants to commit their intentions to paper. But for some time to come we cannot hope that all cohabiting relationships will be self-regulating in this way. We consider the legal status of express contracts in the Appendix.[39]

The more cohabiting couples who make express contracts, the easier it will be for courts to imply contracts in cases where there are no express terms. Bottomley *et al.* see express contracts, however uncommon, as helping to create a climate in which courts will be more likely to imply contracts in other cases.[40] But express contracts will do more than create a climate: they will assist courts to construct contracts because they will become cognisant of common, if not standard, terms in cohabitation contracts.

This raises the crucial question as to whether courts should imply contracts at all. There are two types of implied contract: contracts which are implied in fact and those which are implied in law. Implied-in-fact contracts are the product of conduct, what the parties actually did and said, even though they did not formulate their arrangements in contractual form. Thus, in *Paul v Constance*[41] there were express statements and unequivocal behaviour. In *Tanner v Tanner*[42] the female cohabitant, who had twins by her partner, gave up a small rent-controlled flat at his suggestion and moved into a house he had just bought. The court would not allow him subsequently to turn her out. It held that she had an implied and irrevocable licence to reside in the house so long as the children were of school age.[43] Lord Denning MR put it well (in *Hardwick v Johnson*) when, commenting on the difficulty of ascertaining the parties' intention, he observed: 'the court has to look at all the circumstances and spell out the legal relationship'.[44] Time and time again, he noted, 'courts are called upon to determine what is the true legal relationship'[45] arising from family arrangements. Cases like these show the value of the implied-in-fact contract.

Implying contracts in law, imputing to the parties intentions they did not have, is a more hazardous exercise. The approach employs notions such as *quantum meruit* and unjust enrichment. It constructs what are assumed to be reasonable expectations as to fair dealings in a relationship of the type under consideration. Inevitably it stereotypes and in doing so depersonalises. The danger is that a particular relationship is tested by a stereotypical image of male–female relations. Female cohabitants will then be rewarded insofar as they conform to the 'good wife' image. Questions of conduct and moral blame will inevitably be dredged up. There will be assessments as to how well female cohabitants have performed household services. This, of course, has been happening. There have in American and Canadian cases even been enquiries into the female cohabitant's sexual fidelity.[46] In England no court has gone this far. Nevertheless, they have ranged widely. In *Eves v Eves* the Court of Appeal gave the female cohabitant 'such a share as was fair in view of all that she had done and was doing for [her partner] and the children'.[47] In *Kokosinski v Kokosinski,* the wife (the couple had married after twenty-five years' cohabitation) was said to have 'given the best years of her life'. She had, the judge stressed, been 'faithful, loving and hardworking . . . she has managed his house and been a mother to and helped him to bring up a son'.[48] In these particular cases the decisions, whatever the reasoning, may have achieved rudimentary justice. But the reasoning itself is suspect. Why should a cohabitant receive compensation for household services? A wife, of course, does not, though in England her contribution towards the welfare of the family may be taken into account in assessing financial provision and undertaking property adjustment on a divorce.[49] It may be argued that a wife should also be compensated for household services. But this ignores what paying for services means. It would put the wife, as it does the cohabitant, into a master–servant relationship. The compensation begins to look like a nascent redundancy payment. Such notions, we think, are inappropriate and degrading. If the women in question have been full-time housewives, then they have received, as part of the 'bargain', support as well as benefits – holidays and entertainment for example – that they themselves have not paid for. If they had not been supported in this way, they would have had to support themselves by remunerative employment or sought another man to support them. It may be said that a female cohabitant has expectations of some reward for services rendered. But if this is the case, she ought to be encouraged to stipulate for compensation in an express contract entered into at the outset of cohabitation or, indeed, at some time thereafter.

The problems with contracts implied in law is not so much the fact that they are implied but with *what* is implied. So long as the judiciary is imbued with patriarchal attitudes, it is going to imply contracts in law where women conform to traditional stereotypes. The judiciary clearly sees the growth in cohabitation as a threat to marriage. Its response is, as far as possible, to incorporate the one within the other: cohabitation is to be treated like marriage insofar as it is like marriage. Female cohabitants who do not conform to acceptable stereotypes are penalised; those who do are rewarded. The lesson projected is clear: if you will not marry, then at least behave as if you have married for 'advantages' attach to so doing.

Unlike Deech, we see a place for implied contracts, even contracts implied in law. We too would like to see the express contract as the dominant form. It is clear, however, that only a minority will make express contracts. Weyrauch is surely right to point out that

> express contract and implied contract, although they share the same contractual underpinning, are . . . not necessarily part of the same social frame of reference. In express contract, party autonomy as a middle-class ideal is more or less real or at least a possibility, while in implied contract of cohabitation, party autonomy may have elements of a legal fiction judicially imposed upon parties who often belong to the lower classes.[50]

Not only then is there the danger of stereotypical expectations being imposed on those who do not contract, so that their cohabitations look like marriage even when they do not wish them to do so, but working class cohabitation may be forced into a mould made to fit the property-owning expectations of middle-class quasi-marital unions. We do not wish either of these things to happen, and yet we would argue that implied contracts must still have a part to play.

There are problems with express contracts too. Should parties be held to an express contract, entered into at the start of a relationship, when fundamental changes have occurred in the parties' relationship and their economic situation in the interim period? Eekelaar has expressed concern about this: 'To confine courts to the terms of a contract entered into many years earlier', he writes, 'not only risks overlooking changes in the economic situation of the parties which may have taken place over the years, but also the subsequent introduction of new interests, primarily of the children born to or adopted by the couple, but including those of other adult parties who have become involved in their lives'.[51] Zuckerman's response to this, to the effect that English courts adjudicate disputes 'in the light of the parties' conduct throughout the cohabitation',[52] may be a satisfactory rebuttal of Eekelaar's objection, if one accepts the way that courts take account of conduct. As already indicated, we do not do so.

What those who are concerned with changes overlook is that changes also take place in the situation of parties to commercial contracts, which may be discharged under the doctrine of frustration. It is recognised that if fulfilment of a contract is prevented by some irresistible and extraneous cause for which neither party is responsible, the contract terminates forthwith and the parties are discharged.[53] Parties can exclude the doctrine of frustration by expressly providing for the frustrating event.[54] Much that happens during a cohabitation cannot be said to be unexpected by cohabitants, so that they clearly could provide for many contingencies. These would obviously include matters relating to the custody and maintenance of children, though we would exclude the question of children from the autonomy of the parties. The case for intervention by the courts in matters relating to children is more cogent than matters concerned with the relationship of the parties themselves. But, children apart, why should cohabiting couples who expressly contract at the outset of their relationship be treated differently from other adults who make contracts? If others are limited by the doctrine of frustration, why should a cohabitant be protected against foolishness, lack of foresight or improvidence? There will be situations where, for example, a cohabitant has improved the other's property, but the law of trusts is flexible enough to take care of such cases. We are concerned that cohabitants' rights are subjected to ordinary principles of law and that courts do not interfere with their legitimate expectations because of their relationship.

The directions that the law relating to cohabitation takes are highly significant. Cohabitation is a test-bed for the whole structure of family law – indeed, of male–female relationships – within society. We are concerned that these move in the direction of establishing equality between the sexes in public and private spheres. Current policies in the cohabitation field are oriented to status and dependence. Ostensibly, protection of the weaker party is their goal and this is assumed to be motivated by humane considerations. In reality, the assimilation of cohabitation to marriage is a way of controlling women, a form of moral regulation.[55] It would be better, we think, if marriage were to become more like cohabitation. The future lies with contract rather than status, autonomy instead of supposed protection.[56]

Notes

1 Cf. A. Sachs and J. Hoff, *Sexism and The Law*, Martin Robertson, 1978.

2 Mainly but not exclusively in heterosexual relationships. On homosexual 'marriages', see Comment, 'The Legality of Homosexual Marriages' *Yale LJ* 82 (1973), pp. 573–589.

3 See *ante*, p. 127 *et seq.*

4 See, e.g., Sir P. Devlin, *The Enforcement of Morals*, Oxford U.P., 1965, ch. IV.

5 See, e.g., *Cooke v Head* [1972], 2 All E.R. 38; *Tanner v Tanner* [1975], 3 All E.R. 169. Cf. *Button v Button* [1968], 1 All E.R. 1064.

6 A recent article agreeing with this interpretation is J. Brophy and C. Smart, 'From Disregard to Disrepute: The Position of women in Family Law', *Feminist Review*, no. 9 (1981), pp. 3–16.

7 See H. Land, 'The Family Wage', *Feminist Review*, no. 6 (1980), pp. 55–78.

8 See M. Edelman, *The Symbolic Uses of Politics*, 1964.

9 By D.L. Barker, 'The Regulation of Marriage: Repressive Benevolence', in G. Littlejohn *et al.*, (eds), *Power and the State*, Croom Helm, 1978, pp. 239–66.

10 See M. Mauss, *The Gift*, Cohen and West, 1970, p. 72.

11 *Whigs and Hunters*, Allen Lane, 1975.

12 Sir James Fitzjames Stephen, quoted *ante*, p. 35.

13 Kenneth L. Karst, 'The Freedom of Intimate Association', *Yale LJ*, 89 (1980), pp. 624–92.

14 On the ideal, see M. Poster, *Critical Theory of the Family*, Pluto Press, 1978.

15 *Individualism*, Basil Blackwell, 1973, chs. 7–11.

16 *Idem*, p. 73.

17 'Individualism', in *Encyclopaedia of the Social Sciences*, 1930–5, vol. VIII, p. 676.

18 *The Lonely Crowd*, Yale U.P., 1950, pp. 287, 290.

19 In *Four Essays on Liberty*, Oxford U.P., 1969, pp. 118–72.

20 *Idem*, p. 131.

21 *Idem*.

22 *Idem*, p. 122.

23 *Idem*, p. 129.

24 *Idem*.

25 *On Liberty*, Everyman edition, 1910, p. 75.

26 *Idem*.

27 *Individualism Reconsidered*, Free Press, 1954, p. 27.

28 *Idem*, pp. 37 and 38.

29 *Marriage and Cohabitation in Contemporary Societies*, Butterworths, 1980, Preface.

30 See, e.g., L. Weitzman and R. Dixon, 'The Transformation of Marriage Through No-Fault Divorce: the Case of the United States', in *idem*, pp. 143–53.

31 *Ancient Law*, Oxford U.P. (World Classics edition, 1931), pp. 139–41.

32 On status and contract in relation to cohabitation, see A. Zuckerman, 'Formality and the Family – Reform and the Status Quo', *L.Q.R.*, 96 (1980), pp. 248–80.

33 'The Case Against Legal Recognition of Cohabitation', *I.C.L.Q.*, 29 (1980), pp. 480–97.

34 (1976) 557 P. 2d. 106.

35 *Op. cit.*, note 33, p. 495.

36 Cf. Lord Hodson's remarks in *Pettitt v Pettitt* [1970] A.C. 777, 810.

37 'Metamorphoses of Marriage', *Family Law Q.*, 13, pp. 415–40.

38 *Op. cit.*, note 33, p. 485.

39 *Post*, p. 215.

40 *The Cohabitation Handbook*, Pluto Press, 1981, p. 125.

41 [1977], 1 All E.R. 195.

42 [1975], 3 All E.R. 169.

43 In fact she had left the house but the Court of Appeal awarded her £2,000, the sum which she might reasonably have requested for surrendering the licence.

44 [1978], 2 All E.R. 935, 938.

45 *Idem*. It is notable that he referred to *Balfour v Balfour* [1919], 2 K.B. 571, without dissent but by implication by-passed it.

46 See *Marvin v Marvin*, *op. cit.*, note 34; *Omer v Omer* (1974) 523 P. 2d 957; *Becker v Pettkus* (1978) 87 O.L.R. (3d) 101.

47 [1975], 3 All E.R. 768, 772.
48 [1980], 1 All E.R. 1106, 1117.
49 See Matrimonial Causes Act 1973, s.25(1)(f).
50 *Op. cit.,* note 37, p. 432.
51 *Family Law and Social Policy,* Weidenfeld and Nicolson, 1978, p. 53.
52 *Op. cit.,* note 32, p. 278.
53 See *Denny, Mott and Dickson Ltd. v James Fraser & Co. Ltd.* [1944], A.C. 265.
54 See *Jackson v Union Marine Insurance* (1874) L.R. 10 C.P. 125.
55 See, further, C. Smart and B. Smart, *Women, Sexuality and Social Control,* Routledge and Kegan Paul, 1978; and B. Hutter and G. Williams, *Controlling Women,* Croom Helm, 1981.
56 An excellent recent discussion of contract in marriage is M.M. Shultz, 70 Calif. *L.R.* 204 (1982).

Appendix: Cohabitation Contracts and the Law

Having pinned our faith on contract, we must consider the legal effect of a cohabitation contract in English law. Cretney, writing in 1974, stated that such a contract was 'substantially devoid of legal effect' and 'would almost certainly be illegal and contrary to public policy'.[1] He is now a member of the English Law Commission which is reconsidering this view. This is, we believe, not before time.

To understand why a cohabitation contract is suspect it is necessary to delve into history. There are two lines of thought which must be considered. First, there is the view expressed in many cases from the seventeenth century onwards that a cohabitation contract is contrary to public policy since it is for an immoral purpose.[2] The justification advanced in these cases for not enforcing contracts relating to present or future cohabitation was that often the sole consideration provided by the woman was sexual intercourse. In other cases the man was already married.[3] Sometimes it was said that the woman was little better than a prostitute.[4] Even in the twentieth century courts were expressing their abhorrence of such contracts. This in 1938 in *Fender v St. John Mildmay,* Lord Wright stated: 'the law will not enforce an immoral purpose, such as a promise between a man and a woman to live together without being married or to pay a sum of money or to give some other consideration in return for an immoral association'.[5] As recently as 1959 Ormrod LJ declared in *Diwell v Farnes* that 'even if there was sufficient evidence from which a joint transaction or a joint venture might be inferred . . . such joint venture must depend on a contract express or implied between the parties, i.e. the deceased and his mistress which, being founded on an immoral consideration, would not be enforceable'.[6]

The courts have, however, been prepared to imply trusts, as indeed they did in *Diwell v Farnes.* But these arise only at the date of the separation and cannot therefore, in the eyes of the judges, be said to promote immorality.

In English law contracts require consideration. This has posed problems in the case of cohabitation contracts, since the tendency has been to assume that cohabitation arrangements are agreements merely for the provision of sexual services. But this barrier can be overcome as *Ward v Byham*[7] and *Tanner v Tanner*[8] show. In each case the court was able to find consideration other than the provision of sexual services and was able to uphold contracts relating to aspects of cohabitation. In both cases the contract was at arm's length after separation. The issue of contracting for present or future cohabitation or the consequences of possible breakdown in the future remain unresolved.

There is a second reason why cohabitation contracts cause problems. English law has long demonstrated a reluctance to recognise domestic contracts. Indeed, there is a presumption that domestic arrangements should not be given legal force when made by a husband and wife living in amity.[9] The courts would look askance at an agreement made by a married couple relating to financial support or property distribution upon breakdown at some time in the future. But they are more likely to uphold agreements which were made after the parties' relationship had broken down, provided the agreement was couched in such terms as to indicate strongly the contemplation of legal relations.[10] Even then, as *Gould v Gould*[11] illustrates, the courts evince a reluctance in practice to enforce domestic agreements.

Public policy has changed. Certainly public opinion has and it is generally accepted that cohabitation contracts should not be struck down on the ground that they promote immorality and so are contrary to public policy. Are there any other objections to the legal recognition of such contracts?

An argument sometimes advanced is that cohabitation usually envisages unilateral dissolution, that this encourages the parties to view their relationship as temporary with the result that there is little incentive to overcome problems in the relationship and the economically weaker party feels financially insecure. These factors, it is said, pose threats to social stability.

Marriage, on the other hand, is supposed to be permanent. The three-year bar to divorce[12] is supposed to buttress marriage in the early days; children of such unions are legitimate (a status which produces entitlements from both parents) and the economically weaker marriage partner can rely on divorce legislation to safeguard her future financial position. Cohabitation does not reproduce these same positive reinforcements of the goal of social stability, and it would be unwise to seek to encourage it by recognising cohabitation contracts.

Our position is that these arguments are at best shaky. Marriages can be ended, in fact if not in law, unilaterally and just as quickly as cohabitation. True, if one spouse walks out on the other a divorce, a legal termination of the relationship, may take five years.[13] The three-year bar on divorce has little effect in buttressing marriage and the Law Commission has now recommended that it be reduced to one year.[14] With the introduction of the 'special procedure' for all undefended divorces, many today must feel that marriage is more like a contract, freely dissoluble at the will of either party. But, of course, it is not, for its conditions during its continuance are heavily influenced by tradition and upon breakdown variable only by the state acting through the courts. As far as the status of children is concerned, what was once the trump card in terms of justifying the denial of recognition to cohabitation on social stability grounds, viz: the stigma and disabilities attaching to illegitimacy, may soon disappear.[15] The statistics on the number of divorces and the current rate of divorces (roughly one in three of today's marriages will end in divorce) would also seem to indicate a failure on the part of marriage to live up to its supposed objectives. Further, it seems difficult to argue that the recognition of cohabitation contracts would increase the insecurity of the economically weaker partner. Indeed, we would argue that it would achieve the opposite effect.

The anti-recognition arguments all stem from a fear that recognition of cohabitation contracts will be prejudicial to the status of marriage, despite the fact that marriage itself and the law relating to it reveal grave defects. It is difficult to evaluate the effect that legal recognition of cohabitation contracts would actually have on marriage. It seems unlikely that this alone would lure people away from formal marriage. Marriage remains popular, even with those who have been unsuccessful in previous marriages. The institution of marriage should survive on its own merits and not at the expense of denying the freedom of the individual to make his and her own contracts. The state clearly has an interest in fostering community and family stability but there is no evidence that the recognition of cohabitation contracts threatens such objectives.

If the recognition of cohabitation contracts cannot be shown to threaten the community and family stability, what are the justifications for refusing to recognise the legal effects of contracts containing similar provisions but made between spouses? It is our view that married couples should have the same liberty to make such contracts. However, since most agreements would specifically provide for what happened on breakdown, it is probable that the courts would designate them as being contrary to public policy. But, given the chances that a marriage will break up, there is considerable sense in wanting to provide for such circumstances. An agreement might well reduce the bitterness surrounding a divorce if for no other reason than it might help to avoid lengthy property and custody disputes. If the real reason for refusing judicial recognition to domestic contracts rests on the paternalistic view that the state through its laws and institutions knows best, then this must be made plain. The justification of public policy should not be a cloak for naked state interference in people's lives unless good reason for such intervention can be demonstrated. The present state of family law in England does not indicate that it can.

Examples of cohabitation contracts can be found in a number of places.[16] Space prevents reproduction or analysis of existing model contracts. For these the reader must be referred elsewhere. In England we await the first litigation of an express agreement to share property or assign support duties on breakdown, made by cohabitants at the start of their relationship. Note must, however, be taken of American developments.

Lenore Weitzman[17] has pointed out that the American courts have traditionally been prepared to recognise ante-nuptial and post-nuptial contracts, provided they did not alter the essential elements of the marital relationship and were not made in contemplation of divorce. Closer examination of the two provisos reveals that the essential elements which cannot be contracted out of are the husband's duty to support his wife and the wife's duty to serve her husband. The injustices consequent upon the court's rigid adherence to a strict interpretation of these essential elements are illustrated by two fairly recent cases. In a 1968 North Carolina case,[18] the court held that farm work and caring for the husband's sick relatives were duties for which the wife could not recover payment. In a 1974 Wisconsin case[19] the judge ruled that a business operated by both spouses as a partnership belonged only to the husband, because the wife's efforts were the 'discharge of her wifely obligations' rather than the acts of a business partner. Weitzman has commented: 'although courts have been scrupulous in preventing spouses from contracting to alter the husband's duty to support and the wife's duty to provide domestic services, they have allowed wider latitude with regard to marital property'.[20] Thus, spouses have traditionally been allowed to make contracts about property and to reverse the characterisation of either separate or community property. The American position, therefore, differs significantly from that in England, since the English courts would on breakdown of the relationship have the power to vary any such agreements under s.24 of the Matrimonial Causes Act 1973.

The second proviso relating to the enforceability of nuptial agreements is that they cannot be made in contemplation of divorce. While this corresponds to a similar English proviso, its rationale is somewhat different, in that contracts contemplating divorce in the United States were thought to facilitate collusion in manufacturing grounds for the fault-based system of divorce. But with an increasing number of states adopting no-fault divorce systems, this rationale becomes less valid, and several state courts have recently adopted a much more realistic approach to contracts made between husbands and wives.[21]

A recent decision of the California Supreme Court is illustrative of this new approach. In *Re Marriage of Dawley*[22] concerned the validity of an ante-nuptial agreement made between the father and mother of an unborn child before a marriage, intended by both parties to be temporary and entered into to protect the woman's employment position (she was a school-teacher who feared she would be dismissed as an unmarried mother). The agreement provided for the support of the mother and her child from a previous relationship for fourteen months and support of the unborn child up to the age of twenty-one. Other terms related to earnings and property. In the event the couple lived together for eight years and the trial court found that they had kept to the original provisions of the contract. On divorce, the woman challenged the validity of the agreement, claiming, among other things, that it 'violated public policy by denying her support'. The agreement was upheld. The court openly acknowledged that it was made in contemplation of divorce and that it limited the husband's support obligations. The court said the new test of the validity of these contracts was whether the language of the contract itself objectively promoted dissolution of the marriage. The court declared: 'Neither the re-ordering of property rights to fit the needs and desires of the couple, nor realistic planning that takes account of the possibility of dissolution, offends the public policy favouring and protecting marriage'.[23]

This decision must be applauded as a victory for common sense. The only question which remains is whether courts would take a similar line with a cohabitation contract with identical provisions. As in England, the American courts traditionally refused to enforce contracts between cohabitants on the ground that they would not give effect to agreements for illicit sexual services.[24] Some still do, even today. But state Supreme Courts in Oregon,[25] Michigan,[26] Alaska[27] and California[28] have now taken the initiative in recognising cohabitation contracts. In *Marvin v Marvin* the Californian Supreme Court laid down very clearly the basis upon which it will, and others may, proceed in the future. This, Tobriner J stated that: 'the courts should enforce express contracts between nonmarital partners except to the extent that the contract is explicitly founded on the consideration of meretricious sexual services'.[29] Since by and large an agreement to provide sexual services would be totally alien to the spirit of modern cohabitation, it is unlikely that a contract of this nature would ever be litigated.

Marvin v Marvin has had considerable impact in the United States. In *Re Marriage of Dawley* has also been followed in other states. It is often said that where California leads today, the rest of America follows tomorrow with England following a decade or two later. It is to be hoped that on this occasion English developments will mirror Californian ones without any such lag. In our view the two decisions are of equal importance in recognising the individual's freedom to order his own life. California at least seems to be prepared to acknowledge that no real social harm can result from the recognition of spousal or cohabitation contracts. A desire to make such contracts is a symptom of dissatisfaction with current institutions and laws, and not a cause of it. Once this is recognised, it may be possible to move forward to a new era of reform in family law in which the keynote is less state intervention in the family.

Notes

1 *Principles of Family Law,* Sweet & Maxwell, London, 1974, p. 31.
2 E.g., *Walker v Perkins* (1764) 1 W.B. 517; *Benyon v Nettlefold* (1850), 3 Mac and G. 94.
3 *Priest v Parrot* (1751), 2 Ves. Seb. 160–1.
4 *Robinson v Cox* (1741), 9 Mod. 163.
5 [1938] A.C. 1, 42.
6 [1959] 2 All E.R. 379, 384.
7 [1956] 2 All E.R. 318.
8 [1975] 2 All E.R. 716.
9 *Balfour v Balfour* [1919] 2 K.B. 571.
10 [1970] 2 All E.R. 760.
11 [1969] 3 All E.R. 728.
12 See s.3 of the Matrimonial Causes Act 1973.
13 Though it need not if the deserted spouse takes action.
14 Law Com. no. 116 (1982).
15 We await a final Law Commission report.
16 Three examples are P. Gray, 123 *New Law Journal* 591, 596; A. Coote and T. Gill, *Women's Rights* (3rd ed. 1977), Harmondsworth: Penguin, p. 530; A. Bottomley *et al., Cohabitation Handbook,* Pluto Press, London, 1981, p. 194.
17 'Contracts for Intimate Relationships', *Alternative Lifestyles,* vol. 1, no. 3 (1978), p. 303, 311. See also now L. Weitzman, *The Marriage Contract,* Free Press, New York, 1981.
18 (1968) N.C. App. 143.
19 (1974) 217 N.W. 2d 326.
20 *The Marriage Contract, op. cit.,* note 17, p. 341.
21 E.g., Florida, Illinois, Oregon, Nevada and California.
22 (1976) 551 P. 2d 323.
23 *Idem,* p. 333.
24 E.g., *Vincent v Moriarty* (1895), 31 App. Div. 484.
25 *Latham v Latham* (1974) 274 Ore. 421.
26 *Tyranski v Piggins* (1973), 205 N.W. 2nd. 595.
27 *Levar v Elkins* (1980), 604 P. 2d. 602.
28 *Marvin v Marvin* (1976) 18 Cal. 3d. 660.
29 *Idem,* p. 819.

Index

DATE DUE

RETURNED			
Dec 8 6 RETURNED			
OCT 23 1990 RETURNED			
FEB 01 1995			
81195			